HISTORIC HOUSTON

An Illustrated History and Resource Guide

By Betty Trapp Chapman

Published for the Greater Houston Preservation Alliance

Historical Publishing Network
A division of Lammert Publications, Inc.
San Antonio, Texas

Houston Past and Present, 1836-1996,
needlepoint tapestry designed and created
by the Lone Star Chapter of the American
Needlepoint Guild. Presented to the city
on the occasion of its sesquicentennial
celebration, the 8' ~ 8' artwork hangs
in the the Julia Ideson Building of the
Houston Public Library.

FOREWORD

When Barbara and I moved to Houston 38 years ago, we were immediately impressed by the city that we came to call home. Even as newcomers, we immediately discovered a wonderful sense of community and admired the energy and vision with which Houston's leaders and citizens worked together to build a dynamic city.

Through my travels around the country and the world, I've proudly learned that Houston's reputation for excellence and spirit is widespread. We are known for many things, including world-class medical facilities with their miraculous accomplishments in the field of healing; the Johnson Space Center which has contributed so much to exploration and knowledge of the universe; the incredible man-made port which has made Houston an important trading center; the petrochemical, engineering, and technological industries, which stagger the imagination; the many cultural opportunities, ranging from the ballet and theater to the great rodeo and livestock show; and the wide variety of sports events.

But at the top of this impressive list of assets must be the people themselves. A highly-diverse group of people call Houston home, but they all have at least one very important trait in common: Texas hospitality and friendliness.

The history of Houston stands out as a unique example to the world of what can be accomplished through American enterprise and ingenuity. It is an amazing story that needs to be told and one that every Houstonian needs to know. The importance of the past cannot be overestimated. What has gone before is a foundation for the future. As we prepare for the approaching new century, it is especially important that our past be recognized and preserved for future generations.

I commend the Greater Houston Preservation Alliance for producing *Historic Houston* in order that all Houstonians will have an increased opportunity to learn about the extraordinary heritage that is ours. As we continue along the path blazed by those who have gone before, let us commit to building on our rich history in order to create a stronger, more dynamic, and even greater city for tomorrow.

George Bush

Main Street, 1915.

CONTENTS

6	PROLOGUE	
7	CHAPTER 1	*indians, explorers, and pioneers*
19	CHAPTER 2	*a new town in a new nation*
33	CHAPTER 3	*growth of the commercial emporium*
45	CHAPTER 4	*Houston in the Gilded Age*
61	CHAPTER 5	*black gold on the bayou*
73	CHAPTER 6	*between the wars*
85	CHAPTER 7	*years of triumph and turmoil*
101	CHAPTER 8	*space city USA*
108	EPILOGUE	
109	PRESERVING HOUSTON'S HERITAGE	
118	SHARING THE HERITAGE	

First Edition
Copyright © 1997 by Historical Publishing Network
All rights reserved. No part of this book may be produced in any form or by any means, electronic or mechanical, including photocopying, without permission in writing from the publisher. All inquiries should be addressed to Historical Publishing Network, 8491 Leslie Road, San Antonio, Texas 78254. Phone (210) 688-9008.

ISBN: 0-9654999-1-X

Library of Congress Catalog Card Number: 97-077669

author:	Betty Trapp Chapman
publisher:	Ron Lammert
cover artist:	Grace Spaulding John
designer	Charles A. Newton, III
vice president	
project coordinator:	Barry Black
"Sharing the Heritage"	
representatives:	Barbara Frank
	Rod Ethridge
	Joe Neely
	Gene Peeples
administration:	Dee Steidle
	Debby Smith
contributing writers for	
"Sharing the Heritage":	Anne Feltus
	Dr. Bruce Clark
	Kathleen Morrow

PROLOGUE

On August 30, 1836, an advertisement for a real estate venture appeared in the *Telegraph and Texas Register*. It read:

THE TOWN OF HOUSTON

Situated at the head of navigation, on the West bank of Buffalo Bayou, is now for the first time brought to public notice because, until now, the proprietors were not ready to offer it to the public, with the advantages of capital and improvements.

The town of Houston is located at a point on the river which must ever command the trade of the largest and richest portion of Texas. By reference to the map, it will at this time be seen that the trade of the San Jacinto, Spring Creek, New Kentucky and the Brazos, above and below Fort Bend, must necessarily come to this place, and will warrant the employment of at least ONE MILLION DOLLARS of capital, and when the rich lands of this country shall be settled, a trade will flow to it, making it, beyond all doubt, the great interior commercial emporium of Texas.

The town of Houston is distant 15 miles from the Brazos river, 30 miles, a little North of East, from San Felipe, 60 miles from Washington, 40 miles from Lake Creek, 30 miles South West from New Kentucky, and 15 miles by water and 8 or 10 by land above Harrisburg. Tide water runs to this place and the lowest depth of water is about six feet. Vessels from New Orleans or New York can sail without obstacle to this place, and steamboats of the largest class can run down to Galveston Island in 8 or 10 hours, in all seasons of the year. It is but a few hours sail down the bay, where one may take an excursion of pleasure and enjoy the luxuries of fish, fowl, oysters and sea bathing. Galveston harbor being the only one in which vessels drawing a large draft of water can navigate, must necessarily render the Island the great naval and commercial depot of the country.

The town of Houston must be the place where arms, ammunitions and provisions for the government will be stored, because, situated in the very heart of the country, it combines security and the means of easy distribution, and a national armory will no doubt very soon be established at this point.

There is no place in Texas more healthy, having an abundance of excellent spring water, and enjoying the sea breeze in all its freshness. No place in Texas possesses so many advantages for building, having Pine, Ash, Cedar and Oak in inexhaustible quantities; also the tall and beautiful Magnolia grows in abundance. In the vicinity are fine quarries of stone.

Nature appears to have designated this place for the future seat of Government. It is handsome and beautifully elevated, salubrious and well watered, and now in the very heart or centre of population, and will be so for a length of time to come. It combines two important advantages: a communication with the coast and foreign countries, and with the different portions of the Republic. As the country shall improve, rail roads will become in use, and will be extended from this point to the Brazos, and up the same, also from this up to the head waters of San Jacinto, embracing that rich country, and in a few years the whole trade of the upper Brazos will make its way into Galveston Bay through this channel.

Preparations are now being made to erect a water Saw Mill, and a large Public House for accommodation, will soon be opened. Steamboats now run in this river, and will in a short time commence running regularly to the Island.

The proprietors offer the lots for sale on moderate terms to those who desire to improve them, and invite the public to examine for themselves.

These words were a vivid though perhaps somewhat exaggerated description of what must have seemed to readers an ideal place to settle. They touted the location, climate, natural resources, commercial potential, and recreational advantages of a town which was intended to become the most important trade center in Texas.

The boldness and self-confidence of their advertising matched the optimism and ambition of the proprietors of the proposed town. These traits would be exemplified again and again by Houston's leaders in the years ahead.

The plan of these speculators succeeded far beyond their expectations. Not only did the hamlet on the bayou become a giant among Texas cities; it also grew to become a metropolis of national and international repute.

How this was accomplished is the story of a people with a vision of the future and a conviction that any goal can be achieved. When problems have arisen, they have only stimulated bigger dreams and more vigorous efforts to succeed. This "can-do" spirit has characterized Houston since its founding in 1836, and promises to continue into the twenty-first century. Houston's story is in the best of American tradition.

Carancahueses

Carancahueses by Lino Sanchéz y Tapia,
watercolor, ca. 1835. This representation of
the Karankawas was done by Sanchéz
following an expedition into Texas led by
French naturalist Jean Louis Berlandier,
who documented the many cultures in the
region. This painting is the only known
picture of the Karankawa tribes executed
before they became extinct.
COURTESY GILCREASE MUSEUM, TULSA, OKLAHOMA.

INDIANS, EXPLORERS, AND PIONEERS

At the beginning of the nineteenth century, the bayou country of the Texas coast appeared as a hostile, foreboding region to American and European settlers. The rains and heat were merciless; streams often swelled over their banks and washed across the country-side; storms pulled trees from the ground by the roots and hammered the coast with tidal waves. During warm seasons giant mosquitoes made life miserable. Few settlers of any nationality had ever attempted to live in this environment. Occasional travelers to the area, finding it decidedly inhospitable, had moved on. For the most part, the region was unknown and uninhabited.

The first recorded impression of this swampy marshland was the narrative of Álvar Núñez Cabeza de Vaca, who was shipwrecked on the Texas coast in 1528. The entire Gulf Coast had been mapped earlier by Alonzo Álvarez de Piñeda, who in 1519 sailed along the coast from the Florida keys to Veracruz. There is no evidence, however, that Piñeda and his party disembarked onto Texas land.

This surge of exploration had been fueled by Christopher Columbus's discovery of the New

World in 1492. European nations competed against each other in a global search for riches and a quest for power. Ships and men were sent to establish colonies throughout the world. Spain became one of the most dominant forces in this exploration, soon controlling the Philippine Islands, a large part of North America, and all of South America except Brazil.

From the beginning, the expedition of which Cabeza de Vaca was treasurer and second-in-command was beset by misfortune. Under the command of Pánfilo Narváez, their fleet sailed in early 1528 from Spain to Cuba and then to the west coast of present-day Florida, where they hoped to establish a colony. (At the time of early Spanish explorations, the name "Florida" applied to the entire Gulf Coast area, from the province of Pánuco in Mexico all the way to the Florida peninsula.) After leaving Cuba, a hurricane, desertions, and geographical miscalculations reduced the number of men from 400 to fewer than 250. They abandoned their ships and marched into the interior where they stayed for three months. Beleaguered by hostile natives and suffering a shortage of food, the Spaniards decided to leave and improvised five barges, which they rigged with sails made from their clothing. Three of the barges were lost at sea, and after six weeks the remaining

two went aground on the Texas coast, probably in the vicinity of present-day Galveston.

As the Spaniards struggled ashore, they encountered natives, possibly Karankawa Indians, who claimed as their territory the coastal area from Galveston Bay to the Nueces River. In spite of their savage appearance, the natives proved to be friendly and shared food and shelter with their visitors. Since the Karankawas did not practice agriculture, their food supply depended on the natural surroundings in any given season. During the fall they camped on the offshore islands, catching fish in cane weirs and eating the root of the water chinquapin. By midwinter these underwater plants began to grow, making the roots useless as food. The bands would then move to the mainland shore where they gathered oysters, clams, and other shellfish and hunted wild animals with their chief weapon, a long bow and arrows. In the spring, berries were gathered. During the summer months the Karankawas returned to the lagoons and islands. Occasionally they would wrestle an alligator until it drowned, eat its tail meat, and use the fat as a body oil to repel mosquitoes. No food was continuously plentiful. When the supply was totally depleted, the natives were sometimes driven to eat dirt or animal dung.

Right: Karankawa hut. Based on contemporary accounts, this Karankawa dwelling was reconstructed utilizing materials indigenous to the Gulf Coast: willow, dwarf palmetto, and cattail leaves.

PHOTO BY AUTHOR. EXHIBIT: BAYTOWN HISTORICAL MUSEUM, BAYTOWN, TEXAS.

Below: "Nueva Hispania Tabula Nova," published in Claudius Ptolemy, La Geografia, Venice, 1561. This map of New Spain, improved over previous ones, shows place names revealing the explorations of Cabeza de Vaca and Piñeda.

COURTESY HOUSTON METROPOLITAN RESEARCH CENTER, HOUSTON PUBLIC LIBRARY.

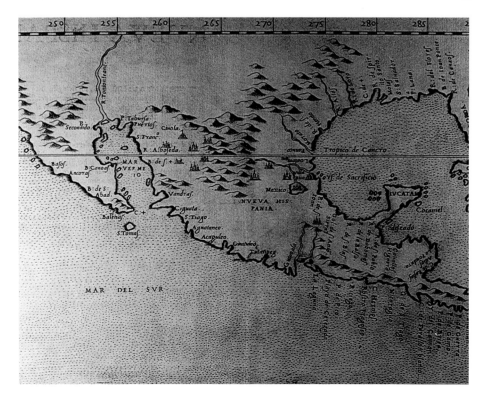

While the Karankawas have often been depicted as cannibals, there is little historical or archeological evidence to support this interpretation. Human flesh may have been occasionally consumed ritualistically, as has been recorded among other preliterate cultures, but it was not a part of their regular diet. Cabeza de Vaca, in fact, noted in his writings that the Indians were shocked and repulsed when the starving Spaniards ate their dead companions.

Since the Indians were constantly moving in search of food, their homes were temporary. Huts consisted of bent-willow poles covered in summer with grass mats and in winter by hides. The floor was made of crushed oyster shell upon which skins were placed as bedding. The mainland was favored in the winter not only because of the food supply but also because the dense forests offered protection from the cold winds, as well as an abundance of firewood.

The Karankawas' nomadic existence was facilitated by the use of dugout canoes fashioned from tree trunks. Families could easily load their few possessions into a canoe and propel themselves to a new location. Labor was strictly divided according to gender. Males hunted and fished; females constructed the dwellings, collected firewood, prepared food, gathered nuts and berries, made animal skins into useful items, and tended the young. Cabeza de Vaca noted in his journal that "their women toil incessantly." He also remarked that "these people love their offspring more than any in the world and treat them very mildly."

The acceptance which Cabeza de Vaca and his companions were accorded turned into a harsh enslavement when many of the natives died of dysentery. Blaming the white men for infecting them with this disease, the Karankawas made slaves of the remaining Spaniards. After a year of near starvation and harsh treatment, made even more unbearable by the bitterly cold weather, Cabeza de Vaca managed to escape the island, which he had named Malhado (Island of Doom), and made his way across the bay to trade with the mainland natives, probably members of the Akokisa tribes.

He described this inland area as having woodlands and rolling plains bordered by flowing rivers with banks lined with pecan trees. Since he was regarded as a neutral by the natives there, he was allowed to have extensive access to the interior lands. He probably traveled across what is presently Harris County and may have gone as far as Oklahoma. From the coastal region he gathered sea snails, conch shells, sea beads, and mesquite beans. Further inland these items were traded for skins, red ochre, hard cane, flint, animal sinews, and tassels of deer hair.

Cabeza de Vaca pursued this trade for many months. Not until 1532, four years after his capture, was he able to leave and begin his flight on foot to Mexico. Accompanied by three other survivors, he reached Culiacán, a Spanish outpost near the Pacific coast of Mexico, in 1536. Cabeza de Vaca's narrative, *La relación*, published in 1542, created an awareness of the vast territory along the Gulf Coast. For the next three hundred years European explorers would periodically seek to tame and exploit the region.

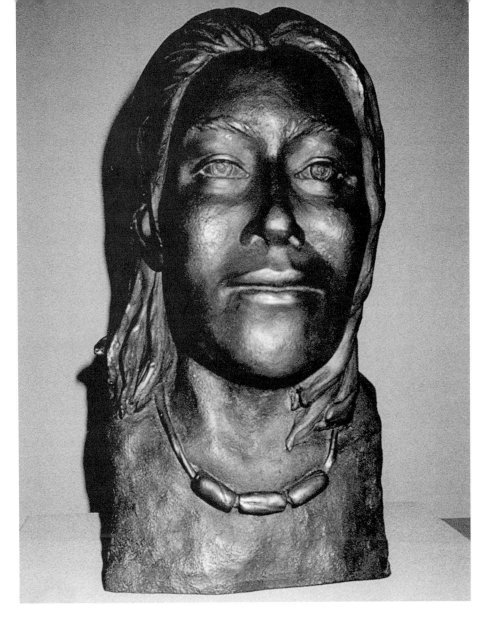

Aboriginal female, Galveston Island, ca. 1500 A.D. Working from a female Texas Coastal Indian skull recovered in archeological excavations in 1962, the face was reconstructed in clay by forensic sculptor Betty Pat Gatliff and then cast in bronze.

PHOTO BY AUTHOR. EXHIBIT: THE HERITAGE SOCIETY MUSEUM, HOUSTON.

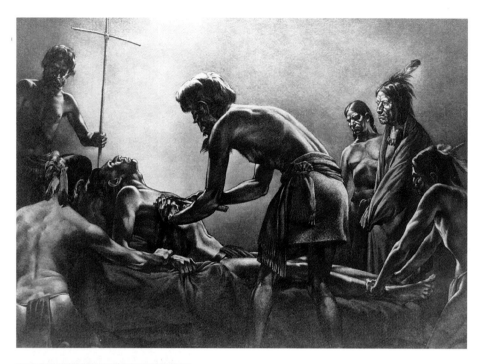

Top: Cabeza de Vaca removing an arrow from the chest of an Indian. *According to his account in La relacion, Cabeza de Vaca, who acted as a medicine man among the Indians, performed surgery by using a needle made of deer bone and sutures made from deer skin. Texas artist Tom Lea commemorated the event in this painting which hangs in medical schools throughout the nation.*

Above: Title page, La relación y comentarios del governador Alvar Nuñez Cabeça de Vaca de lo acaescido en las dos jordanos que hizo a las Indias *by Álvar Nuñez Cabeza de Vaca. Cabeza de Vaca's book was the first published eyewitness account of Texas. This hand-colored woodcut appeared as the title page in the second edition, published in 1555.*

The Spaniards were the most persistent explorers in North America. The *conquistadores* of Francisco Vázquez de Coronado came first in search of the Seven Cities of Cíbola, about which Cabeza de Vaca had told wondrous tales. Coronado and his men then traveled further east seeking Gran Quivira, another area supposedly abounding in wealth. They were unsuccessful in finding riches; but men seeking gold, land, or slaves continued to cross the Rio Grande. They called the new country by various names: Amichel; the New Philippines; and finally Tejas, which in time became Texas. Through the explorations of Piñeda, Cabeza de Vaca, Coronado, and Hernando de Soto, the Spanish claimed this vast territory. However, when they failed to discover gold, they had no reason to explore further. A hundred years would pass before Spain again became interested in its Texas province, and this interest would be spurred by a rival power.

France had established a claim to Texas through the explorations of Rene Robert Cavalier, Sieur de La Salle and his establishment in 1685 of Fort St. Louis on the Texas coast. In the last half of the seventeenth century French traders working their way west of the Mississippi River were attracted by the abundance of game and pelts in this region. They realized that the area was not only rich in natural resources, but it also had natives with whom they could trade.

Spanish rulers, alarmed by the growing French intrusion into the area, tried to assert their authority by encouraging further Spanish settlement. When Franciscan monks from Spain proposed a spiritual conquest of Texas through the establishment of missions, their plan was eagerly adopted with the hope that the natives would become loyal Spanish subjects. By 1756 a dozen missions had been established in Texas, including Nuestra Señora de la Luz north of present-day Trinity Bay. Nevertheless, the upper coastal area remained relatively unexplored and unknown.

In 1767 a special investigator, the Marqués de Rubí, was directed by the Spanish Crown to travel across Texas to evaluate the usefulness of the missions. Finding that most local Indians were uninterested in mission life, he recommended closing all missions east of San Antonio. In his diaries Rubí noted that his group camped on the Rio San Jacinto and the Arroyo Sabino (Cypress Creek) just north of present-day Houston. This was one of the few Spanish expeditions that traversed the coastal region.

The century-long rivalry between Spain and France ended in 1763 when France lost her North American empire at the close of the Seven Years' War, at which time Spanish territory extended eastward to the Mississippi River. A new threat to Spanish sovereignty, however, was poised on the eastern horizon. In 1803, the youthful United States purchased Louisiana without defining its western boundary. The United States suggested that the Louisiana Purchase should extend to the Rio Grande, while Spain insisted that the Sabine River was the boundary. Not until 1819 was the dispute finally settled by the Adams-Onis Treaty, which validated the Spanish claim. By that time, however, Spain was facing a movement by Mexican republicans to gain their independence. Spanish authorities had reason to suspect that the Americans coveted Texas. Scores of United States residents had already entered the territory to trade or to explore, and frequent filibustering expeditions were conducted in an effort to wrest control from Spain.

In 1820, however, Texas was still a relatively empty land. Spain had been unable to recruit permanent settlers to this remote area.

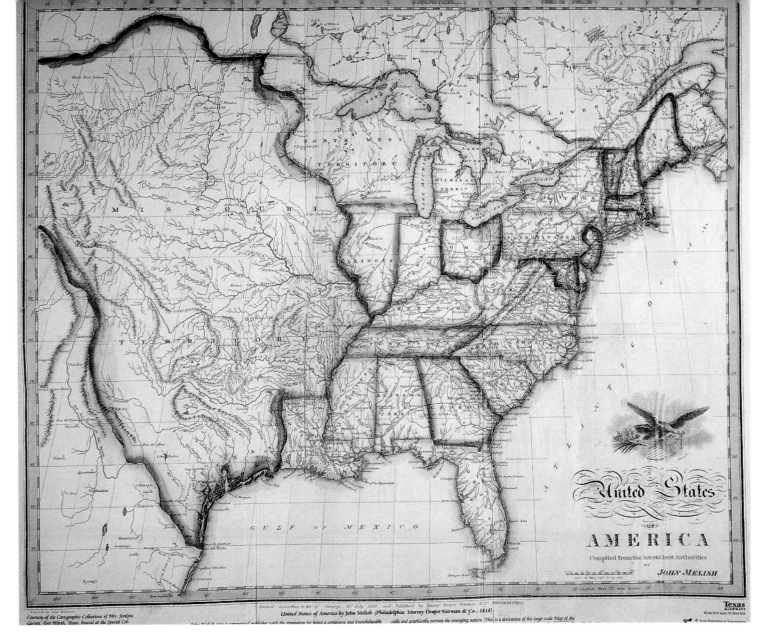

United States of America by John Melish (Philadelphia: Murray Draper Fairman &c., 1818)

The mission system, established to convert and to settle the natives as allies, had failed. The Spanish province still had only a few thousand Mexican and Indian residents clustered around the presidio and missions of San Antonio de Bexar, at the presidio of La Bahía at Goliad, at the village of Nacogdoches close to the Sabine River border with Louisiana, and along the lower Rio Grande River. The Spanish authorities realized that the vast countryside to the north and east provided a buffer zone against foreign incursions; but for it to be an effective tool, a larger population was needed. Reluctantly, they decided to open the area to controlled colonization through the *empresario* system by which individuals would receive land grants for settlement.

The first of these Spanish grants was given to Moses Austin in January 1821. The Connecticut-born Austin, who had been a mining operator in Missouri, was ruined financially in the Panic of 1819. When he learned of conditions in Texas, he applied for a grant to bring colonists into the region. He hoped that the profits from selling the Texas land to immigrants would enable him to regain his financial security. Austin died before he could effect his plan, and the project was then assumed by his twenty-seven-year-old son, Stephen.

Mexico had overthrown its Spanish rulers, and in February 1821 became an independent nation. With the first colonists already on their way to Texas, Stephen F. Austin sought the new government's approval of the grant which had been made by Spain to his father. Austin, one of twenty-six empresarios in early Texas, was uniquely qualified for his role. A graduate of Transylvania University in Lexington, Kentucky, and a student of the law, Austin had served as a member of the Missouri Territorial Legislature and as a cir-

Above: United States of America by John Melish, 1818. The map illustrates the extent of the emerging nation and the close proximity of Texas to American soil.

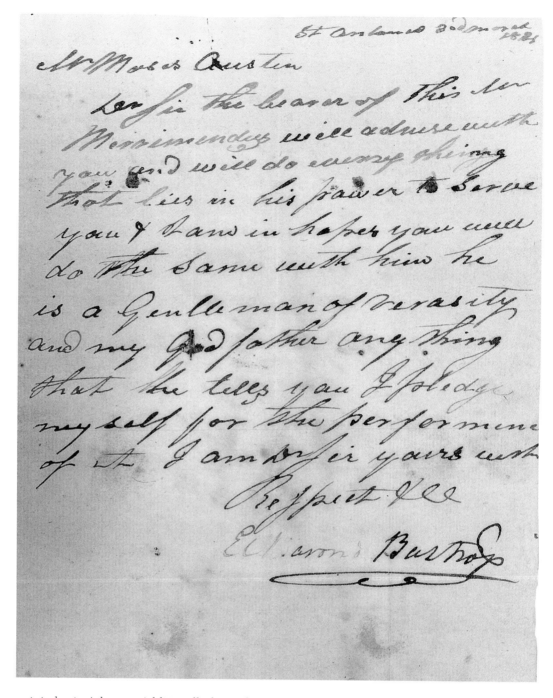

Letter to Moses Austin, March 2, 1821 from Baron de Bastrop, colonial legislator. In the letter Bastrop offers support to Moses Austin in his attempt to receive a grant from the Spanish government. Bastrop later served Stephen F. Austin by traveling across Austin's colony legalizing titles to the colonists' land.

cuit judge in Arkansas. Additionally, he spoke Spanish fluently and was unusually skilled in working with people.

Austin carefully selected the land for his first colony. As he rode between the Brazos and Colorado rivers, he rejoiced at the rich soil, superior pastures, proximity to the sea, and abundance of wildlife. Enthusiastically claiming his grant, he declared that "Texas as a country may be advantageously compared with any portion of North America."

Austin's contract with Mexico stated that a colonizer could bring in persons who would be required to take the oath of Mexican citizenship and to embrace Roman Catholicism, the state religion. For a fee of sixty dollars paid to the state, these newcomers were entitled to a *sitio* (a league or 4,428 acres) to be used for ranching, or one *labor* (177 acres) to be used for growing crops. Most settlers applied for the combined acreage, which equated to little more than one cent per acre. Since land in the United States was selling for $1.25 per acre, Austin had no trouble attracting colonists. Under the terms of the contract he would receive for himself twenty-three thousand acres for every one hundred families he brought.

Immigrants from the United States began arriving at Galveston in 1822, responding to the news of Mexican independence and to advertisements which Austin had placed in Mississippi Valley newspapers. A group of them settled along the east side of the San Jacinto River. After a few months spent struggling to exist, some returned to the United States. One who remained was Jane Wilkins. Mrs. Wilkins apparently decided to travel west on Buffalo Bayou in 1823 to seek a better location. At a bend in the bayou near what would eventually become the center of downtown Houston, she built a temporary dwelling, which she occupied until 1824 when she moved to San Felipe de Austin, a settlement on the Brazos River. John D. Taylor, who also resided first on the San Jacinto River, moved his family up Buffalo Bayou in 1823 and established his residence at a place he called Pine Point (known today as Piney Point Village in the Spring Branch area of Houston). These two families were among the earliest documented residents in the area that would become Houston.

On January 3, 1823, Austin's grant was at long last officially confirmed by the Mexican government. The boundaries were: on the north, the Camino Real (a road from Natchitoches, Louisiana, to San Antonio de

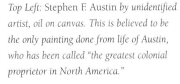

Bexar); on the west, the Lavaca River; on the east, Chocolate Bayou; and on the south, the Gulf of Mexico. The region which would eventually encompass Harris County was initially outside Austin's colony. However, in

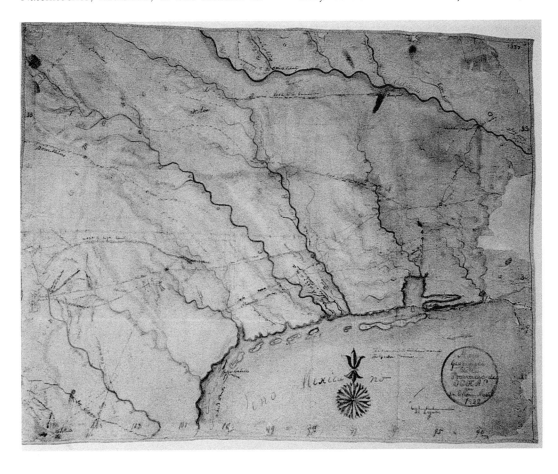

Right: Household items uncovered by University of Houston archeologists at the site of the George R. Brown Convention Center. The teams determined that Jane Wilkins's home was located at that spot in 1822; from the excavated artifacts they were able to document many aspects of life in the Wilkins household.

PHOTO BY AUTHOR. EXHIBIT: THE HERITAGE SOCIETY MUSEUM, HOUSTON.

Below: Cayuga by A. L. Tauch, oil on canvas. The Cayuga, which served as the floating capital of the newly-formed Republic of Texas in April 1836, was the first commercially successful steamboat in Texas. Under the command of Captain William R. Harris, it plied the Brazos River, Galveston Bay, and Buffalo Bayou for several years, leading the way for increased water traffic in the area.

COURTESY BAYTOWN HISTORICAL MUSEUM, BAYTOWN, TEXAS.

1824, Austin received permission to extend his eastern boundary to incorporate the area along Buffalo Bayou and the San Jacinto River into his colony.

Austin's first contract was for three hundred families, later referred to as the Old Three Hundred. Under the terms of the contract, twenty-five families received title to land within the present boundaries of Harris County. Under subsequent contracts, Austin issued twenty-two more patents in Harris County between 1828 and 1832, when the colonial phase ended. In order to perfect the title, each recipient was required to occupy the land and to make improvements to it. In return the settler was exempted from customs duties for seven years and from general taxation for ten years.

Austin was as careful in selecting his colonists as he had been in choosing his land. He adamantly refused entry to any "lawless fugitive," and in order to ensure that his settlers were persons of integrity, he required character references. He expected them to work hard and to cooperate with one another as they established new homes for their families. The aspiring new Texans, many having suffered financial reversals in the United States, were land-hungry and eager to begin anew. As indicated by their ability to survive in an often-hostile environment, they proved to be a tough and hardy lot.

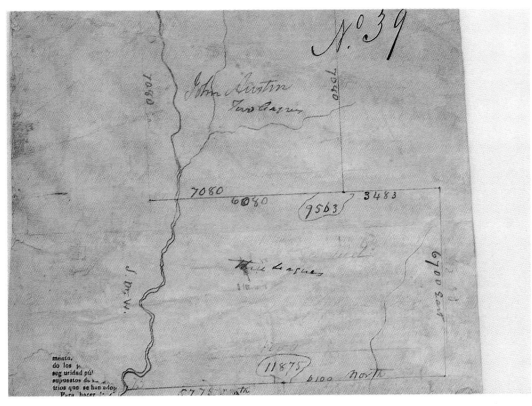

Left: Survey of John Austin's two-league grant, 1824. The map was kept in Stephen Austin's office in San Felipe, pasted to an old Mexican newspaper. Fragments of the newspaper can be seen on the document.
COURTESY TEXAS GENERAL LAND OFFICE.

Below: Certificate of land title to Robert Wilson, 1830. Wilson settled near Clear Creek as an Austin colonist and later became one of Houston's first residents.
COURTESY HOUSTON ENDOWMENT, INC. ARCHIVES.

One who received land was John Austin (who may have been distantly related to Stephen F. Austin). His deed described the site as "two leagues of land in the form of a square on the Buffalo Bayou at the place where the two main branches of said Bayou come together to swell the stream." John Austin was cited as deserving this favor "on account of his qualifications and means, his application to agriculture, rearing of cattle and industry." The time-honored tradition with which Austin received his land is recorded in his grant, which read "The said John Austin, on being given the real and personal possession of said land, shouted aloud, pulled grass, threw stones, planted stakes, and performed the other necessary ceremonies." Unfortunately, records do not reveal what use John Austin made of his 8,856 acres except for his purchase of a cotton gin, which had been established on the land prior to 1824, and which he continued to operate. He established his residence at another location in the colony where he founded the town of Brazoria on land belonging to Stephen F. Austin. John Austin's grant on Buffalo Bayou, however, would receive attention as the site chosen for the town of Houston some years later.

John R. Harris was one of the Old Three Hundred who lost no time in developing his land. He selected his league at the junction of Buffalo and Bray's bayous. Harris considered this locale to be the head of navigation on Buffalo Bayou. He established a trading post there, and a steady flow of goods moved between his business and New Orleans on his fleet of schooners. In 1827 Harris platted the first town in the area, naming it Harrisburg. To facilitate the laborious process of hewing logs for houses, Harris built a steam sawmill. Although the streets were dusty trails and the houses far from permanent, the little community became a thriving port with supplies and new settlers arriving almost every week.

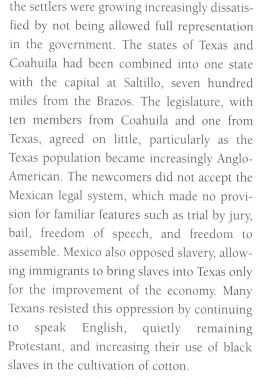

Above: The Old Place. This braced-frame wood dwelling was typical of the homes built by Austin's Old Three Hundred. Originally located on the banks of Clear Creek, it is thought to have been erected by settler John R. Williams in 1823. Today, as the oldest extant structure in Harris County, it is a house museum in Sam Houston Park.
PHOTO BY AUTHOR.

Below: The Dodson Flag, carried into battle in 1835 at San Antonio by the Harrisburg militia unit. Sarah Dodson, whose husband was a lieutenant in the unit, stitched the flag from squares of fabric. As Texas's first "Lone Star" flag, it was later flown at the convention in Washington when independence was declared.
COURTESY GLENDALE CEMETERY ASSOCIATION, HOUSTON.

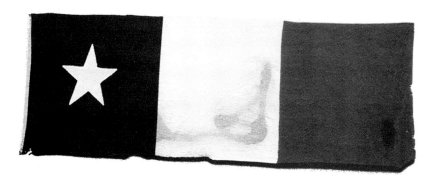

Harris County's other pioneers in the Old Three Hundred included William Bloodgood, Enoch Brinson, Moses Callahan and Allen Vince (unmarried men could jointly receive land), John Brown, Thomas Earle, David Harris, William Harris and David Carpenter, Dr. Johnson Hunter, Humphrey Jackson, Nathaniel Lynch, Luke Moore, Arthur McCormick, Frederick Rankin, William Scott, Christian Smith, James Strange, John Taylor, Ezekiel Thomas, Richard and Robert Vince, William Vince, Amy White, Reuben White, and William Whitlock. Mrs. White, a forty-nine-year-old widow, was one of fewer than a dozen single women who petitioned as household heads to receive land from Austin.

By 1830 Austin's first colony claimed 4,248 residents. Farmers were prospering on the rich soil, and merchants and traders had a steady clientele. Despite the prosperity and outward appearance of tranquility, however,

the settlers were growing increasingly dissatisfied by not being allowed full representation in the government. The states of Texas and Coahuila had been combined into one state with the capital at Saltillo, seven hundred miles from the Brazos. The legislature, with ten members from Coahuila and one from Texas, agreed on little, particularly as the Texas population became increasingly Anglo-American. The newcomers did not accept the Mexican legal system, which made no provision for familiar features such as trial by jury, bail, freedom of speech, and freedom to assemble. Mexico also opposed slavery, allowing immigrants to bring slaves into Texas only for the improvement of the economy. Many Texans resisted this oppression by continuing to speak English, quietly remaining Protestant, and increasing their use of black slaves in the cultivation of cotton.

Recognizing that the Americans in Texas outnumbered Mexicans and that they resisted assimilation, the Mexican government instituted the Law of April 6, 1830, banning further American immigration into the colonies and prohibiting the importation of slaves. At the same time the Mexican government canceled the exemption from Mexican fees and duties, which the colonists had enjoyed, and located customs garrisons at points along the Gulf Coast to ensure the collection of taxes. The settlers along the lower reaches of Buffalo Bayou, accustomed to reasonably unhampered commerce, felt the pinch of new taxes.

As oppressive measures continued, the Texans began more vocally to demand separate statehood for Texas. At a meeting in April 1833, with the Nacogdoches delegate Sam Houston serving as chairman of the drafting committee, a constitution for a separate state was drawn up. The document provided for slavery and established on paper a government much like that of most of the southern United States.

Stephen Austin traveled to Mexico City to present this proposal to the government there. After his arrival, he dispatched a letter back to Texas urging that immediate steps be taken to form a separate state within the Republic of Mexico. The letter was intercepted, and Austin was arrested and held for eighteen

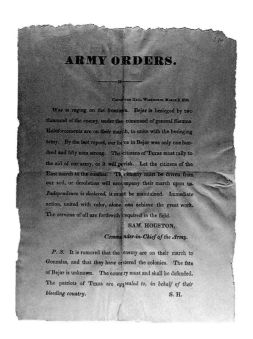

Events of the following month—the disaster at the Alamo, the defeat of Fannin's forces at Goliad, and Santa Anna's pursuit of the Texas army across the Austin colony—are well known in the annals of Texas history. Harrisburg would play a prominent role in the final weeks of the struggle for independence. At the close of the convention in Washington, in the way of Santa Anna's steadily advancing army, the Texas cabinet agreed to move the seat of government to Harrisburg. The home of Jane Harris, widow of John R. Harris, was used as government headquarters. During the next few weeks the *Cayuga* moved up and down Buffalo Bayou and all about the bay taking refugees to Anahuac; men and timber to Galveston, where a fort was being built; and supplies, including whiskey "suitable for genteel men to drink," to the government at Harrisburg.

By this time hundreds of Texans were also fleeing to the safety of the United States. Families, many with husbands and fathers away in the army, packed what belongings they could carry on horseback, wagons, or on foot, and hurriedly left their homes. One refugee vividly described the scene: "Houses were standing open, the beds unmade, the breakfast things still on the tables, cribs full of corn, smoke houses full of bacon, all abandoned." Participants in the Runaway Scrape, as it came to be called, followed Buffalo Bayou to Nathaniel Lynch's ferry landing on the San Jacinto River. Observers estimated that five thousand people arrived at the landing, some waiting as long as three days to cross. One noted that the "prairie near Lynch's resembled a camp meeting; it was covered with carts, wagons, horses, mules, tents, women, and children, and all the baggage of a flying multitude." Some continued by wagon on the road leading to Liberty and on to Louisiana. Others preferred to take a boat to Galveston Island, hoping to find a ship going to New Orleans.

As Mexican forces neared Harrisburg, Mrs. Harris and the remaining government officials abandoned their town and traveled to Galveston aboard the *Cayuga*. When Santa Anna reached the deserted village on April 15, he ordered that it be burned. Three days later the weary Texas army arrived opposite Harrisburg, and there they planned their strategy. On the afternoon of

Above: David Burnet, ad interim president of the Republic of Texas, 1836. Burnet had settled along the San Jacinto River in 1831 after trying unsuccessfully to attract colonists to his own empresario grant near Nacogdoches. Although he served in several government posts while maintaining his residence in Harris County, his politics were not popular in Texas and he never achieved the recognition he sought.

COURTESY BAYTOWN HISTORICAL MUSEUM, BAYTOWN, TEXAS.

Above, left: Army Orders, March 2, 1836. In March of 1836 the Texas cause seemed hopeless. In an effort to rally the people to the defense of Texas, Sam Houston published his Army Orders, which were issued from the convention in Washington just four days before the fall of the Alamo.

COURTESY SPECIAL COLLECTIONS, HOUSTON PUBLIC LIBRARY.

months. During this time Mexico experienced a political change which would profoundly affect Texas. Antonio López de Santa Anna seized power in Mexico, abolished the republican principles of the government by declaring the Constitution of 1824 invalid, and placed control in the central government. By these actions, Santa Anna established himself as a virtual dictator.

In the fall of 1835, the unhappy Texans called for citizens to meet at San Felipe de Austin to determine their course of action. However, before the elected delegates could convene, open warfare erupted. After a clash at Gonzales, a volunteer Texas army formed and marched on San Antonio. The Mexican forces were successfully driven back by this "Army of the People," and Texans now believed that complete independence was their only option.

A convention was called on March 2, 1836, at the town of Washington, located on the Brazos River. The fifty-nine delegates included three from the Harrisburg Municipality: Lorenzo de Zavala, Andrew Briscoe, and John W. Moore. The convention adjourned seventeen days later, having adopted a declaration of independence, written a constitution, and established an executive government for a new nation. David G. Burnet was elected President ad interim with de Zavala as Vice President. Sam Houston was appointed commander-in-chief and was ordered to recruit an army immediately.

Right: General Sam Houston *by Stephen Seymour Thomas, oil on canvas, 1893. The portrait, painted for the Texas Building at the Chicago World's Fair in 1893, depicts Houston at the decisive moment in which he tells his band of rebels to charge the Mexican lines at San Jacinto.*
COURTESY SAN JACINTO MUSEUM OF HISTORY.

Below: The Battle of San Jacinto *by Henry A. McArdle, oil on canvas, 1898.*
COURTESY STATE PRESERVATION BOARD.

the twenty-first, Houston's forces met those of Santa Anna on Peggy McCormick's league of land beside the San Jacinto River. After a battle that lasted only eighteen minutes, the Texans emerged as victors. Independence was now a reality.

The residents of the area did not learn the fate of their property until they began returning home in the weeks following the war. The sawmill at Harrisburg had been burned, as had most homes. Livestock had been stolen and crops destroyed. As families planned their rebuilding in the midst of this turmoil, an idea was born in the fertile minds of two brothers from New York.

A new town would soon emerge in this new nation.

A NEW TOWN IN A NEW NATION

*Presbyterian, Methodist and Baptist
Churches, Houston, Texas, March 20th,
1852 by Thomas Flintoff, watercolor.
The watercolor depicts the meeting places
of three pioneer congregations in Houston:
on the left, Methodist; in the center, Baptist;
and on the right, Presbyterian.*
COURTESY JEAN D. B. SALVADO.

The promise of cheap land had lured Augustus Chapman Allen and his younger brother, John Kirby Allen, to Texas in 1832. Settling in Nacogdoches, they successfully bartered Texas land certificates offered by a New York company. When victory was achieved on the San Jacinto battlefield and an independent nation evolved, the Allens saw an opportunity to capitalize on these events. They envisioned streams of immigrants from the United States and Europe pouring into the fledgling Republic, and they were determined to establish its principal center of trade and commerce.

The young Allens had come from the Mohawk River Valley in central New York. John Kirby brought to their partnership a vibrant personality and uncanny salesmanship, while the more taciturn Augustus, a former bookkeeper and mathematics teacher, was a shrewd planner. Augustus was married to Charlotte Baldwin, whose father had acquired a sizable fortune after founding the city of Baldwinsville in Onodaga County, New York. Having observed that developing a city could be extremely profitable, the two Allens combined their talents in a bold new venture.

John Kirby Allen.

COURTESY HOUSTON METROPOLITAN RESEARCH CENTER,
HOUSTON PUBLIC LIBRARY.

Augustus Chapman Allen.

COURTESY HOUSTON METROPOLITAN RESEARCH CENTER,
HOUSTON PUBLIC LIBRARY.

Above, Right: Buffalo Bayou,
nineteenth century.

COURTESY HOUSTON METROPOLITAN RESEARCH CENTER,
HOUSTON PUBLIC LIBRARY.

Their first task was to select a site on a navigable waterway. Galveston Island with its natural harbor was appealing to the Allens, but they were unable to secure the necessary land title. They next examined prospects along Buffalo Bayou, which emptied into Galveston Bay and extended westward into the most highly developed agricultural region of the nation. The San Jacinto campaign and the flight of the Texas government to Harrisburg had called attention to Buffalo Bayou as a link between the interior and the sea. The burned Harrisburg site attracted the Allens because of its location at what was considered the head of navigation on the bayou. However, the death of Harrisburg founder John R. Harris had so involved his estate in litigation that title to the land could not be readily conveyed. The Allens then looked farther up Buffalo Bayou.

This stream had received little attention during the early settlement of the region, and United States envoy George Graham had made no mention of it in a report to his government in 1818. He had, however, urged the United States to develop the commercial potential of Galveston Bay. Stephen F. Austin also recognized this potential, realizing that traffic could move to Galveston Bay on a stream flowing into it and then across the prairies to the Brazos River farmland. The best description of the bayou was given by Joseph Clopper, a resident of the area, who wrote in his journal in 1828: "We enter the mouth of Buffalo Bayou—this is the most remarkable stream I have ever seen—at its junction with the San Jacinto [it] is about 150 yards in breadth having about three fathoms water with little variation in depth as high as Harrisburg—20 miles—the ebbing and flowing of the tides observable about 12 miles close up to each stream [giving it] the appearance of an artificial canal in the design and course of which nature has lent her masterly hand; for its meanderings and beautiful curvatures seem to have been directed by a taste far too exquisite for human attainment."

The beauty of the bayou was undeniable. Oak, magnolia, cypress, sweet gum, and pine trees grew in dense forests along the banks. Spanish moss hung in clumps amidst the foliage. Where boats had not disturbed the stream, the water was clear and surprisingly clean, revealing the buffalo fish for which, according to legend, the bayou was named. Aside from its beauty, Buffalo Bayou was unusual among Texas streams in that it flowed east and west. This meant that the head of navigation on the bayou was only some twenty miles from the heart of the fertile agricultural region along the Brazos River; and unlike the Brazos and other rivers in the area, Buffalo Bayou appeared to have a deep and swift current.

Augustus Allen set out in a skiff to examine the upper reaches of the bayou. He made surveys and recorded soundings ascertaining that the water was sufficiently deep for navigation. When he reached the junction of the Buffalo and White Oak bayous, he decided that this point was actually the head of navigation on the Buffalo. He knew that other settlements in the area were thriving, and felt that this would be an even more advantageous location for a town. He quickly sought the owner of the land. John Austin, who had been granted the two leagues encompassing the site, had died in 1833. His widow, now Mrs. T. F. L. Parrott, was found in Brazoria.

From Mrs. Parrott, the Allens purchased the south half of Austin's original lower league. The price was five thousand dollars, of which one thousand was in cash and the balance in notes. At the same time, they acquired the western league from William T. Austin, John's brother, for one dollar per acre. The total acquisition was 6,642 acres at an average cost of about $1.42 per acre. The fledgling entrepreneurs, confident that their land speculation would succeed, promised to pay off the entire debt in eighteen months.

The Allens were by no means the only hopeful city fathers on the banks of Buffalo Bayou and Galveston Bay during the 1830s. Speculators hastily laid out Powhatan, Scottsburg, Louisville, San Jacinto, Buffalo, Hamilton, New Washington, and other communities with great expectations, but few, if any, inhabitants. The proliferation of paper cities became a matter of jest to visitors in the area. It seemed to many that almost every enterprising man who came to Texas expected to make a fortune by founding a city. One anonymous visitor observed in 1837: "Should they all succeed, they will no doubt at some day make Texas as famous for her cities as Thebes was for her hundred gates." But while other founders did little more than acquire sites and draw cities on paper, the Allens proved to be shrewd promoters.

They named their town Houston for the hero of San Jacinto who, as the Allens foresaw, would soon be elected President of the Republic of Texas. On August 30, 1836, less than one week after the Allens' purchase of the land, they placed an advertisement in the *Telegraph and Texas Register* and in newspapers as far away as New York, Washington, Mobile, New Orleans, and Louisville. Readers of those papers could not know that the "Town of Houston" existed only in the minds of its founders. They began coming in covered wagons, in schooners and side-wheel steamboats, and on horseback, drawn by the promise of a new town where everyone could begin anew.

One of those attracted to Houston by the advertisement was Francis R. Lubbock. The Allens induced Lubbock to ship a stock of merchandise to Houston, not only preparatory to opening a store, but also to prove that Buffalo Bayou was indeed navigable. The eighty-five-foot steamer *Laura*—the smallest

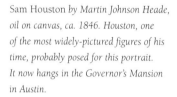

Sam Houston *by Martin Johnson Heade, oil on canvas, ca. 1846. Houston, one of the most widely-pictured figures of his time, probably posed for this portrait. It now hangs in the Governor's Mansion in Austin.*

New Map of Texas with the Contiguous American and Mexican States *by J. H. Young, 1837. Although this map shows the colonial land grants, it also portrays the new republic which emerged after the Texas Revolution.*

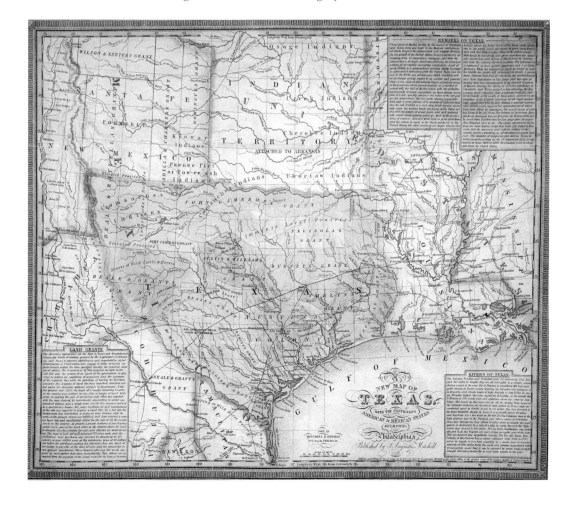

FOR THE CITY OF HOUSTON.

THE REGULAR

PACKET   **STEAMER**

LAURA,

T. W. GRAYSON, MASTER.

WILL leave Marion, on Tuesday, the 21st February, at 4 o'clock, P. M. for the above city, and all intermediate ports. For freight or passage apply on board; or to Aldridge and Davis, Marion, or to Thomas H. Borden. Columbia.

N. B.—The Laura, this trip, will touch at Anahuac.
Columbia, Feb. 20, 1837.   59-1

Advertisement for steamboat trip, February 1837. The Allens hired the Laura to prove the viability of a water route from Galveston to Houston. Upon the Laura's arrival, the headlines of the Telegraph and Texas Register *boldly proclaimed, "The Fact Proved."*

in Texas—was engaged for the trip. The boat reached the site of Harrisburg without mishap, but the twelve miles upstream from there took three days. In his report of the trip, Lubbock wrote, "The slow time was in consequence of the obstructions we were compelled to remove as we progressed. We had to rig what were called Spanish windlasses on the shore to heave the logs and snags out of our way, the passengers all working faithfully.... Just before reaching our destination, a party of us, becoming weary of the steamer, took a yawl and concluded we would hunt for the city. So little evidence could we see of a landing that we passed by the site and ran into White Oak Bayou, only realizing that we must have passed the city when we struck the brush. We then backed down the bayou, and by close observation discovered a road or street laid off from the water's edge. Upon landing we found stakes and footprints indicating that we were in the town tract." When they disembarked, Lubbock and his companions discovered a few tents and several small houses under construction. This was the "Town of Houston" about which they had read.

The newspaper advertisement had suggested that "nature appears to have designated this place for the future seat of government...." John Kirby Allen conducted a persuasive campaign to have his still-unbuilt town selected as the Texas capital. In October 1836, Sam Houston having been elected President a month earlier, the first meeting of the Texas Congress was held at Columbia, the tempo-

rary capital. John Kirby Allen, as a member of the Congress from Nacogdoches, touted Houston as "the most eligible place for the seat of government under the existing state of things." As incentives he promised free land and favorable credit terms, as well as a capitol building, auxiliary government offices, a public house, and a steam sawmill.

Many towns, including Nacogdoches, San Antonio, Goliad, Columbia, Washington, Matagorda, and Velasco, competed for the honor of being named the new capital. When the matter first came before the Congress, the members could not agree on a place. On November 30, upon reconsideration, Houston was selected by a slender majority. Even then, the provisions stated that Houston would be only a temporary capital until 1840, and that the town's proprietors must act on their promise to build a ten thousand dollar capitol building at their own expense. Congress voted to convene in its new capital on April 1, 1837. Step by step the Allens were succeeding in their plan.

Gail and Thomas Borden, publishers of the *Telegraph and Texas Register*, were hired to lay out the city. An assistant, Moses Lapham, did the surveying while the Bordens prepared and printed the maps. Although most of the purchased land lay north of Buffalo Bayou, the Allens decided to locate their town on the south bank. They wanted to use the grid system of streets, a plan popular in the United States and one particularly suited for commercial purposes. The focal point was usually a central street, and in Houston the Bordens made Main Street the principal thoroughfare. Since the boat landing was to be the town's busiest commercial site, Main Street began there and the sixty-two blocks of the original plan extended in an orderly manner from that artery. The Bordens, despite the ridicule of many observers, laid out streets eighty feet wide, asserting that "great steam vehicles will someday traverse the streets of the Town of Houston."

The Allens carefully selected names for their streets. Many of the names chosen—San Jacinto, Fannin, Milam, Travis, Louisiana, Austin—were reminders of the Texas War for Independence. Others—Commerce, Congress,

THE ORIGINAL PLAN OF HOUSTON

Left: Plan of the City of Houston, Gail and Thomas Borden.

COURTESY HOUSTON METROPOLITAN RESEARCH CENTER, HOUSTON PUBLIC LIBRARY.

Below: "Grocerie, 1837" by Mary Austin Holley. Mrs. Holley made the first-known sketches of Houston during a trip in December 1837. The conical structure in the center of this sketch was Henry Kesler's Round Tent, the busiest saloon in town. During this period, grocery and bar room were synonymous.

COURTESY THE CENTER FOR AMERICAN HISTORY, UNIVERSITY OF TEXAS AT AUSTIN.

Brazos, Franklin—reflected aspects of the town's commercial and political activity. The Allens shrewdly named some—Preston, LaBranch, Carolina—for prominent public figures or states who might support the annexation of Texas by the United States. Four blocks were designated for specific purposes: the halls of Congress, the courthouse, a church, and a school.

The Allens also donated land to attract notable prospective residents. Town lots were given to the heroes of the revolution, lawyers, the members of Congress who had provided the slim margin of victory in selecting Houston as the capital, and other influential men from the United States and abroad. Sam Houston was the recipient of an entire block. The framework was in place for the "great interior commercial emporium of Texas," which the Allens had promised.

The first lot was sold by the Houston Town Company on January 1, 1837, for seven hundred dollars. In spite of primitive living conditions, sales were brisk. Although oak, cypress, and cedar trees were plentiful, lumber frequently had to be imported because the new sawmills experienced difficulties in operating. Since both milled lumber and labor were scarce, many new residents were forced to sleep in tents or barrels while others simply camped on the open prairie. Many of the early houses were crudely built by setting frameworks of poles into the ground and covering them with split-pine boards. Few of these primitive constructions were painted or had glass windows. One traveler to Houston described them as "merely patched up shantees of rough boards." Construction began on the temporary capitol, but the lumber ordered from Maine was slow in arriving. As a result, Congress could not meet until May 1, 1837, a month later than had been planned. Even then, there was still no roof on the structure at Main and Texas, so branches were thrown over the top to provide some shelter for the delegates.

In their advertisements, the Allens had

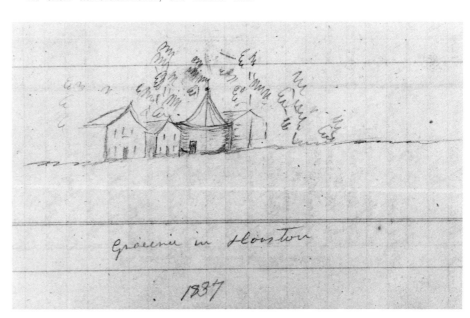

Right: Executive Mansion at Houston, 1837-38. This small, crude frame building with the attached lean-to served as Sam Houston's residence while Houston was capital of the Republic.

accurately described their prospective town as "well watered." Rains were frequent, and mud was deep. Oxen often became bogged in the mire. Standing water bred mosquitoes which were reported to be as large as grasshoppers. In May 1837, the celebrated naturalist, John James Audubon, visited Houston. Arriving on Buffalo Bayou, which was then at flood stage, he described the surrounding area as having "a wild and desolate look." After wading through knee-deep water to visit President Sam Houston, Audubon found "the floors,

benches, and tables of both houses of Congress as well saturated with water as [my] clothes had been in the morning."

Though Houston was frequently plagued by more water than it wanted, little of it was potable. The only drinking water was then found in a few cisterns, at Beauchamp Springs which lay north of the city, or at spots in the bayou. An 1837 visitor noted that "the water in Buffalo Bayou is dirty, filthy, miserable stuff covered with a green scruff."

Despite the rawness and lack of conveniences, Houston continued to attract new residents. Within a few months of its founding, it was home to more than five hundred inhabitants.

In spite of the Allens' statement that "vessels from New Orleans or New York can sail without obstacle to this place," there were many who felt that Buffalo Bayou was not living up to its expectations. The schooner *Rolla* had made the journey up the bayou from Florida, and the *Laura* ran regularly scheduled trips from the

Spotted Sandpiper *by John James Audubon, engraving and watercolor, 1837. On his journey to Texas, Audubon sketched these birds with Buffalo Bayou in the background. Audubon recorded in his notebook how he managed to draw, make notes, and secure specimens as he carried his drawing board strapped about his waist, notebooks in his pocket, and a gun on his shoulder.*
COURTESY LIBRARY OF CONGRESS, WASHINGTON, D. C.

Yellowstone. *Built in 1831 for John Jacob Astor for use in the fur trade on the Missouri River, the Yellowstone was brought to Texas in 1835 for service in the war for independence. After the war it carried cargo and passengers up and down Buffalo Bayou between Houston and Galveston.*
COURTESY SAN JACINTO MUSEUM OF HISTORY.

CHAPTER TWO

25

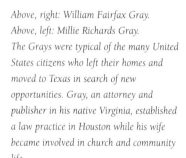

Brazos River farmlands to Houston. Bayou navigation, however, did present problems. The waterway was sometimes impassable because of dense foliage, and the abrupt turns in the bayou required great skill and precision by pilots. Boats frequently ran aground.

To quell complaints about the obstacles to transportation, the Allens arranged to have the 150-foot steamboat *Constitution* visit Houston. Although the vessel arrived safely, the captain found, after pocketing his thousand-dollar fee, that there was not room to turn his vessel around. He could navigate a turn only after backing down the bayou to a bend near Harrisburg. That spot became known as Constitution Bend (and years later would become the Turning Basin of the Houston Ship Channel). Within a year, however, boats were making daily runs between Houston and Galveston Island. A round trip took thirty hours. Realizing that the bayou had become the lifeline of the town, city fathers gradually began making improvements on the waterway.

The bayou was of great importance because survival of the town depended on trade. Houston merchants exchanged such goods as furniture, clothing, farm tools, books, medical supplies, and groceries for produce of the countryside, principally cotton, lumber, livestock, and hides. In 1837 a wholesaler, George Fisher, advertised the arrival on the *Sam Houston* of a stock of shelled almonds, New Orleans sugar, marbled paint, starch, sweet oil, ginger, sweetmeats, honey, Havana leaf tobacco, beans, lard, pork, mackerel, blankets, grass, and gunny sacks as well as general groceries, liquors, and clothing.

Some merchants maintained permanent places of business and cultivated a regular clientele, but auction sales were also common. Real estate, dry goods, and slaves were sold at auction during the trading season, which lasted from September until April. Country produce came into Houston by wagon, though in bad weather the trip could take as long as two or three weeks. The goods were purchased by local merchants and then sent down Buffalo Bayou to Galveston for transfer to oceangoing ships. To complete the cycle, Houston merchants frequently journeyed to Mobile, New Orleans, and New York to purchase new merchandise and arrange for its shipment to Houston.

Cotton remained the principal item of trade. The extraordinary soil of the coastal plain between Galveston Bay and the Brazos River produced some of the richest yields in the entire cotton kingdom of the South. Trains of oxen carried cotton from plantations along the Brazos and Colorado rivers to stores at the foot of Main Street, where the wagons would be reloaded with goods bound for the interior. Cotton, shipped down Buffalo Bayou to Galveston and from there to northern ports, provided an economic link between the Republic of Texas and the United States. The Allen brothers' dream of making their city an important cotton market was within sight.

As business boomed during 1837 and 1838, the population increased rapidly. "No place has ever within my knowledge improved as this has," President Houston wrote less than a year after the *Laura's* first visit. "I presume not less than one hundred souls arrive by sea each week that passes, and generally of the better sort of folk—bringing wealth, worth, and intelligence into the country." In April 1839, the *Morning Star* gave the population as 2,073 of which only 453 were female.

Despite its increasing population and prosperity, Houston was not without its adversities. John Kirby Allen, the staunchest promot-

William Marsh Rice at the age of 34 years.
COURTESY WOODSON RESEARCH CENTER, FONDREN LIBRARY, RICE UNIVERSITY.

James Holman, the first mayor of Houston. Holman, an agent for the Houston Town Company, had strong ties to the city's business establishment—a trait which would become common among Houston's mayors.
COURTESY HOUSTON METROPOLITAN RESEARCH CENTER, HOUSTON PUBLIC LIBRARY.

er of the town, had died of yellow fever in the summer of 1838. The reality of the hot and humid coastal climate was far different from the healthy climate the Allens had extolled in their advertisement. Excessive rainfalls collected into pools of stagnant water, and the plains drained badly. Cholera, influenza, pneumonia, and malaria afflicted the population. Yellow fever was a prevalent and persistent scourge. "Yellow jack" struck suddenly and killed relentlessly. Without knowing the cause of the disease, the *Telegraph and Texas Register* cautioned that it could best be prevented by "tranquility of mind, regularity of habits, and the conscientious discharge of public and social duties." No one thought of draining the breeding places of mosquitoes. During a devastating epidemic in 1839, Millie Gray recorded in her diary: "Sickness—Sickness—Sickness all around and many deaths… Summoned early in the morning to see Judge Humphreys who is dying. Over there nearly all day… There are a fearful number of new graves… This is an awful disease and does not seem to be understood by the physicians." Out of a population of slightly more than two thousand, there were 240 deaths and perhaps as many as a thousand cases of yellow fever that summer. The disease would continue to plague the city.

Houston suffered another blow when the government decided to relocate the capital. Lawmakers had become increasingly dissatisfied with the lack of accommodations, unpleasant weather, the ever-present mud, and the constant threat of disease. One unhappy legislator referred to Houston as "this detested, self-polluted, isolated mudhole of a city." Mirabeau B. Lamar, who in 1838 succeeded Sam Houston as President, disliked the city of Houston almost as much as he detested Houston the man. As a result, he persuaded the Congress to select a new location for the capital. Waterloo, a Colorado River settlement with four families, was chosen and renamed Austin. When the wagons pulled out of Houston in September 1839 carrying the government archives, many residents followed, and much of the vitality left town with the wagons. No longer would there be the steady stream of office seekers, immigrants,

lawyers, speculators, and settlers seeking to do business with the government. But those citizens who remained, especially the strong nucleus of merchants, were determined that Houston would survive.

The businessmen who had moved to Houston in its infancy had a great deal at stake in the survival of the town. They had come to this raw frontier as young men bent on building their future and, in the process, had invested their money and their energy. Such men as British immigrants Charles Shearn and Thomas House had established their stores in the young town. Erastus Perkins and Ebenezer Nichols were New Yorkers who, like the Allens, brought visions of urban entrepreneurship with them as they started their mercantile operations. William Marsh Rice put down his commercial roots in spite of having lost his entire stock of merchandise at sea while en route from Massachusetts. This strong entrepreneurial vision in the face of hardship would become a trademark of this town on the bayou. Moreover, the merchant class firmly entrenched itself in the leadership roles within the community.

Businessmen realized that Houston was facing competition from a rebuilt Harrisburg and from Galveston, a thriving seaport that had been founded in 1838. Spurred by a sense of urgency to preserve the position of Houston as the leading trade center in southeast Texas, business leaders formed a Chamber of Commerce to work with city officials to initiate improvements. They realized, however, that the real key to commercial success lay in upgrading the transportation arteries. Not yet the waterway that had been touted by the city's founding fathers, Buffalo Bayou was so filled with snags and brush that boats frequently sank. Not only did the sunken vessels choke the stream, but they also raised complex legal questions concerning jurisdiction to remove them. This issue was not resolved until June 8, 1841, when a municipal ordinance created the Port of Houston. The port included all of the bayou within the corporate boundaries of Houston, and vessels of more than ten tons were required to dock at the municipal wharf. Charges ranged from one to six dollars per

day, depending on the size of the ship. Rates for cargo ranged from one dollar for a "pleasure carriage" down to a cent each for hides. During the first year of operation 4,260 bales of cotton, 72,816 feet of lumber, and 1,803 hides were shipped down the bayou from Houston.

The Allens had predicted on August 30, 1836, that railroads would come to their new town, bringing trade from the upper Brazos into Houston. Two early attempts at establishing rail lines in the area failed; and when actual track was finally laid in 1841, it was not intended to benefit Houston but rather to revive Harrisburg. With financial backing from investors in both Harrisburg and Galveston, Andrew Briscoe, the first chief justice of Harris County, received a charter for the Harrisburg Railroad and Trading Company. His plan was an ambitious one in which rail would extend from Harrisburg to the Pacific Coast. Two miles of roadbed were completed before the Harrisburg project col-

lapsed. The Allens' vision of rail transportation would not become a reality for another fifteen years.

When the capital was moved, city leaders turned their attention to the much-neglected municipal government. The town had been incorporated in the summer of 1837; and in an election in which thirty-three votes were cast, James S. Holman was elected mayor. By 1840 Houston encompassed nine square miles. An amended city charter provided for four wards, each electing two representatives to the City Council. Main and Congress Streets formed the innermost boundaries of the wards, which extended outward to the city limits. The county courthouse was considered to be at the very center of Houston.

The municipality was initially given few powers other than keeping peace and order, maintaining public improvements, and receiving revenues from taxes levied on an ad valorem basis. Officials could require citizens to keep fire-fighting equipment on hand, and the

Market Place and Gaol, Houston, Texas, March 20th, 1852 *by Thomas Flintoff, watercolor. Congress Square on the Bordens' map became the site of Houston's first market house and city hall. It became the heart of the city's commerce and trade and soon earned the designation of Market Square.*

municipality could establish a school if it chose to do so. Municipal functions were broadened during the first years to include public health, issuance of money, control of the public market and the port, fire regulations, licensing of occupations, erection of public improvements, and the protection of citizens against fraudulent or tainted merchandise and services.

Since Congress had earlier designated Houston as the seat of Harrisburg County, two log structures were built on Courthouse Square, one of the blocks on the Borden map designated for a specific purpose. These were to serve as courthouse and jail. John W. Moore, the first sheriff of what was renamed Harris County, meted out justice frontier style. After one of the first trials held in the county, the defendant, who had been convicted of theft, was not only fined but also received thirty-nine lashes on his bare back, and his right hand was branded with the letter "T." Duels, brawls, and general disorder were prevalent. Saloons abounded, as did

gambling operations. A local attorney branded the city as "the greatest sink of dissipation and vice that modern times have known."

Yet in the midst of this disorder and violence, culture was not ignored. Houston supported a dancing academy, a French restaurant, and a portrait gallery. General education was promoted through a philosophical society; a thirteen hundred volume circulating library, and a debating society which considered such questions as "Have theaters an immoral tendency?" Although the outcome of that debate is unknown, theaters flourished in the city. John Carlos brought troupes of actors from London, New York, Boston, and New Orleans to perform in such productions as *Romeo and Juliet* and *Othello*, while his competitor, Henri Corri, provided a major social event with the opening of his theater. Houston playhouses presented not only drama but also entertainment by ventriloquists, comedians, minstrels, trained animals, singers, local amateurs, bellringers, and phrenologists.

Religion was much slower to make an appearance in Houston. In June 1839, the *Morning Star* lamented, "It is a source of much astonishment, and of considerable severe comment upon the religious character of our city, that while we have a theater, a courthouse, a jail, and even a capitol in Houston, we have not a single church." Itinerant preachers frequently stopped in Houston, conducting services wherever they could gather a crowd. However, churches were slow to organize and even after formal organization, they grew slowly. Ministers cooperated with each other, preached in the Capitol building, boarded among the people, and shared communicants. Finally, in 1841, the Presbyterian congregation erected a structure which served the entire community until others were built.

In addition to freedom of religion, the 1836 Texas Constitution guaranteed freedom of education. To ensure the necessary funds, Congress passed a bill in 1839 granting each county the proceeds from the sale of four leagues of land (17,712 acres) for the creation and upkeep of public schools. The institutions would be administered by county school boards, which were empowered to establish courses of study and to set qualifications for teachers.

However, real estate was so abundant in Texas and was of such little sales value, that most counties did not even attempt to survey their designated land. As a result, schools were usually established privately. Less than a year after Houston was founded, this ad appeared in the *Telegraph and Texas Register*: "Mrs. E. A. Andrews… gives notice that she will open a school… on the first Monday in November next, principally for young ladies, yet a few boys under the age of 12 will be received until further notice. The various branches of English education will be taught."

In addition to the schools taught by women for girls, young ladies, and small boys, several outstanding private schools taught by men were established, including the Houston Select School, the Select Classical School, and the Houston Academy. The curriculum at the Houston Academy offered a beginning course of reading, writing, and orthography; a secondary course in arithmetic, grammar, and geography; and a final course in Latin, Greek, philosophy, and "higher matter." Boys and girls were instructed in separate rooms, and advertisements assured the public that profane language would be prohibited. Houston attracted more teachers than any other Texas town and established the only public schools in the Republic. However, schools were often of short duration and, in the absence of mandated public education, students frequently did not receive high-quality instruction.

The issue of annexation to the United States had been present in Texas ever since independence was achieved in 1836. A great majority of the Republic's electorate favored becoming a part of the United States. However, political trends varied with each election. The continued threat of invasion from Mexico initially caused leaders in the United States to reject the idea of statehood for Texas, and northern states vehemently objected to the admission of Texas as a slave state.

After extensive negotiations and lengthy debate in the United States Congress, a bill for the annexation of Texas was passed on

February 26, 1845. By the terms of this bill, the State of Texas was permitted to retain title to its public lands; slavery would continue as a legal institution; and Texas received the right to divide itself into as many as five states, with slavery outlawed in any state north of the 36° 30′ line. A Texas convention accepted the offer in July; the voters of Texas ratified the action in October; and the new state formally entered the Union on December 29, 1845.

Houstonians overwhelmingly supported union with the United States. The *Telegraph and Texas Register* reported the local sentiment in an editorial comment: "The news of the passage of the annexation resolutions was hailed with a burst of enthusiasm by our citizens that has never been exceeded…. The sound of the drum and other musical instruments, the roar of the cannon, the loud shouts of the multitude resounding long after midnight, indicated the ardent longing of our citizens to return… under the glorious eagle of the American union."

On February 19, 1846, Anson Jones, the last president of the Republic of Texas, lowered the Lone Star flag with the words, "The final act in this great drama is now performed. The Republic of Texas is no more." Houstonians were officially citizens of the United States, many for the second time. Their town had survived its infancy in a fledgling republic. Now it was ready to mature in an established nation.

GROWTH OF THE
COMMERCIAL EMPORIUM

The Terry Rangers *by Carl G. von Iwonski,*
oil on canvas, ca. 1862.

COURTESY THE WITTE MUSEUM, SAN ANTONIO, TEXAS.

Before Houston could enjoy its new status as part of the United States, war clouds began to gather. Mexico viewed the annexation of Texas by the United States as a seizure of Mexican soil and had warned that such action would lead to war. When the annexation was finalized, Mexico immediately severed its diplomatic relations with the United States. After a skirmish along the Rio Grande between Mexican and American troops, the United States Congress on May 11, 1846, declared war on Mexico.

Between 125 and 150 Houstonians volunteered for military action in the Mexican War, and wartime activities increased traffic to the Port of Houston. Tons of arms, cotton, and foodstuff passed through the port, boosting the city's growth.

After almost two years of fighting, the war ended with the signing of the Treaty of Guadalupe Hidalgo. The United States gained vast territories, including not only all of present-day California, Nevada, and Utah, but also parts of what would eventually become Arizona, New Mexico,

Colorado, and Wyoming. The Spanish West had become the American West.

Houstonians then turned their attention to Galveston, the rapidly developing city south of Houston. During their early years the two cities had enjoyed a symbiotic relationship in order to maintain the flow of trade. Bulky four-hundred-pound bales of cotton, brought overland to Houston by ox teams, were loaded onto flat-bottomed steamers for passage to Galveston where they were then transferred to oceangoing vessels. Houstonians regarded the Galveston harbor as peculiarly their own and the island as a depot from which merchandise destined for Houston could be reshipped.

The amiable relationship between the two towns soon deteriorated, however, into one of intense rivalry. As Houston began pushing for direct deepwater navigation, Galveston was working for direct connections to the interior. The struggle to achieve primacy in establishing rail transportation would occupy the efforts of leaders in both towns for years to come. In the race to become the most important center of commerce on the Gulf Coast, Houston developed a distinctive group of city builders, who would eventually determine the winner of the competition. In the 1850s, a farsighted business elite emerged, eager to control the future of the town.

Thomas W. House personified this generation of successful Houston businessmen. Born in Somerset, England, House immigrated to New York in 1835 and began working as a baker. Three years later he came to the new town of Houston, where he established his own bakery. The young entrepreneur's business quickly expanded into banking, commission sales of cotton, and a thriving real estate business in which he extended credit to farmers in exchange for liens on their crops and land. By the mid-1850s, House transformed these diverse but related activities into an economic empire. He managed the largest wholesale firm in the state, major warehouse facilities in both Houston and Galveston, and substantial investments in water transportation, toll roads, and railroad corporations. At the same time he was active in such civic undertakings as helping organize the city's first volunteer fire department, serving as an alderman, and occupying the mayor's office in 1862.

House and his fellow members of this commercial-civic elite realized that the public welfare and their private interests were deeply intertwined. As a result, wholesale and

commission merchants—such men as House, William R. Baker, Cornelius Ennis, William M. Rice, William J. Hutchins, Paul Bremond, and B. A. Shepherd—in order to expand the city's commerce, turned their attention to developing the infrastructure of the city rather than to erecting elegant buildings and participating in an urbane life style.

As the editor of a Galveston newspaper noted in 1858, "In Houston everything is business.... Our merchants are spending their thousands in building handsome stores with iron fronts, while the merchants of Houston are doing a much larger business in the same buildings they have been occupying for years." Indeed, the monuments left by the "daring plungers of Houston," as *Telegraph and Texas Register* editor E. H. Cushing described the merchant class in 1859, were not to be found in mansions or impressive storefronts, but in the town's thriving commerce.

These leaders realized that adequate transportation was imperative if Houston was to continue to thrive. Roads to and from the city were still in much the same condition as they had been in 1836. In dry weather they were passable, but in rainy seasons freight wagons loaded with cotton could travel only six to eight miles a day, frequently having to wait several days at flooding streams. Ferdinand Roemer, a German who traveled in Texas from December 1845 to April 1847, wrote of a six-mile trip during which the wagons were repeatedly mired in deep black mud and frequently had to be unloaded in order to be freed. Sometimes teamsters were forced to dump bales of cotton beside the road, leaving them to rot. Poor road conditions caused high freight rates, which in turn resulted in exorbitant prices on merchandise both bought and sold in the interior.

Houstonians periodically attempted to improve their wagon roads. Attention was first directed to the west of Houston. During the Gold Rush of 1849, the road toward the Santa Fe and Chihuahua trade was promoted as the best route to California. This road also led to Austin, the state capital. Mail from Houston sometimes took four weeks to reach Austin, and twenty days was considered good time for freight wagons traveling between the two cities.

To build a more adequate route, some of the wharfage fees collected at the Port of Houston were used to begin construction of a turnpike.

In the meantime the Buffalo Bayou, Brazos and Colorado Railway Company had begun laying track from Harrisburg to Richmond, completely bypassing Houston. The company had been chartered by Sidney Sherman at the urging of Boston capitalists who were financing the railroad for the Harrisburg Town Company. By 1853 the first locomotive, the *General Sherman*, was running between Harrisburg and Stafford's Point. Construction was slow, and the tracks did not reach Richmond and the Brazos River until January 1, 1856.

Disgruntled by being bypassed, city leaders obtained authorization from the Texas legislature for Houston to build a line from its business district to the tracks of the Buffalo Bayou, Brazos and Colorado. By October 1856 the Houston Tap, as it was called, was completed; Houston had its first railroad.

Realizing that rail transportation was necessary for primacy as the commercial center of southeast Texas, Houston and Galveston initiated a battle to become the railroad center. The business leaders of the rival cities approached this issue from very different perspectives. Galveston interests proposed a network of railroads leading fanlike from the island city to bring the produce of the state to Galveston wharves for shipment abroad. In opposition to the Galveston plan was the "corporate plan," supported by railroad capitalists in the United States and by Houston merchants. Under this plan Texas railroads would become a part of the transcontinental system running east and west across the United States. If this plan were adopted, Houston would become the railroad center of Texas, and the

~

Above: Thomas William House.

Opposite Left: Pillot Building. This iron-fronted brick structure was erected near the courthouse in 1858 for retail businesses and offices. The large barrel supported by a pole on the corner may have been an early cistern installed for fire protection. A reconstruction of the building is on the site today.

Below: Erastus S. Perkins home. Perkins, a Houston merchant, built this unusual octagonal house on a full block in the 1860s. It was the only known residence built here in this style.

NEW ROUTE
TO
New Orleans!

TEXAS & NEW ORLEANS R. R. CO.'S

SHORE LINE.

THROUGH TO NEW ORLEANS IN 26 HOURS!

No Exposure to Sea Sickness!

ONLY TEN HOURS AT SEA!

Baggage Checked Through
TO NEW ORLEANS.

THE PASSENGER TRAIN
WILL LEAVE
Houston for New Orleans
DAILY, (EXCEPT SUNDAY.) AT 6 O'CLOCK, A. M.

This line is the quickest, safest, and most comfortable route
to New Orleans, and is A TEXAS INSTITUTION.

For Through Tickets apply to
C. R. GENTRY,
Through Ticket Agent,
No. 62 Main Street, Houston, Texas.

Above: Advertisement, Texas and New Orleans Railroad Co., Houston City Directory, 1866. When this ad appeared, travelers made segments of the trip by boat and stagecoach, in addition to rail. Through rail traffic from Houston to New Orleans did not begin until 1881.

COURTESY HOUSTON METROPOLITAN RESEARCH CENTER, HOUSTON PUBLIC LIBRARY.

Right: Houston & Great Northern Railroad Co. Bond, February 15, 1872. The Houston & Great Northern Railroad Co. was chartered in 1866 to build a line from Houston to the Red River, then on to Canada. In 1873 when the line reached Palestine, it acquired the Houston Tap and Brazoria Railway and the Huntsville Branch Railway. That same year it became a part of the International-Great Northern System.

COURTESY THE TORCH COLLECTION, HOUSTON

trade of the state would be routed not to the sea, but through the rail centers of St. Louis and Chicago.

Proponents of the Galveston plan realized that financing could not be obtained from Eastern sources if their tracks did not connect with the transcontinental system. They advocated, therefore, that the railroads be built not by private capital but by the state; and their plan became known as the "state plan." The summer of 1856 was spent in a battle to decide the issue, and the attention of the entire state focused on it. A group of Houston merchants toured the state promoting their plan. The issue was decided on August 13 when the legislature passed a bill favoring the "corporate plan" and granted generous assistance in the form of loans and land grants to private builders. The decision gave Houston a clear victory over Galveston in the battle for interior routes and in large measure determined the future of the two cities.

The railroad that brought the most activity to Houston was the Houston and Texas Central. Although it had been chartered in 1848 as the Galveston and Red River Railway Company, no construction began until Paul Bremond acquired the ownership in 1855 and changed the name of the line. Bremond, a Houston merchant who believed in supernaturalism, thought that he had received ghostly advice to build a railroad system. However, despite his business acumen and financial backing, construction was tediously slow. Finally, track was laid northwestward from Houston and hamlets began to spring up along the roadbed. By June 1858, the road had reached the fifty-mile post, at which the company laid out the town of Hempstead. Within three years the line reached Navasota and Millican.

The last railroad to be built out of Houston before the Civil War was the Texas and New Orleans Railroad Company, meant to connect Houston with New Orleans. This road was simultaneously built east and west from the banks of every stream to which supplies could

be shipped; and bridges were built across the San Jacinto, Trinity, and Neches rivers. On May 25, 1861, track was completed all the way from Houston to Beaumont.

On the eve of the Civil War 450 miles of railroad track had been laid in Texas, with more than 350 miles passing through Houston. The Allen brothers' prediction that their town would become a center of rail transportation had come true.

City leaders knew, however, that rail transportation alone was not enough to ensure Houston's commercial leadership. Buffalo Bayou, the commercial lifeline of Houston, was still narrow and sinuous, but pilots had learned to run side-wheelers up and down the stream with few accidents. The only obstructions were Clopper's Bar, where the bayou emptied into Galveston Bay, and Red Fish Bar, which bisected the bay. When the north winds blew water from the bay into the gulf, ships often went aground on these two obstacles. In the late 1850s, the state appropriated money for the improvement of navigable streams, and the funds permitted the cutting of a channel through both bars. A short time later, a dredge was used in the bayou itself.

Steamboat traffic between Houston and Galveston was dominated by the Houston

Navigation Company, whose principals were Houston merchants and a number of bayou pilots. Company steamers left Galveston and Houston at three o'clock every afternoon except Sunday, and made the run in eight hours. Though enjoying a virtual monopoly of the bayou trade, the company kept its tariffs reasonable and operated with a high degree of safety and efficiency.

The bulk of the cargo moving downstream was cotton on its way to world markets, while most of the upstream cargo was manufactured goods. Ice may have been the best indicator of the efficiency of the transportation system. Packed in sawdust, it was brought from New England rivers and lakes, stored briefly in Galveston, and placed on sloops or schooners bound for Houston. With an increase in the demand for this product, an icehouse was built in the city in 1858. Soon afterward a newspaper reported that 540 tons of ice was on its way to town. Because of the high price, many individuals never used ice except during times of fever or for an occasional churn of ice cream. It made frequent appearances, however, in the town's numerous barrooms.

Although some observers suggested that Buffalo Bayou trade was becoming obsolete in view of railroad development, community leaders saw a danger in giving the railroads a monopoly over transportation. The *Telegraph* editor, E. H. Cushing, warned that outside capitalists owned a controlling interest in the railroads and that Houston would be at the mercy of outsiders if it abandoned the bayou trade. To save this trade, Cushing urged the repeal of Houston's wharfage fees, which he called "highway robbery." Influential merchants backed Cushing in this fight, and the fees were repealed in a special election in May 1860.

In contrast, the Galveston Wharf Company—known by its detractors as the Octopus of the Gulf—held monopolistic control of the Galveston port and exacted what Texans from the rest of the state called "tribute" on all goods passing through Galveston. As a result, Houston interests began seeking ways to bypass the island. They decided that cotton could be compressed in Houston, put on barges for the journey downstream, and

loaded on oceangoing vessels without touching the island. When barges actually began unloading in mid-channel, the Galveston Wharf Company retaliated by levying an additional charge on these vessels when they docked at Galveston to take on return cargo. The battle lines were clearly drawn between the two coastal cities.

Houston business leaders were not only involved in developing improved transportation facilities; they were also participants in every aspect of commercial activity. Many cotton merchants also operated cotton compresses and could therefore handle, store, compress, and sell the staple. Since the Texas Constitution of 1845 forbade banks, cotton factors performed all banking operations except the issuance of notes. They advanced cash to planters at the beginning of the cotton season, sold them equipment and supplies on credit, and honored their drafts. For a commission, they would also import for the planters manufactured goods not stocked by local shops. The scope of these businesses is indicated by an entry in the 1858 ledger of R.G. Dun & Company (the nineteenth century ancestor of the modern credit reporting agency, Dun & Bradstreet): "W. M. Rice & Company... doing a large trade and have been

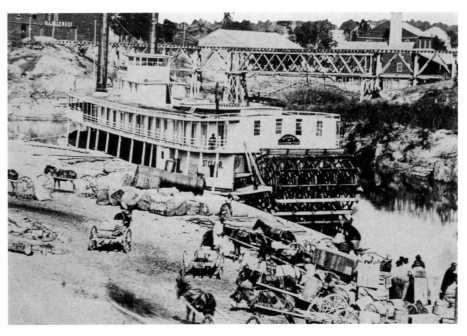

Seal, City of Houston. The current seal for the City of Houston, designed over one hundred years ago, prominently displays a rail locomotive, signifying the importance of the railroad industry to Houston's development. The other important component in the city's economy at that time was agriculture, as indicated by the plow.

REPRINTED WITH PERMISSION BY STECK-VAUGHN COMPANY. COPYRIGHT DATE: 1993.

St. Clair. The St. Clair is shown loading cotton at the foot of Main Street. This sternwheeler carried passengers as well as freight. On one trip it transported the Stonewalls, a Houston baseball team, to the San Jacinto Battlefield where they met and defeated a Galveston team.

COURTESY HOUSTON METROPOLITAN RESEARCH CENTER, HOUSTON PUBLIC LIBRARY.

for years… are sound and solvent… do an annual business of $400,000."

Houston's thriving commerce was reflected in the fortunes accumulated by its merchant princes. According to the 1860 census, the richest man in Houston (and second in the entire state of Texas) was William Marsh Rice with holdings of $750,000. He was followed closely by William J. Hutchins, Thomas W. House, Cornelius Ennis, and Paul Bremond. The aspirations that these men brought with them to the infant city of Houston a quarter of a century earlier had unmistakably been achieved.

On the eve of the Civil War, Houston had grown to become a prospering community with a population of 4,845. Advertisements for Texas had continued to attract newcomers throughout the republic and early statehood years. Thousands of immigrants came to Texas, many of them landing in Galveston and making their way up the bayou to Houston. John and Anna Margaret Bering and their eleven children arrived in 1846, intending to join a German settlement in central Texas. When their oxcart broke down, however, the Berings remained in Houston and later established the first lumber yard in the city. Others also chose to settle in the city despite warnings such as this letter written in 1848: "Immigrants will not take advice—seem to prefer the marsh prairies along the Buffalo Bayou near Houston where all of them will soon perish like flies."

The United States Census of 1860 reflected that in Houston there were numerous Germans, Irish, English, and French; a few Scots, Swiss, Poles, Hungarians, Danes, Swedes, Italians, Belgians, Cubans, Spaniards, British West Indians, Mexicans, and Madeira Islanders; and one native each of Holland, Algiers, and Malta. German immigrants outnumbered those from all other countries. The population of the city was young; more than two-thirds of the residents were less than thirty years old.

The census also listed 1,069 slaves and eight free blacks. Slavery figured significantly

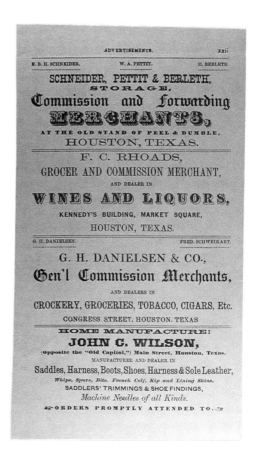

in the economic life of Houston. The city's economy was based mainly on cotton and to a lesser degree on sugar, and the production of these commodities depended on slave labor. Slaves also worked as teamsters and dock workers in town, helped build the plank roads and railroads that were vital to the prosperity of the city, and assisted in much building construction. While most performed unskilled labor, some slaves were skilled craftsmen.

Most Houston slave owners possessed two or three adult slaves; few had more than six, and only three are known to have owned as many as twenty. Slaves in Houston were purchased through a slave depot or merchant house, which accepted consignment of slaves from their customers for resale or in default of payment for goods. A slave might sell for as much as fifteen hundred dollars.

Some owners leased their slaves to others. While many slaves were hired out as domestic servants or journeymen, they could not accept outside work without the consent of their masters. The city enacted strict measures to control slaves, requiring them to be off the streets by eight o'clock in the evening and prohibiting them from gambling, carrying weapons, buying liquor, or selling anything without their masters' permission.

Although few free blacks lived in Houston, their lives were also restricted. When freed by their owners, ex-slaves were required to petition the Texas legislature for permission to remain in Texas. Fannie McFarland, who had been emancipated by her owner in 1835, stated in her petition that she had "put together a little property by her industry, prudence, and economy." While most free blacks who lived in Houston had been denied permanent residence by the legislature, they nevertheless found means of supporting themselves and continued to live in the city, undisturbed by public authorities. Fannie McFarland engaged in a number of real estate transfers and profited from her investments.

Although there were fewer slaveholders in Houston than elsewhere in Texas, urban slavery was a stable institution and a permanent part of Houston's social structure. Slavery, however, was rapidly becoming an issue that would divide the country and lead to sectional war.

As dissension grew between northern and southern states, the threat of war increased. Some Houstonians opposed secession, while others advocated restoring the Texas Republic. The overwhelming majority, however, favored seceding from the Union. Early in 1861, Governor Sam Houston visited the city in an effort to quiet the fervor for secession. Although he spoke dramatically from the balcony of the Perkins Theater, the governor's pleas went unheeded. On March 23, 1861, the state of Texas officially ratified the Constitution of the Confederate States of America. Harris County had voted for secession by a 1,084 to 144 majority. Sam Houston, proclaiming "I love Texas too well to bring civil strife and bloodshed upon her," refused to swear allegiance to the Confederacy and stepped down as governor.

By the time war broke out, several military companies, composed of more than five hundred Houstonians, had been organized and were conducting daily drills. On May 31, 1861, a company of about fifty soldiers under Captain Thomas S. Lubbock departed Houston for the war in Virginia. Each man paid his own way, furnished his own horse and saddle, and took $250 in cash with him. On the day of their departure, the *Weekly Telegraph* predicted, "Daring enterprise and bold strokes are in reserve for this company."

At the battle of First Manassas in July, Lubbock and his fellow Houstonian, Benjamin Franklin Terry, conceived the idea

Above: "Houston," engraving, Illustrated London News, *January 4, 1845. Images identified as Houston circulated throughout the eastern United States and Europe, and were used by immigration societies to encourage settlement in Texas. The creator of this illustration, obviously ignorant of Houston's topography, must have used his imagination to embellish accounts of the city's bayou location.*

COURTESY HOUSTON METROPOLITAN RESEARCH CENTER, HOUSTON PUBLIC LIBRARY.

Below: Richard W. "Dick" Dowling and wife, Elizabeth Ann. Dowling, an Irishman, typified the immigrant who came to Texas seeking new opportunities. Settling in Houston in the late 1850s, he became a successful businessman by operating the Bank of Baachus saloon as well as a liquor-importing business.

COURTESY ARCHIVES & INFORMATION SERVICES DIVISION, TEXAS STATE LIBRARY.

Above: "Battle of Galveston," Harper's Pictorial History, 1866. The Confederate vessel, Bayou City, *succeeded in capturing the Union gunboat,* Harriet Lane, *and destroying the* Westfield *on January 1, 1863. As a result, Galveston remained free throughout the remainder of the war.*

COURTESY HOUSTON METROPOLITAN RESEARCH CENTER, HOUSTON PUBLIC LIBRARY.

Below: Bell from Harriet Lane. *The bell was salvaged from the Union gunboat and was taken to Houston. For many years it tolled the opening and closing of Sam Houston Park. Today the bell is exhibited in the Museum of Southern History, Richmond, Texas.*

PHOTO BY AUTHOR.

of organizing a regiment of Texans for service in the war. Upon returning to Houston to recruit for the new regiment, Lubbock and Terry had no difficulty in enlisting twelve hundred eager young men. They set up headquarters in Houston and began training their new recruits. Within one month, the Eighth Texas Cavalry Regiment, more commonly referred to as "Terry's Texas Rangers," was mustered into the Confederate service and sent to Kentucky. Only three months after entering battle, Terry was killed, but his Rangers fought on.

Back home, Houston bustled with activity. Throughout 1862, Confederate soldiers streamed into town to numerous training camps. The city also bulged with displaced Galvestonians fleeing the Federal blockade that had been imposed the previous July. Refugees from Louisiana, Mississippi, Arkansas, Tennessee, and even as far away as Virginia, also arrived in Houston to distance themselves from the battle sites. The local newspaper declared that "every hotel was filled from garret to basement." The increased population pushed prices upward and forced a shortage of food and supplies. Citizens learned to be resourceful by substituting dried okra for coffee, castor bean oil as fuel for their lamps, and wrapping paper for stationery. As the war progressed, paper stock became so scarce that the local newspapers printed on any color paper available.

The people of Houston fervently raised funds for the war effort by holding concerts, fairs, and festivals. Many families donated cherished possessions to be sold at lottery to aid the confederacy. One such function featured two sewing machines, a five-octave melodeon, a guitar, a white crepe shawl, two acres of land near town, a gold watch and chain, a model ship, and an oil painting. Citizens also donated linen cloth to be used as bandages and allowed their carpets to be cut into blankets for the soldiers.

Throughout 1862 war news flooded the city. Upon the arrival of newspapers from Richmond, Atlanta, Charleston, Mobile, Vicksburg, or other areas close to the action, articles were reproduced in extras put out by the *Telegraph*. Although the papers were generally a week or two old when they arrived, they nonetheless informed Houstonians of the progress of the war. As battles were lost and casualties mounted, many Houstonians began to question the wisdom of secession, and the populace grew increasingly apprehensive when eight Union vessels appeared off the Galveston coast. By the end of October, Federal troops had moved ashore at Galveston but were able to hold the city for only a little more than two months. On January 7, 1863, the headlines of the *Galveston Daily News* read: "Glorious News! Recapture of Galveston from the Yanks!" General J. Bankhead Magruder had gathered a small force in Houston and outfitted a strange array of vessels with bales of cotton as armor, a varied collection of guns, and an eager group of fighters who wanted to end the war immediately. This odd flotilla proceeded down Buffalo Bayou and caught the Federal defenders by surprise. Although Galveston was returned to Confederate control, the blockade of the coastline continued.

Six ships were captured by the Confederate forces. One of these, the *Harriet Lane*, was stripped of armament and sold to Houston commission merchant, Thomas House, for use as a blockade runner. House sent the ship through the Galveston Island blockade with a load of cotton bound for Havana. Although the *Harriet Lane* made only one trip after its capture, blockade running became a regular venture. Several times each week runners left from Galveston under cover of dark and fog. Small ships, loaded with cotton, sailed to Havana, Matamoros, Veracruz, or Nassau, returning with trade goods, munitions, and Enfield rifles. Runners made immense profits. House alone, by the end of the war, had converted the profits from his covert operation into more than three hundred thousand dollars in gold.

Hope was again planted in the hearts of Houstonians when they received news of the rout of Federal forces on September 7, 1863, at Sabine Pass, where Houston saloon owner Dick Dowling led the Davis Guards (a unit of forty-seven fellow Irishmen recruited by Dowling) in an astonishing defeat of a strong Federal fleet consisting of five thousand troops on four gunboats and twenty transports. Confederate President Jefferson Davis called it "an unparalleled victory in military history."

In spite of wartime hardships, business remained good in the city. At the outbreak of the war, Harris County had only twenty-one manufacturers in contrast to more than 150 mercantile establishments. Most of the manufacturing firms were small businesses like Bartholomew Tuffly's confectionery and the town's two bakeries operated initially by John Hermann and Peter Floeck, and later by John Kennedy and Henry Stude. Three Germans operated breweries; the largest was owned by Peter Gabel who made beer, ale, and wine. There were also two leather-working businesses, a wagon-making concern, and five tin

and sheet metal shops. The most energetic mechanical enterprise was Alexander McGowen's foundry, which provided the entire area with castings and machine parts.

By 1862, however, local businessmen were beginning new industries to fill the needs of both the military and civilian populations. A soap and candle factory and two flour mills were constructed. Two iron and brass foundries were started. A large Quartermaster Depot was located in Houston and produced shoes, uniforms, tents, tin goods, and wagon equipment. The most productive tannery in the entire military District of Texas was located in Houston. Three hundred hides per week were processed for manufacturing harnesses, shoe leather, and glue. Wartime activity unquestionably spurred the industrial development of the city.

In August 1863, news reached the city that Sam Houston had died after a lingering illness. Although he still commanded the love and the respect of many, much of the hero worship following his 1836 defeat of Santa Anna had fallen away. His stand against secession had caused many admirers to turn away from him. On the day of his death, the town that bore his name was a key military center in a war he had opposed.

Soldiers were much in evidence on the streets of Houston. The city served as headquarters for the Confederate army's District of Texas, New Mexico, and Arizona. As such, it became the nerve center of the Trans-Mississippi Department. Fifteen thousand soldiers were stationed in the Houston-Galveston area. The wounded and the sick were brought into the military hospital at Houston where local citizens volunteered as nurses.

When rumors of General Robert E. Lee's surrender at Appomattox Courthouse on April 9, 1865, reached Houston, residents reacted with disbelief. Information about the war had always been inconsistent, and for four years Houstonians had vacillated between optimism and despair as they received reports of each campaign. The

Left: "All slaves are free," notice printed in the Galveston Tri-Weekly News, June 21, 1865. Newspapers across the state printed Union General Gordon Granger's order declaring all slaves free.
COURTESY THE CENTER FOR AMERICAN HISTORY, UNIVERSITY OF TEXAS AT AUSTIN.

Above: Davis Guards medal, September 8, 1863. Fearing that Maximilian would intervene in the Civil War, the Union wanted to establish sovereignty in Texas by taking Sabine Pass. From there, Union troops could capture the railroad to Houston, the state's capital. Lt. Richard W. Dowling and his troops, the Davis Guards of the First Texas Heavy Artillery, repulsed the Union advance down the Sabine River. The citizens of Houston commissioned this medal in gratitude for the Guards' bravery. It is the closest thing to a Confederate battle medal ever issued.
COURTESY THE TORCH COLLECTION, HOUSTON.

Above: Richard Allen. During Reconstruction, Allen—a freedman—was involved in all aspects of Houston affairs: political, business, civic, religious, and fraternal. He represented Harris and Montgomery counties in the 12th Texas legislature, where he worked diligently for the passage of the first comprehensive bill for free schools in the state.

Below: Jack Yates. A former slave who moved to Houston after the war, Yates became a leader among the black population as minister of Antioch Baptist Church and as a strong advocate for education.

Weekly Telegraph, however, finally reported that the end had in fact come and that the war was over.

Early in June a new flag flew over the courthouse in Houston, and Federal soldiers marched in the streets that had once buzzed with Confederate military activity. On June 19, 1865, United States Army troops landed at Galveston and proclaimed in the name of President Andrew Johnson that the authority of the United States over Texas was restored, all acts of the Confederacy were null and void, and all slaves were free. This was the first "Juneteenth," celebrated by Texas blacks as Emancipation Day.

Although Houston escaped the devastation of battle, it shared the general economic ruin that the war brought throughout the Confederacy. The transportation system had deteriorated severely. Some of the railroads that had brought prosperity to Houston in the late 1850s were abandoned, and the others were in disrepair. Buffalo Bayou, having been largely neglected for four years, was also in a deplorable condition and the hard-won improvements of previous years had virtually disappeared. Shoals had formed near the city, snags had accumulated, and the bars had returned to their natural state.

As Houston began to repair its transportation arteries, economic rivalry with Galveston resumed. Local businessmen made plans once again to bypass the island to avoid the exorbitant fees still imposed by the Galveston Wharf Company. Another concern was the high freight rates imposed by Commodore Charles Morgan, who owned most of the vessels plying the bayou.

For immediate relief City Council encouraged the organization of a company to put barges on the bayou to load and unload ocean vessels in mid-channel, and local merchants organized the Houston Direct Navigation Company. By the spring of 1868 this company had negotiated a shipping agreement with the New York steamship company of C. H. Mallory and was advertising "through bills of lading from Houston to New York and from New York to Houston without touching Galveston, at a saving of 20% to 40% to the shipper."

During the same year, company profits were so substantial that a luxury boat was built for the bayou. Named the *T. M. Bagby*, it and another of the company's vessels, the *Diana*, were described as "floating palaces" and were widely acclaimed as being as fine as any on the Mississippi River. The steamboat trip between Galveston and Houston became popular with both vacationers and businessmen. One traveler noted, "A trip to Galveston was a delightful experience. You started late in the afternoon, had a fine supper, listened to the band, danced or played cards, had a good sleep, breakfast the next morning, and landed at Galveston in ample time to attend to any business you might have and take the return boat late in the evening."

Although the Houston Direct Navigation Company successfully navigated the bayou, carrying both freight and passengers, long-term improvements were still foremost in the minds of local businessmen. City Council, on October 19, 1865, had approved an ordinance authorizing the mayor to accept voluntary loans from citizens for work on Buffalo Bayou. In the spring of 1867 the council took the further step of commissioning a survey of the proposed channel and calling for public subscriptions in the amount of seventy-five thousand dollars for the purpose of opening Red Fish and Clopper's bars. Before these plans could be effected, Reconstruction politics intervened when the commander of the United States military district governing Houston replaced city officials with his own appointees. Reconstruction government replaced channel repair and improvement as the primary preoccupation of the city.

The appointment of Andrew Jackson Hamilton as provisional governor of Texas on July 21, 1865, introduced Reconstruction into Texas. Since the state had seceded from the Union when it joined the Confederacy, Texas, in order to regain its status within the United States, had to repeal its act of secession, repudiate all debts incurred in the cause of the Confederacy, and draft a new constitution excluding slavery. When the new state constitution was ratified in 1866, it appeared that Texas would rejoin the Union without major difficulties. A local election in which

Alexander McGowen was chosen mayor generated so little activity that the *Telegraph* commented: "What a quiet and peaceable city Houston has become. But few cities of the size and population of Houston can boast such a record the day after a city election." During the next three years, in spite of financial problems in the municipal government, the city's general prosperity increased.

The political climate changed dramatically in January 1870 when Edmund J. Davis became governor. The Radical Republicans had gained control of Congress four years earlier. Believing that the ex-Confederate states were restricting the status of freedmen, they replaced state and local officeholders and forced the adoption of still another state constitution. Davis became a virtual dictator, and through his appointments sought to implement his own policies.

One of Davis's appointees was Thomas H. Scanlan as mayor of Houston. Scanlan, a native of Ireland, had come to Houston in 1853 and established himself as a general merchant. After the war he declared for the Radical Republican cause, and enjoying the backing of the occupation forces, rose rapidly in municipal politics. He was dedicated to improving the lot of freedmen, and during his years in office blacks served for the first time on City Council and the police force. His administration also extended the sidewalks, built a market house, constructed a large sewer, and improved roads and bridges. Despite these improvements, Scanlan was accused of financial mismanagement and personal graft, the new market house being a source of much discontent. The handsome building had cost about four hundred thousand dollars but was insured for only one hundred thousand. When it was destroyed by fire, the city found itself in financial straits. A new, less pretentious structure was built for one hundred thousand dollars, but the indebtedness on the old one still had to be

paid. This incident was widely used against Scanlan as an example of his extravagance. However, when Houstonians were allowed to elect their own officials for the first time in six years, they returned Scanlan to office, and corruption was never proved against him or his administration.

In 1872, Texas Democrats regained a majority in the state legislature, and a year later Democrat Richard Coke was elected governor. Scanlan was removed by Governor Coke, and Houston received a new charter. With the passage of a new state constitution in 1876, Reconstruction officially came to an end in Texas.

Although Reconstruction slowed improvements to the bayou, a significant step toward deepwater transportation had been taken in 1870 when Congress designated Houston a port of delivery and provided that a surveyor of customs should reside there. The United States Army Corps of Engineers approved work to increase the width of the channel to a hundred feet and its depth to six feet. Two years later, Congress made an appropriation for this work in the amount of ten thousand dollars, which was applied to the improve-

Above: Main Street, 1865. These substantial buildings replaced those which had burned in 1860. The imposing Morris Building in the middle of the block was Houston's first four-story structure.

COURTESY HOUSTON METROPOLITAN RESEARCH CENTER, HOUSTON PUBLIC LIBRARY.

Below: Market House, 1876. This structure housed not only market activities and city government offices, but also the first telephone exchange and an early library facility. The fountain in front of the building graces the entrance of Glenwood Cemetery today.

COURTESY HOUSTON METROPOLITAN RESEARCH CENTER, HOUSTON PUBLIC LIBRARY.

CHAPTER THREE

43

kets. Thus, cheap water transportation was important to the cotton industry.

The biggest boost to Houston's deepwater aspirations, however, came from an unlikely source. Commodore Charles Morgan, whose company had monopolized commerce on Buffalo Bayou, became dissatisfied with the Galveston Wharf Company over its excessive wharfage rates and lengthy quarantine periods during which his ships sat idle. When Morgan was approached by the hard-pressed Buffalo Bayou Ship Channel Company about taking over its operations, he readily consented. On July 1, 1874, in exchange for stock in the company, he signed a contract agreeing to construct a channel at least 120 feet wide from Galveston Bay to the environs of Houston. His first act was to dredge the bayou to a depth of twelve feet, thus enabling any ship that could cross the Galveston bar to proceed to Houston. Morgan selected a point opposite the junction of Buffalo and Sims Bayous as the terminal point for ship traffic and began construction of a railroad to connect the shipping terminal, which he named Clinton, with the railroads at Houston.

On September 22, 1876, a ship carrying seven hundred tons of cargo came up Buffalo Bayou. The *Daily Telegraph* editor exulted, "This is a practical result beyond quibble and doubt of the success of the Ship Channel and proves its reality to the understanding of all. The merchants are free of the extortions of Galveston's *bete noir*, its hideous wharf monopoly." Buffalo Bayou was beginning to look like the superior waterway so highly touted four decades earlier by the Allen brothers.

By the mid-1870s, Houston was a well-established commercial town with a network of railroads and a navigable bayou. It had grown in population, survived the Civil War, and witnessed the decline of yellow fever. The approaching decades would be a period of transition from a struggling community on the western edge of the South to a city poised to become the metropolis of the southwest.

Above: $3.00 note, Briscoe, Harris & Co., 1867. The earlier practice of private firms issuing their own currency reemerged after the Civil War and was prevalent in Reconstruction Texas. This note was issued by a firm in the town of Harrisburg.

COURTESY THE TORCH COLLECTION, HOUSTON.

Below: Bird's-eye View of the City of Houston, Augustus Koch, 1873. Koch prepared a map of Houston as if viewing it from 2,000 to 3,000 feet above. Artists walked the streets to accurately sketch the buildings, trees, and other features. This section of the map details the waterfront area of the city.

COURTESY HOUSTON METROPOLITAN RESEARCH CENTER, HOUSTON PUBLIC LIBRARY.

ment of Red Fish Bar. The Buffalo Bayou Ship Channel Company, which had been organized in 1869 and was the chief participant in channel improvements, was already at work cutting across Morgan's Point to avoid Clopper's Bar. Houstonians expended two hundred thousand dollars on the channel before the Panic of 1873 threw the Buffalo Bayou Ship Channel Company into dire financial straits and halted its work on the channel.

On June 12, 1874, a group of cotton factors and businessmen established the Houston Board of Trade and Cotton Exchange, an organization that would exert profound influence on the commerce of Houston and on the future of the channel. The Cotton Exchange, as it was commonly called, was designed to regulate and systematize the cotton business. Cotton was still the major export from Houston with much of it going to foreign mar-

Houston in the Gilded Age

Railroad yard at Grand Central Station. On the afternoon of October 22, 1894, the Grand Central depot area was filled with flatcars loaded with bales of cotton shipped in from the small farms and gins of the Coastal Bend and East Texas.

Throughout America the last quarter of the nineteenth century has often been called the Gilded Age. While Texas did not share in the opulence to which this appellation referred, the state did grow in population and in production as it became more urbanized. Communities acted to solve their major problems, and society and culture matured. Houston, guided by determined and farsighted leaders, reflected these trends, growing rapidly in population and importance.

The growth of railroads continued as a stimulus to Houston's development. The Houston and Texas Central was the first line to resume building after the Civil War. When it reached Denison in north Texas in 1873, it connected with the Missouri, Kansas and Texas Railroad, establishing a through connection to St. Louis. Pullman service, new to Texas, was provided all the way. In 1876 the line changed to the standard 56fi" gauge, providing other sections of the nation with easy access to Houston.

In 1875, Paul Bremond interested a group of enterprising Houston capitalists in chartering the Houston East and West Texas Narrow Gauge Railway. The line, nicknamed "Hell Either Way

Taken," was designed to extend from Houston to the Piney Woods of east Texas. The *Houston Daily Post* reported in 1881 that the three-foot-gauge railroad was transporting twenty carloads of lumber daily to Houston. Two years later the railway had reached Nacogdoches, providing additional access to the timber-producing belt of Texas.

Houston had become the railroad hub of the Southwest. Nine railroads with more than twenty-two hundred miles of rail converged on the city, and eighteen hundred more miles were under construction. With the railroad industry came associated enterprises, includ-

ing timber, law, and banking. Both blue and white-collar workers were in demand, and the population of the city grew accordingly.

As early as 1871 local real estate agent William Brady, glimpsing Houston's future in the lumber industry, had reported, "Houston situated in an intermediate position with the vast timber lands of Texas east of her parallel, and the vast expanses of country where that timber can and will be utilized west of that parallel, must become the great central depot for the lumber trade of Texas."

By 1885, when the Houston East and West Texas reached its ultimate destination, the Sabine River, Houston was realizing Brady's prediction. In 1899, 420 million feet of lumber passed through Houston railroad terminals on the way to other parts of the state as well as to national and international markets.

John Henry Kirby epitomized the entrepreneur in the growing lumber industry. In the 1880s Kirby, a Woodville attorney, persuaded Boston capitalists to invest four hundred thousand dollars in the forests of east Texas and to build a railroad to the outside world. Kirby himself eventually controlled more than a million acres in east Texas. In 1890 he moved to Houston, making it the center of his growing lumber, railroad, and real estate empire. By 1901, Kirby was reported to be the "wealthiest man in town," and his adopted hometown had become the hub of the lumber industry in the state.

The rapidly developing railroad industry in Texas significantly affected the growth of the legal profession. Railroads needed more capital and greater professional coordination than traditional businesses, resulting in new legal issues in the areas of finance, corporations, and interstate commerce.

Before the advent of railroads, the legal profession in Texas had been loosely organized. The 1866 Houston City Directory listed twenty-two attorneys, most of whom practiced independently. The oldest firm in the city, Gray and Botts, had evolved from the solo practice of Peter Gray, who was joined in 1865 by Walter Browne Botts. A short time later, Judge James A. Baker moved from Huntsville to join the firm, which acted as general attorneys for the Missouri, Kansas and

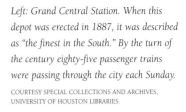

Texas, an important line in the northeastern part of the state, and for the Houston and Texas Central. By the 1880s the firm had achieved national prominence and served as counsel for railroad magnate Jay Gould's Missouri Pacific line.

A new era in Texas railroading began in 1893 when the state legislature created the Texas Railroad Commission as a regulatory agency. At the same time, Collis Huntington, one of the builders of the transcontinental system, had begun to consolidate his many holdings in Texas, placing them under his Southern Pacific Company and designating Houston as the company's regional headquarters. Baker, Botts, Baker and Lovett became

general counsel in Texas for Southern Pacific and was soon acknowledged as the regional leader in railroad law.

By 1900, Houston had more than two hundred lawyers. Recognizing their role in an increasingly urbanized and middle-class society, they organized the Houston Bar Association in 1904, and the legal profession entered a new stage, playing an important part in Houston's development.

Banking, which had previously been a privately controlled function of the city's mercantile class, emerged as an established commercial venture during these years of industrial growth. The Civil War had greatly altered the Houston economy. Many Texans, whose wealth consisted of Confederate money, bonds, or cotton receipts, were left penniless. During the war, European mills

had learned to rely on producers outside the South for cotton. Since control of railroads, manufacturing, and finance was centered in the North, the South had to cope with discriminatory freight rates, higher prices for manufactured goods, and lower prices for farm products. Substantial amounts of investment capital and a banking system were needed to rebuild the economy.

In 1863 and 1864, Congress had passed legislation allowing the chartering of national banks. Although the law did not immediately affect the South because of the war, a group of Houston businessmen established the First National Bank in 1866. A year later, merchant B. A. Shepherd, the first person in Texas to act exclusively as a banker, became the president and merged his private banking operations with those of the new organization.

As Houston's economy improved, other nationally chartered banks were formed. The Commercial National Bank, established in 1886, was closely tied to the cotton trade. Early directors included Henry Gardes, a New Orleans cotton factor and banker, and local cotton merchants William B. Chew, who served as president of the bank, and William D. Cleveland. Commercial National also had connections to the railroad industry.

In the last two decades of the nineteenth century as the lumber industry became a major economic base in east Texas, Houston acted as the regional financial center for lumbering activities. The South Texas National Bank was organized in 1890 with lumber interests dominating its direction. Martin Tilford Jones, president of the M. T. Jones Lumber Company, served as its first president.

By 1900, Houston had five national banks, the private banking firm of T. W. House, and one trust company. The local banking industry would soon enter a period of growth as Houston's increasing population created a greater demand for consumer goods.

It was apparent to at least one city visitor in 1879 that, while Houston's commercial progress might be exemplary, its living conditions were less than adequate. Upon returning to his hometown the traveler wrote: "Houston is the great railroad center of Texas... besides this it is the harbor of the

Morgan line of steamships, running to New Orleans, Havana, Brownsville, and Santa Cruz.... It has some good looking stores... and, I am told a good cotton press. But the city looks shabby. There is not a paved or macadamized street in the town, and but few decent sidewalks, and no system of sewers at all. Wooden troughs are placed in the gutters in some places, and waste water from houses is conducted into them through other wooden troughs. This water does not run off, but stands and emits an unhealthful odor. If such a want of cleanliness does not breed disease, it is only because the day of wrath is being put off.... The city is beautiful for situation and were it paved, painted and polished up, it would shine like a star."

Although the original city charter and its subsequent amendments clearly placed

responsibility for health, education, fire protection, and public improvements with the municipality, these issues had been addressed only superficially during Houston's formative years. Much needed to be done if the quality of life in the city was to keep pace with commercial advancement. During the last quarter of the nineteenth century, considerable progress was made toward this end.

A Board of Health had been formed in Houston as early as 1839. However, other than occasional reports to City Council about "spreading lime, firing off cannons, and searching out nuisances," little is known about its function. By 1865, Houston claimed only a handful of physicians, one charity institution, and a facility serving railroad workers. Several attempts at forming a medical association had been short-lived. Clearly, health care for the general public was grievously deficient.

It was left to the private sector to remedy this situation. Two nuns from Galveston's Congregation of the Sisters of Charity of the Incarnate Word traveled to Houston in March 1887 to find quarters for a general hospital. Three months later St. Joseph's Infirmary opened in a deserted frame building in downtown Houston. A nursing staff and a single physician administered the forty-bed facility.

Above: Joseph F. Meyer. An active member of Stonewall No. 3 Company, Meyer served in the 1870s as chief of the city's Volunteer Fire Department. The trumpet he is holding was used primarily for ceremonial purposes, such as parades.

COURTESY THE HERITAGE SOCIETY, HOUSTON.

Below: The Ladies' Reading Club. Despite much ridicule from the male population, a group of women formed the club in 1885 for serious study. It still exists after 112 years.

COURTESY HOUSTON METROPOLITAN RESEARCH CENTER, HOUSTON PUBLIC LIBRARY.

Since local residents remained suspicious of hospitalization, the patient census for the entire first year was only thirty-nine. The staff, however, continued to promote quality health care, and within ten years Houston's first general hospital had expanded and relocated. The organization of the Harris County Medical Association in 1903 signified the developing commitment to health care in Houston.

Education had been addressed in the community just as sporadically as health care. From the time of Houston's founding, private schools had provided most of the city's educational offerings. In the years before the Civil War, two especially distinguished schools opened. The Houston Academy, the city's first chartered educational facility, was a source of pride for Houstonians as was Miss Mary B. Brown's Select School for Young Ladies, referred to by the *Houston Post* as the "Vassar of the South." These schools, however, served only the more affluent white families in the city.

Shortly after the war, the Freedmen's Bureau established schools for recently freed slave children. By 1870 the three Freedmen's Bureau schools had been replaced by Gregory Institute. Still, many of Houston's young were offered no formal education.

During the 1870s, the movement for free public education gained momentum in urban areas all across the United States. Harris County established a free county school system in 1873. Ashbel Smith, a physician educated at Yale University, was a strong advocate of educational reform and became superintendent of county schools.

The 1876 state constitution provided additional funds for public education and gave control of public schools to the local government. After receiving approval from property owners, City Council began to provide free schooling for all children eight to fourteen years of age. On October 1, 1877, more than twelve hundred students enrolled in the system of fourteen schools. The *Houston City Directory* praised these facilities, boasting that "To Houston belongs the honor of having first successfully established the system of graded schools in Texas."

The educational system, however, was not in every way exemplary. Only half of the eligible children in Houston actually attended, and, inasmuch as the system was racially segregated, no high school for black students was provided until 1892. Moreover, the black schools usually suffered from substandard facilities and inadequate funding.

Since 1854 the only library in the city had been owned by the Houston Lyceum. The Lyceum's constitution had declared, "The objects of this association shall be to diffuse among its members intelligence and information, by a library, by lectures upon various subjects, and by discussion of such questions as may elicit useful information...." In spite of several interruptions of its activities through the years, the Lyceum continued to build its library. By 1880 there were twenty-four hundred volumes on the shelves; but circulation was low, since the only eligible users were dues-paying members of the Lyceum, all of whom were white males. Houston clearly needed a free public library to complement the educational system.

Again the private sector, this time represented by women's clubs in the city, stepped forward. In the late nineteenth century women's clubs had been formed in almost every American community. The first such club organized in Houston was the Ladies' Reading Club. Frustrated in their intellectual pursuits by the lack of a public library, these women began a decade-long campaign to establish one. Finally in 1899, the city administration assumed control of the Lyceum, which was housed in inadequate quarters. The same year, at the request of The Woman's

Club, Andrew Carnegie gave fifty thousand dollars to erect a suitable building. The city administration then voted an annual appropriation of four thousand dollars to support the library once the proposed building was opened. Club women, led by Adele Looscan, Elizabeth Ring, and Belle Kendall, headed a drive to raise funds for a library site. On March 2, 1904, The Houston Lyceum and Carnegie Library opened, providing a free public facility for the first time. Six years later Andrew Carnegie answered another appeal to establish a library for black Houstonians.

Women were to be a potent force in improving other aspects of the quality of life in Houston. As clubs organized among both white and black women, they addressed issues that were often ignored by city fathers. Their work targeted sanitation, child welfare, education, beautification, and labor conditions. Tireless campaigning won new provisions for garbage collection, kindergartens, art education in the schools, additional park land, health clinics, and improved working conditions in industry.

Fire control had been a volunteer effort in Houston since Protection Company No. 1 had been founded in 1838. Shortly after organizing, the company had purchased a small hand engine. When an alarm was sounded by the bell atop Saint Vincent de Paul Catholic Church, volunteers would race toward the designated ward where the fire had been reported. Citizens who kept leather fire buckets and had cisterns on their property assisted the volunteers by a bucket brigade.

In subsequent years additional companies were formed. Eventually, in order to combat fires more efficiently, all of the volunteers united to become the Houston Volunteer Fire Department. On May 2, 1862, the city government officially recognized the department by ordinance.

As Houston expanded, more new companies were added to the department. Each had a distinct personality and held monthly meetings, which were usually high-spirited social

Above: Houston Fire Department.
Firefighters at Station No. 5 enjoyed all the
comforts of home. An interesting feature of
their quarters was the mosquito netting on
the beds, a necessity in Houston before the
advent of window screens.
COURTESY THE HERITAGE SOCIETY, HOUSTON.

Below Right: Advertisement, Eugene Heiner,
Houston City Directory, 1884. After being
apprenticed to an architect in Chicago,
Heiner established his practice in Houston
in 1878. He achieved special prominence as
the architect of county courthouses
and jails, but he also designed many major
commercial buildings and large private
homes in Houston.
COURTESY HOUSTON METROPOLITAN RESEARCH CENTER,
HOUSTON PUBLIC LIBRARY.

gatherings. The expenses of manning a station were often staggering for a group of private citizens to assume. Yet these volunteers continued because of the social status they enjoyed and because they knew they were providing a vital service to the community.

By the mid-1890s, as the city population approached thirty-five thousand, Houstonians began to clamor for a full-time paid fire department. Backed by many local businessmen, City Council voted to make the change; and at one minute past midnight on June 1, 1895, the Houston Fire Department became operational.

As the city grew in size and importance, its outward appearance changed. In Houston's early years most of its buildings were plain two and three-story frame or brick commercial and public buildings and modest wooden houses. Houston businessmen, for the most part, had invested their money in improving commerce rather than in erecting ostentatious buildings.

By the last quarter of the nineteenth century, however, new ideas, new technology, and new money combined to produce a demand for new buildings. Romantic Idealism, a movement that embodied a glorification of nature, imagination, and emotion, had swept the country. Architectural trends responded to these new ideas, and by the 1870s professional architects were practicing in Houston. Men like Eugene Heiner, George Dickey, Olle Lorehn, and J. Arthur Tempest left their imprint on the face of the city.

A grand Victorian Gothic courthouse replaced the modest structure on Courthouse Square, while a block away an elaborate Moorish building housed the post office and federal courts. The old Capitol Hotel (originally the capitol building of the Republic of Texas) was razed for a modern five-story Renaissance Revival structure, and the Cotton Exchange erected an impressive facility near the bayou. Downtown Houston assumed a more urban appearance as these larger buildings were constructed.

In affluent neighborhoods, new homes following the same elegant and imaginative styling were designed to display the owners' wealth and standing in the community. As a variety of building materials and ornamental elements became locally available, houses became more individualistic, ranging in style from the square-towered Italianate villa to the turreted Queen Anne mansion.

Houses in middle- and working-class neighborhoods were designed for economy, shelter, and comfort and tended toward stylistic uniformity. Hundreds of small, simply decorated Victorian cottages were constructed in the Sixth Ward neighborhood, and rows of shotgun houses sprang up in the Fourth Ward Freedmen's Town.

Regardless of where people lived or worked, they nevertheless shared a common problem: streets which more often than not were mired in mud. The *Houston Daily Post* acknowledged this problem by describing Houston in 1882 as "a huddle of houses arranged on unoccupied lines of black mud." The condition of Houston streets even received notice by a columnist for the *Galveston Daily News* who wrote, "Houston is celebrated for the luxuriant beauty of her private gardens and for the fluent muddiness of her streets. The main thoroughfares have not been improved by the labor of man since their foundations emerged out of the profundity of chaos on the date of creation." Conditions became so intolerable that in 1882 the city's Fifth Ward unsuccessfully petitioned the local government for the right to secede and found the "City of North Houston."

The first attempt at paving occurred that year when property holders along Main Street had limestone squares installed over a gravel base. The experiment failed when the mud seeped over both the gravel and the limestone. Cobblestones were next used as a paving material. When they, too, proved unsatisfactory, the city tried using wooden blocks of bois d'arc and cypress. After every rain, the wood would swell, rise to the surface, and float away.

In the early 1890s City Council seriously addressed the muddy-street problem. An intensive study of drainage methods and paving materials used in other cities resulted in the first brick paving being laid in 1894 and the first asphalt paving three years later. By the turn of the century, Houston had twenty-five miles of paved streets.

While the streets were still mired in mud, public transportation had been initiated in the city. As early as 1868 mule-drawn streetcars were operating on a few downtown streets. Soon after service began, the *Weekly Telegraph* reported, "There were twenty-three persons on the car which was drawn by one mule with perfect ease at the rate of fully ten miles an hour." By 1874 the Houston City Street

Railway was not only serving the important
business thoroughfares of Main Street and
Congress Avenue, but it was also extending
lines out to new residential areas.

In time, however, animal-powered cars were
replaced across the nation with newer electric
streetcars. Recognizing the potential value of
an improved transit system for Houston, a
group of investors led by Oscar M. Carter of
Omaha, Nebraska, purchased the local company in 1890 and immediately began to rebuild it
for electric operation at an estimated cost of
five hundred thousand dollars. When the electric streetcar routes were established, suburban
development began in earnest.

Oscar Carter saw an opportunity to plan a
suburban community on a scale unprecedented in Houston. The Omaha and South Texas

Land Co., which Carter headed, platted
eleven thousand lots on acreage west of the
city. Named Houston Heights for its altitude
which was twenty-three feet higher than that
of downtown Houston, it developed into a
self-contained community with homes, businesses, industries, schools, churches, and
even an opera house. Streetcars ran regularly
from downtown along Heights Boulevard. As
the suburb developed, the Heights streetcar
line became one of the most heavily used in
the city.

Other suburban developments followed
the extension of the street railway system. The
Brunner suburb north of Buffalo Bayou, and
the Fairview, Fairgrounds, and Westmoreland
additions to the south of the business district
were real estate ventures spurred by the transit system. This pattern of growth would continue into the twentieth century.

As Houston expanded in size and importance, cultural activity kept pace with the
growth of the city. The arts continued to flour-
ish. European opera troupes and the internationally famous Jenny Lind had visited the
city prior to the Civil War. The first grand
opera presented in Houston was at the
Perkins Theater in 1867 when *La Traviata* and
Il Trovatore were performed by a visiting
troupe. In 1870 the Perkins was completely
refurbished and the seating capacity optimistically expanded to one thousand.

Shakespearean plays, especially *Romeo and
Juliet*, *Julius Caesar*, and *Othello*, were favorites
with Houston audiences. The highlight, however, was the appearance of Edwin Booth in
Hamlet at Pillot's Opera House. The performance was sold out for months before Booth's
arrival. On the day of the event, February 23,
1883, disappointed ticket seekers were offering as much as twenty dollars for seats that
had originally sold for two dollars. The performance lived up to expectations, and the
Houston Daily Post drama critic delivered a
glowing review the next day. Other notable
performers who appeared at the Pillot were
Lillie Langtry, Otis Skinner, and Maurice
Barrymore.

In 1889 the opulent Sweeney and Coombs
Opera House was erected facing Courthouse
Square. Its grand opening featured Gilbert

and Sullivan's operetta, *The Gondoliers*, which had been written less than two years earlier, and had been performed in England only the previous season. In the next decade, the Sweeney and Coombs was famed for its lavish productions.

To provide another venue for cultural activities the Winnie Davis Auditorium, named for a daughter of the former Confederate president, was built in 1895. John Philip Sousa's band played the opening concert. The Polish pianist, Ignace Paderewski, was warmly received there and was paid the then remarkable sum of twenty-five hundred dollars for one concert. The Winnie Davis Auditorium would be the site in 1901 for a landmark event, the Metropolitan Opera's first visit to Houston. Though their city had a relatively small population, Houstonians were resolute in bringing the finest cultural events into their midst.

By the 1880s, the city's business and political leaders envisioned Houston as the "Chicago of the South." Yet they had made only tentative steps toward the creation of a modern city. Areas such as public utilities, environmental engineering, and municipal reform had received little attention.

The blueprint for local government had been drawn early in Houston's development and reflected the tremendous business commitment to growth. City leaders were most often drawn from the elite of the business community. During the years of rapid urbanization the mayor's post was filled by James T. D. Wilson, Andrew J. Burke, and William R. Baker—all prominent business leaders. One interruption in the control of city govern-

ment by the business elite occurred when mechanic Daniel Smith was elected mayor. Smith's council was more representative of the working-class population and succeeded in expanding public works projects into all areas of the city. This was in sharp contrast to City Hall's previous approach of focusing on improvements meant to benefit the economy. How to provide basic services while best serving public welfare would remain a controversial issue for the remainder of the nineteenth century.

The municipal government experienced severe financial problems during these years. Emerging from the Panic of 1873 with a heavy debt, the city was pushed into virtual bankruptcy. Economic recovery was not achieved until commerce was revived and the city's revenues began to increase.

In 1884, the *City Directory* admitted that "there have occurred periods in Houston's history when internal improvements seemed to be at a stand and its pulse as a city presenting urban facilities and advantages of life beat with a very feeble stroke. The shadow of its

Above: Houston Heights. Large, stylish homes were built along Heights Boulevard. Advertisements enticed buyers by saying: "Come out to the beautiful Houston Heights where pine trees grow so high they tickle the toes of the angels...." Houston Heights became an incorporated town in 1896 and remained so until 1918, when it was annexed by Houston.

COURTESY HOUSTON METROPOLITAN RESEARCH CENTER, HOUSTON PUBLIC LIBRARY.

Bottom, left: Westheimer Co. wagon. Westheimer's wagons were a common sight on Houston streets as they proudly posted their telephone number and advertised, "We move anything."

COURTESY HOUSTON METROPOLITAN RESEARCH CENTER, HOUSTON PUBLIC LIBRARY.

great debt darkened its future and enforced a current of economy which was painfully realized in darkness and mud." Yet, it optimistically predicted, "The boon of a great population is in the air, and the whir of machinery, the shrieks of locomotives and the din of workshops tell the story of progress and prosperity."

An indication of that progress was the introduction of public utilities as they became available. Telegraph service had been established between Houston and Galveston by 1860. A line laid along the Galveston, Harrisburg and Houston Railway allowed Houstonians to receive reports from the island about weather, ship arrivals, and prices in New Orleans. By 1869, this system had consolidated with the Western Union Telegraph Company.

Ten years later Western Union brought telephone service to Houston by running a line from the *Houston Daily Telegram* building to an encampment of the Houston Light Guards a mile away. The *Telegram* reported that conversations could be "distinctly heard." Houston's first commercial telephone exchange began operation with twenty-eight subscribers. In 1882, the first private branch exchange in the United States was installed in the Capitol Hotel. The following year the first long distance service in the state was instituted between Houston and Galveston. As novel uses continued to be found for this new invention, Christ Episcopal Church broadcast its services to parishioners who could not personally attend. The *Houston Daily Sun* reported that Pillot's Opera House had installed a telephone and was announcing the racing results from the local track to audiences between acts at the matinee performances. The telephone was soon considered a necessi-

ty by some Houstonians, and by 1900 there were two thousand subscribers in the city.

The Houston Electric Light and Power Company received its franchise in 1882. On December 13 the bar of the Capitol Hotel became the first place in Houston to be electrically lighted. Two years later five 2,000-candle-power arc lights strung twenty-six feet above the ground sputtered to life on Main Street. The *Houston Daily Post* reported, "The view from the head of Main Street, taking in five lights in a line is very fine, producing a beautiful effect." Gas lighting, however, remained much in evidence in the business district and in selected residential areas. The Houston Gas Light Company, in operation since 1868, continued to service customers by extending its network of pipes and mains to residential neighborhoods of the working class.

Providing an adequate, clean water supply proved to be much more difficult than furnishing electricity, gas, or telephone service. In 1878 the city authorized a New York firm to build waterworks to supply the city with water from Buffalo Bayou. Pipes were laid before the operation was sold to a group of Houstonians in 1881. Under local ownership, the Houston Waterworks Company ran into severe problems. Several fires devastated major areas of the city because the water pressure was inadequate. Additionally, drinking water from the bayou was polluted. Even after

artesian wells were drilled to provide pure water, contamination occurred each time water was drawn from the bayou to fight fires. The polluted waters of Buffalo Bayou would remain as a continuing problem.

Opinion among city leaders was divided over the best method of financing city improvements. One faction favored private franchises; the other favored municipal ownership of public facilities. Samuel Brashear, a strong advocate of public ownership, was elected mayor of Houston in 1898 and

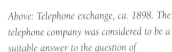

Above: Telephone exchange, ca. 1898. The telephone company was considered to be a suitable answer to the question of respectable employment for young women.
COURTESY HOUSTON METROPOLITAN RESEARCH CENTER, HOUSTON PUBLIC LIBRARY.

Left: City Park. Band concerts were a popular Sunday afternoon event in City Park, later renamed Sam Houston Park. Houston's first zoo was also located in the park.
POSTCARD FROM AUTHOR'S COLLECTION.

promptly hired a civil engineer from New York to produce a comprehensive plan that included an electric power plant, waterworks, a sewage treatment plant, and a garbage incinerator. By the time the plan was presented in February 1899, the city charter had been revised to provide funding for the massive public works project.

Mayor Brashear also believed that the city should own and operate parks for its residents. In 1899, he purchased eleven acres along Buffalo Bayou for the city's first public park. The Noble home on the property became the park headquarters, and new improvements included a small lake with a conservatory nearby, a bandstand in the center of the park, a pavilion, and an arbor. City Park, soon renamed Sam Houston Park, became a popular gathering place.

The one project which had most consistently engaged the energies of Houston's leaders throughout the city's existence was the development of a viable waterway. This remained a vital concern of the community in the latter decades of the nineteenth century.

The years after Charles Morgan sent his first vessel to the terminal at Clinton were busy ones for the channel. By 1880 the Morgan line was transporting approximately 286,000 tons of cargo annually on Buffalo Bayou. The increase in traffic on the channel was accompanied by improvements in related facilities. With the encouragement of the

Houston Cotton Exchange, several new cotton compresses were erected. All were conveniently located between the bayou and railroad connections so that cotton could be received from the interior, compressed, sent down a chute to barges on the bayou, and then placed on oceangoing vessels. By 1883 Houston was surpassed only by New York City in cotton sales. Some enterprising Houstonians also saw the potential of their town as a grain market since railroads to the north connected Houston with grain-producing areas. Their vision resulted in the construction of a grain elevator with a capacity of 150,000 bushels.

With the increased activity, the inadequacies of the ship channel became more obvious. Although a federal survey in 1871 had recognized the potential of the channel, Congress appropriated little money for improvements. Even after work finally began on deepening the channel and planning a route across Galveston Bay, the army engineers still had misgivings about further development of the channel, because the Morgan interests had diverted most water-borne cargo to their recently completed railroad line between Houston and New Orleans. Even more damaging to Houston's aspirations for a deepwater channel were renewed efforts at Galveston to increase the depth of water over the outer bar in the harbor there.

Although some work continued on the stretch of bayou between Clinton and Houston during the 1880s, more and more of the water traffic was limited to low-grade freight. The passenger boats which had produced so much activity in the previous two decades passed into oblivion.

However, a dedicated group of Houstonians still believed that Buffalo Bayou could accommodate oceangoing vessels. Eber Worthington Cave and George W. Kidd began collecting data which they sent to Washington as a show of support for the channel. They were assisted in these efforts by William D. Cleveland and H. W. Garrow, both active in the Houston Cotton Exchange; attorney John T. Brady; Captain R. B. Talfor with the United States Army Corps of Engineers; and Joseph Chappell Hutcheson, who represented Houston in Congress.

The devotion of these and other men to their city became a matter of jest to some visitors. One humorist wrote, "After you have listened to the talk of one of these pioneer veterans for some time, you begin to feel the creation of the world, the arrangement of the solar system, and all subsequent events, including the discovery of America, were pro-

visions of an all-wise Providence, arranged with a direct view to the advancement of the commercial interests of Houston."

The same humorist made a great show of looking for the Port of Houston. When at last he found it, he gave a description calculated to amuse Galvestonians: "The Houston seaport is of a very inconvenient size—not quite narrow enough to jump over, and a little too deep to wade through without taking off your shoes. When it rains, the seaport rises up twenty or thirty feet, and the people living on the beach, as it were, swear their immortal souls away on account of their harbor facilities. The Houston seaport was so low when I saw it, that there was some talk of selling the bridges to buy water to put in it."

On the other hand, deepwater improvements at Galveston were no jesting matter to Houston leaders. In 1896 Galveston harbor, with a depth of twenty-five feet, officially opened as a deepwater port. Refusing to be defeated by this economic crisis, Houstonians launched their own deepwater movement. Representative Hutcheson, just before retiring from Congress, introduced a bill requesting a survey for a twenty-five-foot-deep channel to Houston. Hutcheson arranged for members of the Rivers and Harbors Committee to visit the city to inspect Buffalo Bayou.

As the day of the visit approached, local leaders became apprehensive. The year 1896

had been one of unusual drought, and Buffalo Bayou had dwindled to a mere trickle. However, as the Congressmen were en route, heavy rains descended on Texas. The bayou rose in its banks and then overflowed. The congressional committee was duly impressed and reported favorably on the channel project.

A board of engineers met in Houston in late July 1897 to consider the work. Houston business leaders presented statistics supporting the economic value of the channel, reporting that over a half-million bales of cotton were being transported each year. In addition to cotton and cotton products, coal, lumber, building materials, and general merchandise were also cargo items.

After their inspection of the bayou and the Houstonians' presentation of its advantages, the engineers recommended the adoption of the project. They estimated that the initial cost of upgrading the channel would be $4 million. However, in spite of the engineers' approval and the ongoing support of Congressman Tom Ball, who had replaced Hutcheson in the House of Representatives, the channel received only small appropriations, and the work proceeded slowly. By 1900 the proposed depth of twenty-five feet had been modified to eighteen-and-one-half feet.

On September 8, 1900, nature intervened when a hurricane with winds estimated at 120 miles per hour and an accompanying six-foot tidal wave struck Galveston Island, taking six thousand lives and destroying much of the city. This tragic event made obvious the advantages of a port protected from the sea. Houstonians began new negotiations to ensure that their city would emerge as the preeminent port on the Gulf Coast.

As a new century dawned, Houston, with 44,653 residents, was seventy-fifth in population among American cities. It was the nation's largest railroad center south of St. Louis; the second-largest manufacturing center in Texas; and, exceeded only by New Orleans, the South's second-largest city in bank clearings. Houston was on the brink of soaring to new heights, and a rich discovery in the earth would speed that journey along.

BLACK GOLD ON THE BAYOU

January 10, 1901, was a cold, clear day in southeast Texas. About half past ten that morning a gusher erupted in the Spindletop oil field near Beaumont. For nine days it poured out seventy to one hundred thousand barrels of oil each day, making it the largest producing well in the world outside the Baku field in Russia. The largest daily flow from any previous site in the United States had been six thousand barrels.

Texas settlers had often observed crude oil seeping from the earth. As early as September 13, 1847, Andrew Briscoe wrote from Houston that "about 74 or 75 miles east of this… on the low coast prairie, there is a shallow pond" from the bottom of which rose "sulphurous gas bubbles… and British oil or something very like it… this place is called Sour Lake." During his visit to Texas in 1854, Frederick Law Olmsted had also noted a slight odor "of sulphurrated hydrogen" at Sour Lake. Shortly after the Civil War, Dick Dowling, the hero of Sabine Pass, had acquired a consider-

able oil lease near Houston but was unsuccessful in his exploration.

The first economically significant discovery came in 1894 near Corsicana. The Corsicana field developed gradually, peaking about 1900. It was there that the first modern refinery in Texas was operated by the J. S. Cullinan Company.

One of the most active areas for exploration in Texas was the upper Gulf Coast near Beaumont, where drilling began in 1892.

Speculator Pattillo Higgins spent several years in shallow drilling. In 1899, after frequent futile efforts, Higgins appealed to Captain Anthony F. Lucas for assistance. Lucas, the nation's leading expert on salt dome formations, was convinced that there was oil in the vicinity of the large salt dome known as Spindletop; and he readily negotiated a lease with Higgins's Gladys City Oil, Gas, and Manufacturing Company. After an unsuccessful well was abandoned, a new one was started in the fall of 1900. When it reached a depth of 1,139 feet, mud began bubbling from the hole. Soon gas, and then oil, was shooting a hundred feet into the air. A new age was born.

Beaumont became a boom town, but the discovery of the Spindletop field had a tremendous effect on Houston as well. Businessmen immediately recognized opportunities in a fledgling industry and sprang into action. Peden and Company, a local hardware concern, began to advertise "Oil Well Casing and Pipes, Drilling Cable, Etc." and Hugh Hamilton of the Houston Ice and Brewing Association journeyed to Beaumont to negotiate for one hundred thousand barrels of fuel oil. By the end of the year, fifty industrial plants in the city had converted to oil-fueled energy systems, and the first local freight train utilizing oil rather than coal was being operated by the Houston and Texas Central Railroad.

Four hundred companies were organized at Spindletop during the first year. An oil stock exchange was established in Houston to offer stock in these companies to an eager investing public. Between June 1, 1901, and February 1, 1902, the Houston exchange transacted sales totaling over seven million shares. Because most of the smaller companies were not successful, many investors lost money.

Of greater significance to Houston's future were the major oil companies that evolved after the discovery at Spindletop. Three of these companies—the Texas Company, Gulf, and Humble—would eventually move their principal offices to the bayou city.

Joseph S. Cullinan, who had learned the intricacies of the oil industry by going to work as a young man for Standard Oil of

Pennsylvania, had been a pioneer in the Corsicana oil fields. Moving to Beaumont following the discovery at Spindletop, Cullinan, with the financial backing of former Governor James Hogg and a group of New York investors, founded the Texas Fuel Company to buy oil and sell it to northern refineries. In 1902, the company was reorganized as the Texas Company and began expanding its operations by utilizing subsidiary companies for production. Subsequent production at the Sour Lake and Humble fields near Houston provided the company with a secure financial basis. In 1905, the Texas Company linked these two fields by pipeline to its new refinery in Port Arthur. In the same year Cullinan had written to a business associate, "Houston seems to me to be the coming center of the oil business." Three years later the Texas Company moved its central offices from Beaumont to Houston. This was the first step toward Houston's becoming the center of the oil industry in the Southwest.

John H. Galey and James M. Guffey, who had backed Anthony Lucas financially, persuaded the Mellon banking interests of Pittsburgh to support them in further Spindletop ventures. In May 1901, they organized the J. M. Guffey Petroleum Company as a fuel marketing firm. The company soon began construction of a field collecting system

and a pipeline to link Spindletop to the extensive storage and loading facilities at Port Arthur. By June it had decided to expand operations by construction of a refinery at Port Arthur. Work on the refinery, later incorporated as a separate entity and designated the Gulf Refining Company, began July 13, 1901. By the next spring, the refinery was in operation. Gulf Oil Corporation moved its offices to Houston in 1916.

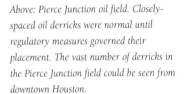

Above: Pierce Junction oil field. Closely-spaced oil derricks were normal until regulatory measures governed their placement. The vast number of derricks in the Pierce Junction field could be seen from downtown Houston.

COURTESY HOUSTON METROPOLITAN RESEARCH CENTER, HOUSTON PUBLIC LIBRARY.

Left: Dixie Filling Station, 1919. The first filling station which Humble Oil and Refining Company built in Houston contained such decorative elements as art glass and mosaic tiles. This elegant styling was intended to convey the elevated status of automobile owners.

COURTESY HOUSTON METROPOLITAN RESEARCH CENTER, HOUSTON PUBLIC LIBRARY.

In 1905, as Spindletop began to decline in production, a location nearer Houston became the largest oil-producing site in southeast Texas. A field near the little community of Humble, eighteen miles northeast of Houston, was soon producing about three million barrels of oil a month. The village of eight hundred attracted ten thousand people to the area, and the price of real estate soared to twelve thousand dollars per acre within a week's time.

Two of the more successful drillers in the Humble field were William Stamps Farish and Robert E. Blaffer. Farish, an attorney, and Blaffer, a purchasing agent for Southern Pacific Railroad, had met in a boarding house in Beaumont during the oil fever days after the Spindletop discovery. In 1906, they moved to Houston to concentrate on the nearby Humble field. To expand their operations, in 1911, Farish and Blaffer formed the Humble Oil Company with Ross S. Sterling, an independent oil operator, and Walter Fondren, one of the most skilled rotary drillers in southeast Texas. The company made Houston its headquarters in 1912 as it added drilling operations in Oklahoma and at the Sour Lake and Goose Creek fields between Houston and Beaumont. In just five years, Humble Oil Company had 217 wells in production. As its operations expanded, the company, with a capitalization of a million

dollars, reorganized in 1917 as the Humble Oil and Refining Company.

In 1918 Humble deeded Standard Oil of New Jersey a half interest in the growing Humble organization in exchange for $17 million as capital for the construction of new pipelines and refineries. Humble Oil and Refining Company exemplified a company that began as a relatively small operation and achieved recognition as an integrated organization that produced, transported, refined, purchased, and marketed petroleum.

As exploration surged, Houston found itself in the middle of an emerging oil region. Goose Creek had begun to produce in 1908. Discoveries followed at Damon Mound, Barbers Hill, West Columbia, and Blue Ridge. By 1919 three-quarters of Gulf Coast oil was from fields in the Houston area.

The increase in oil production spurred the development of the related oil tool industry. Howard R. Hughes, Sr., an Iowa attorney who had migrated to the Texas oil fields, realized that a special drill bit was needed to penetrate the surface of very hard rock. Hughes successfully designed a bit that would penetrate medium and hard rock surfaces ten times faster than any equipment previously employed. In 1909, Hughes and Walter B. Sharp organized the Sharp-Hughes Tool Company to manufacture the bit on a large scale. By 1914 Hughes's drill bit was being used in eleven states and thirteen foreign countries. James Abercrombie, who had been a driller-contractor in both the Spindletop and Humble fields, invented a device to prevent well blowouts caused by excessive pressure. H. S. Cameron, who serviced Abercrombie's equipment, began producing the device. As a result of this collaboration, Cameron Iron Works, an oil field equipment manufacturer, came into existence.

Houston's business leaders firmly believed that their city could become the focal point of the oil industry in southeast Texas. An important component of this goal was deepwater shipping, preferably in a protected harbor. Thus, efforts were continued to enlarge Houston's ship channel. It soon became apparent that the $4 million appropriated by Congress in 1897 was inadequate to complete the work, and the issue arose again as to the best and most cost-efficient site for a terminus. The location of the head of navigation on Buffalo Bayou had been debated since 1836 when the Allens declared that the head should be the intersection of Buffalo and White Oak bayous. Some old-timers continued to support that idea, which would still place the terminal point at the foot of Main Street. Others favored a location farther downstream.

After conferring with his colleagues in Congress, Representative Tom Ball advised Houston's port proponents that a downstream terminus should be selected in order to eliminate the costs of straightening the sharp bends in the upper bayou. A section of the bayou located just above Lynchburg and known as Long Reach was chosen as the most feasible location. When work began in March 1905, surveyor Charles Crotty described the area as still having a primitive appearance with the sloping south banks lined by large magnolia, pine, and oak trees, and the steep north bank covered with heavy underbrush.

The project was almost completed by 1908, when financial constraints caused a sharp reduction in all river and harbor appropriations. For the next four years, as tugs and barges continued to carry most of the traffic, little was done on the channel except maintenance.

Impatient at the slow progress on the channel after 1908, a group of deepwater support-

ers met at the office of the Houston Business League to hear a proposal by Congressman Ball that the city complete the project. The mechanism for doing this would be a navigation district, which would issue bonds to pay for the improvements. Not only did Ball recommend the creation of the navigation district, but he suggested that the city offer to share with the federal government the cost of a deepwater channel. A local delegation, headed by Mayor Horace Baldwin Rice, traveled to Washington and appeared before the Rivers and Harbors Committee with their offer. After receiving assurance that the facilities would be publicly owned, the committee voted unanimously to accept the proposal. The Houston Plan established the precedent, which would be followed routinely in the years ahead, of cost-sharing between local and federal government.

Left: The William C. May *being escorted by tugs on the Houston Ship Channel. The first oceangoing vessel to make its way up the channel after it officially opened in 1914, the* William C. May—*a 184-foot schooner—brought a load of pipe from Philadelphia.*

COURTESY HOUSTON METROPOLITAN RESEARCH CENTER, HOUSTON PUBLIC LIBRARY.

Below: No-tsu-oh Court, 1902. King Nottoc, Jesse H. Jones, and Queen Claire Robinson ruled over the annual festivities.

COURTESY HOUSTON ENDOWMENT, INC. ARCHIVES.

Above: Advertisement, Houston Packing Company. The largest independent packing plant in the southwest, it was located on six acres along the Houston Ship Channel. It advertised that Houston was the only city in the South in which canned meats were processed.

COURTESY HOUSTON METROPOLITAN RESEARCH CENTER, HOUSTON PUBLIC LIBRARY.

Right: Advertisement, Magnolia Park Subdivision.

COURTESY HOUSTON METROPOLITAN RESEARCH CENTER, HOUSTON PUBLIC LIBRARY.

Below: Opening Ceremony of Houston Ship Channel, November 14, 1914. Sue Campbell, daughter of Mayor Ben Campbell, dropped white roses into the water and declared, "I christen thee Port of Houston and hither the boats of all nations may come and receive hearty welcome." Standing with her are Texas Governor Oscar B. Colquitt and Captain A. W. Grant of the battleship Texas.

COURTESY HOUSTON ENDOWMENT, INC., ARCHIVES.

The delegation returned home to persuade the citizens of Harris County to create the Harris County Houston Ship Channel Navigation District and to approve the issuance of bonds in the amount of $1,250,000 to pay for the District's share of the waterway. Rallies were held throughout the city with dozens of prominent citizens presenting the project as critical to the progress of the region. The *Houston Daily Post* reported that the election was the "most momentous epoch in the history of Texas since the Battle of San Jacinto." Mayor Rice even declared a half-holiday on election day, January 10, 1911, to enable voters to go to the polls.

Although the issue was approved by the voters, the bonds were difficult to sell, and it appeared that Houston would not be able to match the federal appropriation. Jesse H. Jones, a director and major stockholder of Union National Bank, offered to ask Houston banks to purchase the bonds in proportion to their capital and surplus. Seven banks agreed to jointly purchase $750,000 of the bonds. The remaining bonds were purchased by the city and county governments or were sold to

MAGNOLIA PARK
SUBDIVISION OF
HOUSTON, TEXAS

PRESENTED BY
MAGNOLIA PARK LAND CO.
916 TEXAS AVE.   OLD PHONE 2600
HOUSTON, TEXAS

investors. With the money raised, work on the ship channel began the next year.

In 1913, the citizens of Harris County approved another $3 million in bonds for port improvements, and work on the channel was completed by September 1914. Houston now had a waterway fifty-one miles long and twenty-five feet deep.

The formal opening of the Ship Channel was incorporated into the annual No-tsu-oh Carnival that year. No-tsu-oh, a Mardi Gras-like festival, had originated in 1899 to stimulate business for Houston merchants. Using a vocabulary with backward spelling, the businessmen founders devised a fable surrounding the legendary King Nottoc (Cotton) and his annual return to his capital city of No-tsu-oh (Houston) in the mythical realm of Saxet (Texas) in the land of Tekram (Market). The week of gaiety was filled with parades, balls, and sporting events. The 1914 celebration was designated as the No-tsu-oh Deepwater Jubilee, ruled over by King Retaw (Water).

On November 10, celebrants gathered at the new Turning Basin. Arrangements had been made for President Woodrow Wilson to fire a cannon on the banks of the Channel by pushing a button in Washington. As the cannon boomed, Houston was officially designated a deepwater port.

Before the end of 1915, ships were traveling regularly between Houston and east coast ports. On January 13, 1917, the *Baltimore*, the first ship to sail from Houston to a foreign port, departed for Havana. Once again the vision and persistence of Houston leaders had paid handsome dividends for the city.

Two other major projects had a significant effect on Houston. The Gulf Intracoastal Waterway provided an inland route from Galveston Bay to New Orleans. Together with the Houston Ship Channel, it linked Houston suppliers to inland consumers through the

Mississippi River System. The recently completed Panama Canal provided Houston shippers easier access to the Pacific Ocean and to markets of the Far East.

The opening of the Houston Ship Channel spurred the development of oil refineries in the area. The Galena Signal Oil Company, constructed in 1916, was the first; and numerous other regional companies built refineries within the next two years. Throughout the 1920s, the Shell Petroleum Corporation, Humble Oil, the Texas Company, the Gulf Refining Company, and most of the other oil interests in southeast Texas expanded their facilities along the channel.

Other industries also located their operations in the ship channel area. In 1914 Armour built a plant to produce twenty thousand tons of fertilizer per year, and the Texas Portland Cement Company began to operate in 1916 with shell from Galveston Bay, clay from Pasadena, and oil brought via the channel on barges. Flour, steel, and chemical companies were also attracted, and in the next decade more than fifty businesses had located along the channel.

As new industries were established, Houston entrepreneurs rushed to the area with schemes to provide housing for the new, large labor force. Planned communities sprang up on both sides of the channel. Magnolia Park, Central Park, Houston Harbor, and Port Houston became thriving neighborhoods offering industrial laborers homes near the workplace. At the same time,

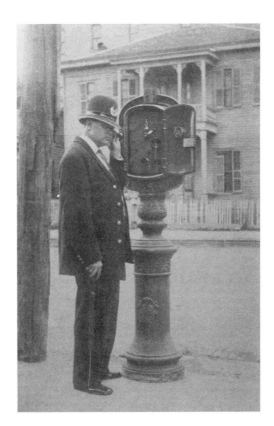

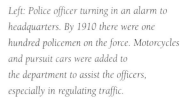

the streetcar line made the city readily accessible. Magnolia Park became a lively *barrio* for many immigrants from Mexico. These newcomers established a wide range of community institutions, including mutual aid societies, religious organizations, and theatrical groups. The communities eventually became part of the city of Houston.

Houston's municipal government continued to play a major role in the city's development, although some Houstonians questioned its actions as an instrument of the business community. At the turn of the century the city government had been embroiled in a struggle between business leaders, who favored granting services to spur the economic growth of the business community, and ward-based politicians concerned with the delivery of services to the neighborhoods. In particular, municipal services were denied to black neighborhoods. In 1900 the ward system of elections was replaced by the at-large system, and in 1903 the imposition of a state poll tax had the effect of further disenfranchising poorer citizens.

By 1905, the business elites were in complete control when a commission form of government was created. Under the new structure, four aldermen would be elected at large,

Above: George Hermann. A native Houstonian, Hermann was deeply interested in the welfare of his fellow citizens. He not only gave park land to the city but his will provided for a charity hospital, which finally opened in 1925.

COURTESY HOUSTON METROPOLITAN RESEARCH CENTER, HOUSTON PUBLIC LIBRARY.

Right: Gold medal awarded at the World's Industrial and Cotton Centennial Exposition to Thomas William House, Jr. for sugar production, 1884.

COURTESY, THE TORCH COLLECTION, HOUSTON.

Below: South Main Street at Hermann Drive, 1928. Hermann Park was laid out according to landscape architect George Kessler's plan. The area plantings were carefully developed, as indicated by the gardens leading to the park and the double rows of live oak trees placed on both sides of Main Street.

COURTESY HOUSTON METROPOLITAN RESEARCH CENTER, HOUSTON PUBLIC LIBRARY.

while other officers would be appointed by the mayor with the consent of the aldermen. On June 5, 1905, Horace Baldwin Rice became Houston's first full-time mayor.

The new government proved to be a reasonably efficient one. It solved the city's water problem by purchasing the privately owned water company and purifying the contaminated water. In the area of finance, the government reduced taxes and eliminated the floating debt. For the first time, a city administration took an interest in general planning. While early attempts had been made to enhance the beauty and order of the town by planting trees and assigning street names and numbers, Houston's general appearance was still not pleasing, and citizens were becoming more vocal in their complaints. *Progressive Houston*, a City of Houston publication billed as a "Journal for the Advancement of the City," addressed this need in its August 1911 issue by stating, "We believe that the movement for the refinement of urban life… is inspired by a genuine desire for a softer and more exalting environment." In a more practical vein the article added that these improvements would also be advantageous in providing desirable publicity for the city.

In view of these public sentiments, Edward A. Peden, president of the Chamber of Commerce, urged that the city undertake more extensive planning in order to build a more habitable community. In the spring of 1912, Arthur C. Comey, a landscape architect from Cambridge, Massachusetts, spent several months in Houston and drew a developmental scheme for the City Park Commission. His suggestions included an encircling band of parks following the bayous, an outer railroad belt to break the vast number of lines crossing the city, zoning to protect land values, a civic center, and a commission which would prepare and enforce an official plan for Houston. Of Comey's recommendations, the only one adopted was that a park be developed across from Rice Institute, which was then being built on Main Street at the southern edge of the city. In 1914, George Hermann, who had assembled a real estate empire after the discovery of oil on his land at Humble, donated 285 acres along Bray's Bayou near the South Main site. Following Hermann's death later that year, additional

acreage was acquired from his estate, and in 1915 the Board of Park Commissioners retained George E. Kessler of St. Louis as its consulting landscape architect. Kessler drew plans for Hermann Park and designed a park-like boulevard by planting double rows of live oak trees on the part of Main Street fronting Rice Institute. Progressive Houston approved such planning as an affirmation that the great city of the future must be "a thing of beauty and joy forever."

About the same time, Mayor Rice and the City Council sponsored a study of European cities in order to plan for Houston's future. In Frank Putnam's 1913 report, he commented: "Six years ago, viewing Houston for the first time, and observing that this city had nearly if not quite a hundred excellent churches, but had very few sewers, less than one-half the necessary water service that was needed for people then here, a scant one-eighth of the needed pavement, and only a small percentage of scattering sidewalks, I gained the impression that while people of Houston were admirably equipped for living in Heaven, they were rather poorly equipped for living in Houston." Putnam proposed, among other things, the establishment of a planning commission. However, no systematic form of planning would be considered by the municipal government until the 1920s.

The absence of certain amenities did not lessen Houstonians' enthusiasm for their growing city. Civic boosterism became a popular means of selling the city to interested capitalists as well as to prospective residents. Slogans were used to create a favorable impression. In 1891 Houston had been labeled the "Hub City" for its railroads, the "Bayou City" for its location near navigable water, and the "Magnolia City" for its natural beauty. In 1905, the *Chronicle* referred to Houston as the "Queen City of the Southwest." The most lasting label, "Where Seventeen Railroads Meet the Sea," became a trademark phrase and was used for decades to promote the city.

Local boosterism was also utilized in the movement to diversify Texas agriculture and to portray the Texas Gulf Coast as ideal for

Above: Market House, 1904. This structure was the fourth one to occupy Market Square. The bell in its lower tower served as fire alarm for the entire city, while the Seth Thomas four-sided clock could be seen a mile away. When this building burned in 1961, the square became a public park.

COURTESY HOUSTON METROPOLITAN RESEARCH CENTER, HOUSTON PUBLIC LIBRARY.

Below: Promotional brochure, prominently displaying one of the city's most popular logos—"Where Seventeen Railroads Meet the Sea."

COURTESY HOUSTON METROPOLITAN RESEARCH CENTER, HOUSTON PUBLIC LIBRARY.

truck farming. Harris County had long been known for its fertile soil. Now that the extensive rail transportation network was in place, agricultural products could be shipped to Midwestern and Eastern markets. The area around Houston soon became nationally recognized as a source for two commodities, sugar and rice. Sugar cane, an important local crop prior to the Civil War, regained its prominence after the turn of the century through the use of prisoners as farm laborers, and through the establishment of sugar mills. In 1909, seven mills operated in the region, and the American Sugar Refining Company at Sugar Land was the largest producer of refined sugar in the state.

Rice farming became profitable in the area when improved methods of irrigation were developed. One of the earliest rice growers in

Above: Display in Main Street store, 1917. This clothing display not only reflected the patriotism of Houstonians but also showed the profound effect the war had on fashion.

COURTESY HOUSTON METROPOLITAN RESEARCH CENTER, HOUSTON PUBLIC LIBRARY.

Right: Camp Logan, World War I. The camp eventually trained more than 30,000 soldiers, including both infantry and artillery.

COURTESY HOUSTON METROPOLITAN RESEARCH CENTER, HOUSTON PUBLIC LIBRARY.

Below: Rice cultivation. Kiyoaki Saibara stands with other workers in a rice field owned by his father, Seito Saibara. This land is now part of the NASA facility in southeastern Harris County.

COURTESY MAY, JULIA, AND NINA ONISHI, U. T. INSTITUTE OF TEXAN CULTURES, SAN ANTONIO, TEXAS.

Harris County was Seito Saibara, who immigrated from Japan in 1903 with the idea of establishing a Japanese colony in Texas. Although the colony did not materialize, Saibara successfully introduced rice cultivation; and by 1909 Texas had become the foremost supplier of rice to the nation. Four rice mills operated within the city of Houston.

While no other crops approached the national importance of sugar and rice, promotional literature extolled the profits to be made from growing oranges, figs, and strawberries. Indeed, the Pasadena area became known as the strawberry center of the Gulf Coast. As a result of the constant boosting of the area's agricultural potential, large numbers of immigrants were attracted to Houston and the surrounding countryside.

The most active boosters in the city were members of the business community. The Business League, created in 1895 to promote civic involvement, was renamed the Chamber of Commerce in 1910 since the earlier Chamber had faded from existence many years before. By 1911 the organization, with twelve hundred members, began discussing requirements for Houston to become a major metropolis. They reported that "the world is now a neighborhood, made so by rapid transit and competition in the carrying trade by rail and water." Their vision for a "Greater Houston" was a rapidly expanding one. Little

did Houstonians realize that their city would soon emerge onto the worldwide stage.

The assassination of Austrian Archduke Franz Ferdinand at Sarajevo on June 28, 1914, plunged the major nations of Europe into war. Although Houstonians, along with the rest of America, tried to remain neutral and hoped that the conflict would not involve their country, they nevertheless became very conscious of the war. The city's first "preparedness" parade was held in June 1916. In the same year a local chapter of the American Red Cross was organized in the event wartime disasters should occur.

When the United States entered the war on April 6, 1917, Houstonians were eager to do their part. By June more than twelve thousand men were enrolled in local selective service registration, and Liberty Loan subscriptions totaled more than $2.5 million. Citizens enthusiastically participated in the food conservation program known as "Hooverizing," which called for wheatless Mondays and Wednesdays, meatless Tuesdays, and porkless Thursdays and Saturdays; fat and sugar were to be conserved every day. Heatless days and lightless nights were also encouraged as a show of patriotism.

The United States government, having recognized the usefulness of airplanes for both reconnaissance and bombing, initiated a major pilot-training effort. The government's search for training sites prompted Houston leaders to bid for a base. A bond issue was used to purchase approximately two thousand acres of low-lying pasture land seventeen miles south of downtown. The business community united behind the effort, and the Houston site was selected. The Army pumped $5 million into construction of its first aerial bombing school.

The field, which was officially opened on November 27, 1917, was named for Lt. Eric Ellington, who some years earlier had trained in Texas City prior to being killed in a flight

accident. During the next year, young pilots from Ellington Field were the first to fly at night, to make long distance flights, to establish an aerial gunnery range, and to implement an aerial ambulance.

A National Guard training facility was also placed in Houston. Construction began in the summer of 1917 on Camp Logan, situated about three miles west of downtown. The business community had lobbied for Camp Logan, knowing that it would be an economic boon for the city. At the same time a potentially explosive situation was developing. The all-black Third Battalion, Twenty-fourth United States Infantry arrived in July to assume guard duty at the construction site. Races were rigidly segregated in Texas, and in Houston hostilities quickly arose between white residents and the black troops.

On the night of August 23, 1917, a confrontation erupted between a black military policeman from the Third Battalion and two city policemen over the arrest that day of a soldier from Camp Logan. Amidst accusations of police brutality and rumors of mob attack, a massive altercation resulted in the deaths of two black soldiers, five police officers, and thirteen white civilians. In the aftermath of this disturbance, which would come to be known as the Riot of 1917, the entire Third Battalion was transferred to New Mexico where the largest court martial in American military history convicted 110 soldiers of murder and mutiny, and nineteen were eventually executed. Although a tragic chapter in Houston's history came to a close, the underlying issues were yet to be resolved.

The war did, however, have a positive effect on Houston's economy. The demand for cotton and oil, both vital to the war effort, stimulated business both during and after the war. Cotton was needed for the manufacture of smokeless powder, as well as for military clothing, medical supplies, and tenting. As the demand grew, cotton prices spiraled from less than seven cents to more than thirty-five cents per pound. As the United States was transformed from a debtor to a creditor nation through Allied purchases of American goods and supplies, bank deposits in Houston increased dramatically from $32 million in 1915 to more than $94 million in 1919. This influx of capital into Houston banks enabled local cotton merchants to become more directly involved in the growing, ginning, and milling of cotton and to expand their compresses, storage, and wharf facilities along the Ship Channel, making Houston more attractive as a seaport.

Above: Foley Bros. Store, 1907. Brothers Mike and Pat Foley opened their dry goods store on Main Street in 1902. The proceeds from their first day of business totaled $129.27. Their venture expanded into the present day merchandising giant, Foley's.

Below, left: Streetcars lined up on a downtown street, early 1900s. A local magazine calculated in 1907 that a streetcar passed the corner of Main and Congress every fifty six seconds.

Anderson, Clayton and Company, a cotton firm which had been founded in Oklahoma City by Frank E. Anderson, Monroe D. Anderson, and William L. Clayton, moved its headquarters to Houston in 1916 and designated the Houston Ship Channel as the primary clearinghouse for its cotton. Will Clayton, president of the company, explained the move, stating that "Houston was the little end of the funnel that drained all of Texas and the Oklahoma territory.... We were at the back door, and we wanted to be at the front door." Houston emerged from the war as the largest spot cotton market in the world and the largest inland seaport in the nation. Anderson, Clayton and Company eventually became one of the world's largest cotton brokerage firms.

The war also profoundly affected the oil industry. As the use of such land vehicles as trucks, tanks, and automobiles increased, demand for petroleum products also rose, and modern navies and the airplane augmented the consumption of oil. Shipments of petroleum products from the Port of Houston increased dramatically from 31,584 tons in 1915 to 293,400 tons in 1916. Gulf Coast oil prices rose from forty-eight cents per barrel in 1915 to $1.70 per barrel by 1919. The growth of the oil industry during the war greatly accelerated the industrialization which would occur in Houston in the 1920s.

Further improvements to the Ship Channel also resulted from the war experience. With the advent of war, business and civic leaders stressed the advantages of a deeper channel, emphasizing that petroleum could more easily be shipped to the Allies, and that improved waterways would relieve the nation's congested railroad system. Their lobbying paid off, and with appropriations of both federal and local funds, the Houston Ship Channel by 1925 was deepened to thirty feet.

While the war in Europe did benefit the city economically, it nonetheless had tragic consequences to the general public as more than five thousand Texans died. Thus, the news of the armistice on November 11, 1918, was received with great relief and was cause for celebration in Houston. The next day the *Houston Post* described the local reaction: "At 4:15 the *Post* was on the street and then the city rubbed its eyes and awoke. First the cry of the newsboys, then the honking of automobile horns, then far out in the city came the rattle of the city's private arsenals of light-pocket artillery. The locomotives then got into action and gradually all the factory whistles and sirens for miles around. No one able to get up remained in bed. Lights gleamed in every dwelling and people poured down into the business district. Until late in the day the revelry continued."

As Houstonians returned to peacetime activities, their city experienced unprecedented growth and acquired a new prominence on the national and world scenes. Stimulated by the oil industry and to a lesser degree by the cotton and lumber businesses, the economy seemed secure and the future bright. The next two decades, however, would not be free from trouble. Economic depression, racial unrest, labor conflicts, and natural disasters would pose problems.

BETWEEN THE WARS

I n April 1921, a thirty-two-year-old businessman, Oscar F. Holcombe, was elected mayor of Houston. He would serve eleven terms in the post during the course of his political career, and his tenures would be marked by numerous municipal improvements. At the same time, he set in place the strong-mayor form of government that would become the Houston standard in years ahead.

In his first campaign, Holcombe promised better business administration, reorganization of city departments, new schools, and paved streets. The growing number of automobile owners were already placing a burden on city thoroughfares. The first automobile, an electric "horseless carriage" had appeared on Houston streets in 1897. By 1922, there were thirty-five thousand gasoline-powered vehicles in the city, with a large number being produced in the area. The Ford Motor Company was assembling 350 cars per day in a factory in nearby Harrisburg. In addition to Ford, name brand cars being sold in Houston included Stutz, Overland, Maxwell, Winton, Packard, Buick, Cadillac, and Hupmobile. To control traffic, hand-operated signals were installed in 1921 at eleven downtown intersections. These were replaced six years later by fully automated traffic signals, making Houston the second city in the country to have such an advanced system.

The problems related to the increase in traffic, and in a more general way to Houston's rapid growth, once more raised the issue of city planning. In 1924, Mayor Holcombe appointed a permanent City Planning Commission. The firm of Hare and Hare, consultants from Kansas City, presented a comprehensive plan, which was ignored when the commission's appropriations expired. In 1927, the City Planning Commission was reestablished and Will C. Hogg was appointed chairman.

Oscar Holcombe. Known as "the Old Gray Fox" for his political acumen and his prematurely gray hair, Holcombe served as mayor of Houston for a total of twenty-two years between 1921 and 1957.

Above: William Clifford Hogg.
COURTESY MUSEUM OF FINE ARTS, HOUSTON ARCHIVES.

Below: 1920s traffic on Main Street. As evidenced by the lone policeman in the middle of the street, automatic traffic signals had not yet appeared.

SAN JACINTO MUSEUM OF HISTORY, CECIL THOMSON COLLECTION. COURTESY HOUSTON METROPOLITAN RESEARCH CENTER, HOUSTON PUBLIC LIBRARY.

An interesting blend of private businessman and public-minded citizen, Hogg was the oldest child of former Texas governor James C. Hogg, and he felt a keen sense of responsibility for civic welfare. Personal wealth, made possible by real estate and oil, enabled him to pursue this responsibility as a private citizen. Hogg saw the planning commission as the agency through which a merger of the "city efficient" and the "city beautiful" could be effected.

The concerns expressed earlier by Hare and Hare were once more addressed. After two years of work, the City Planning Commission presented its report, which included a detailed plan for improving thoroughfares, developing a network of highways and a transit system, expanding parks, and instituting zoning ordinances. Other sections of the report focused on waterways, aviation, the civic center, and schools. The report concluded: "Houston's growth has been rapid and promises to increase. It is the purpose of this plan to provide for the welfare, convenience and happiness of present and future citizens. In adopting the provisions of the plan, the people of Houston and their officials will have to decide whether they are building a great city or merely a great population."

To inform the public of the need for comprehensive planning and to stimulate pride in the city, Hogg formed the Forum of Civics. Through the Forum, the efforts of some three hundred private civic clubs, public officials, professional societies, and public utilities were coordinated. In spite of favorable public

sentiment, none of the proposals except for the civic center were even considered. A small but vocal anti-zoning element, along with the sudden death of Will Hogg and an approaching economic depression, brought the city's efforts at planning to an end.

Will Hogg's legacy to city planning is to be found in the private sector rather than in the public one. In 1924 Hogg, his brother Mike, and Hugh Potter developed River Oaks, a subdivision on eleven hundred acres at the western edge of the city. In keeping with his principles of urban planning, Hogg incorporated underground utilities, numerous small parks, abundant landscaping, and carefully laid-out streets. All nonresidential facilities were placed on the periphery of the development. Although River Oaks grew slowly, it became a prime example of what careful planning could accomplish.

At the same time, the Hogg family made possible a major park when they sold to the city at cost the 1,503 acres of land which had contained Camp Logan during World War I. Intended to honor those soldiers who perished in the war, the deed stipulated Memorial Park as the name and provided that, should the land be used for anything other than park purposes, it would revert to the Hogg heirs. Will Hogg's passion for planning a well-ordered environment had been partially fulfilled.

Education, one of the proposed components of a comprehensive urban plan, continued to be a concern to Houstonians. In 1920 the Houston public school system had twenty-eight thousand students. As the need for additional funding became critical, the school system moved away from municipal control and toward an independent district with a separate taxing authority. In 1923, city voters authorized an elected school board, and a year later the Houston Independent School District began to operate with Dr. E. E. Oberholtzer as superintendent of the system.

Dr. Oberholtzer expanded the concept of public education in 1927 when funding was provided for a junior college system that would operate as a component of the Houston public school system. Its two racially segregated branches used local high school facilities at night. Houston Junior College began

meeting at San Jacinto High School while Houston Colored Junior College held classes at Jack Yates High School. The schools continued as junior colleges for seven years. However, by 1933 there was strong support to expand to four-year colleges, still to be administered by the Houston School Board.

The University of Houston—formerly Houston Junior College—began operating in June 1934. Permanent facilities were subsequently built on the southeastern edge of the city. The first building was provided by oilman Hugh Roy Cullen, who felt strongly about "education for the children of working folks," which he saw to be the purpose of the University of Houston. At this point, Cullen began a life-long association with the university, both as board chairman and generous philanthropist. Houston Colored Junior College, which had been renamed Houston College for Negroes and would later become Texas Southern University, moved in 1946 to a permanent campus on land also donated by Hugh Roy Cullen.

The philanthropy of another Houstonian had provided several years earlier for the city's first institution of higher education. William Marsh Rice, whose entrepreneurial ventures in Houston had made him immensely wealthy, decided in 1891 that he wanted to create a school "dedicated to the advancement of art, literature, and science" in his adopted hometown. With this in mind, he established

a trust and stipulated his desires in his will. In 1900 while living in New York, Rice met an untimely death at the hands of his valet, who chloroformed him. After a widely publicized trial that revealed evidence of forged wills, the guilty parties were sentenced and Rice's original will was validated.

However, the will became involved in complicated litigation, and plans for developing Rice's vision were delayed. In 1907 the board, whom Rice had appointed years earlier, selected Princeton University professor Edgar Odell Lovett as the first president. Dr. Lovett toured universities all over the world seeking both ideas and an illustrious faculty for the school. In 1912 fifty-nine students entered the William M. Rice Institute for the Advancement of Letters, Science and Art.

To promote the recognition of Rice Institute as an educational facility of the first rank, as Lovett clearly intended, invitations were sent to educational institutions all over the world to send representatives to the opening ceremonies. One hundred seventy-five institutions, foreign and domestic, responded by sending biologists, physicists, mathematicians, philosophers, poets, historians, engineers—all outstanding scholars. A local newspaper reported, "Truly, as emphasized by the prominence of the men attendant upon them, these inaugural ceremonies usher in a season epochal in our history." William Marsh Rice's dream had materialized in the true spirit of accomplishment so characteristic of Houston.

As in the area of education, arts in Houston were enriched by the contributions of civic-minded citizens. In 1913 a group of women had organized the Houston Symphony Association. Thirty-three musicians were employed for an opening concert, which was held on a Sunday afternoon in June under the baton of cellist Julian Paul Blitz. In the succeeding years, three concerts were presented each season, all underwritten by local patrons who donated twenty-five dollars each. Although performances were discontinued during World War I, the Association remained intact, first under the leadership of Mrs. Edwin

CIVICS FOR HOUSTON

January 1928

B. Parker, and later with Miss Ima Hogg as president. During the 1920s, the group continued to meet regularly and to lay the groundwork for the eventual 1930s renaissance of the orchestra.

At this same time, a young Houstonian moved into a public role that she would occupy for the next half-century. Edna Woolford Saunders, a trained musician and an active member of the Women's Choral Club, became booking agent for the City Auditorium, built in 1910 as the South's largest auditorium and convention hall. In this capacity, Saunders became the most successful impresario in the entire Southwest. In 1920 she brought world-famous tenor Enrico Caruso to Houston where he appeared before six thousand persons, one of the largest audiences of his entire career. Subsequent performers appearing under "Edna Saunders Presents" were Serge Rachmaninoff, Fritz Kreisler, and Amelita Galli-Curci, as well as Al Jolson, Will Rogers, Jeanette McDonald, and Nelson Eddy. The Metropolitan Opera Company and the Ballet Russe de Monte Carlo became annual visitors to the city as Edna Saunders brought the very best in cultural experiences to Houstonians.

During the 1930s, Houston became recognized as a regional hub in the world of jazz. A multitude of dance halls and clubs provided opportunities for jazz musicians to develop their talent while entertaining the city's residents. Clubs such as the Eldorado Ballroom, Harlem Grill, and Pilgrim Temple provided venues for Milton Larkin, I. H. Smalley, Daisy

Richards, Arnett Cobb, and other musicians, many of whom attained national prominence after beginning their careers in Houston.

Another group of citizens was active in the field of visual arts. The Pubic School Art League had been formed in 1900 to introduce Houston's school children to great works of art. After placing reproductions in the city's classrooms, the group turned its efforts to educating the adult population. Rechartered in 1913 as the Houston Art League, the organization began acquiring a collection of art that was housed in the mayor's office and in members' homes. To provide a permanent home for the League, a site was secured through the generosity of Joseph F. Cullinan and the George Hermann estate. Extensive fundraising for a building followed. The entire community responded with individual gifts ranging from two dollars to thirty thousand dollars. On April 12, 1924, the Houston Art League opened the first municipal art museum in Texas. The next year, with the formal reorganization of the League, the name was changed to The Museum of Fine Arts, Houston.

The first museum director, Rice professor James Chillman, began building a collection to exhibit in the new building. His efforts were enhanced by the gifts of Annette Finnigan, who had long been interested in a Houston museum that would be comparable to those in Europe. Finnigan provided the museum's first collections in Egyptian, Greek, Roman, and Byzantine art. These early acquisitions were joined by significant pieces given by Ima Hogg. Slowly the museum's collections began to grow.

The 1920s were years of unrest for the city's minorities. The Ku Klux Klan, which had been active during the Reconstruction period but had since been dormant, reawoke after World War I and directed its hatred against the city's blacks, foreign-born, Catholics, and Jews. Strident propaganda and terrorist campaigns were used to curb involvement in community affairs or politics by groups the Klan deemed "un-American or immoral." But the Klan failed in its effort to control Oscar Holcombe during his first term and was also unsuccessful at defeating him in his reelection campaign. By 1923 the Klan

had lost much of its support and ceased to have a significant effect on the city.

The Klan's existence, however, had underscored myriad problems associated with runaway growth. Houston's population jumped from 78,800 in 1910 to 138,276 in 1920, making it the fourth fastest growing city in the nation. This pattern would continue as Houston, with a population approaching three hundred thousand in 1930, became the largest city in Texas.

The city's minority population, especially its black residents, were subjected to severe discrimination. School segregation had been in place since the Texas Constitution of 1876, and state laws had segregated railroads in 1891. A 1903 city ordinance had separated the races on Houston streetcars, and in 1907 City Council had enacted a law segregating hotels, restaurants, theaters, and other public facilities, including rest rooms and drinking fountains.

Occupational status remained low for the city's black population throughout the 1920s, and the Depression compounded its economic problems. Houston was, however, home to a small but substantial community of black professionals and business owners. In 1929 Houston had the thirteenth largest black population in the nation, and it ranked tenth in the number of black-owned businesses and seventh in average amount of sales for such businesses. Although the Houston Negro Chamber of Commerce was organized in the mid-1930s to promote black enterprises in the city, it achieved little success.

While Houston experienced no racial violence during these years, not all blacks complacently accepted subservience. Their exclusion from participation in primary elections

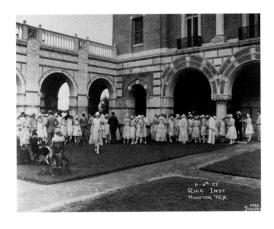

in a one-party state, as Texas was in the 1920s, effectively negated any potential political power.

In 1921, the Harris County Democratic Executive Committee passed a resolution expressly prohibiting blacks from voting in the next primary election. C. F. Richardson, editor of the *Houston Informer*, condemned the decision as a direct violation of constitutional rights, and a group of local black leaders filed suit against the chairman of the Harris County Democratic Party. This suit was the first step in a legal battle that would last almost a quarter of a century and would involve the city's black newspapers, many of its black civic leaders, and the National Association for the Advancement of Colored People (NAACP).

Houston's Hispanic population, who originally were mostly of Mexican descent, experienced many of the same obstacles as their numbers grew to approximately six thousand in 1920 and to 14,500 in 1930. While many found employment with the railroads and on the waterfront, others worked in a variety of service-oriented establishments. Still others opened their own businesses and developed a thriving shopping district east of downtown. In the ensuing economic depression, however, many of these businesses failed, increasing economic hardships within the city's Latin community.

In addition to widespread poverty,

Above: City Auditorium, constructed 1910. The City Auditorium was not only the site of musical performances, but it was also used for such events as poultry shows, hardware exhibits, boxing matches, and church conventions. The site is occupied today by the Jesse H. Jones Hall for the Performing Arts.

SAN JACINTO MUSEUM OF HISTORY, CECIL THOMSON COLLECTION. COURTESY HOUSTON METROPOLITAN RESEARCH CENTER, HOUSTON PUBLIC LIBRARY.

Below Left: Graduation day, Rice Institute, June 6, 1927.

COURTESY HOUSTON METROPOLITAN RESEARCH CENTER, HOUSTON PUBLIC LIBRARY.

Below: Edna Woolford Saunders.

COURTESY HOUSTON METROPOLITAN RESEARCH CENTER, HOUSTON PUBLIC LIBRARY.

Mexicans also suffered from discrimination in housing, education, and employment. To counter some of the racism, a local unit of the League of United Latin American Citizens (LULAC) was organized in 1934. The organization's activities focused on incidents in which the rights of people of Mexican descent were infringed upon by both employers and the police. A second group, the Latin American Club of Harris County (LAC), was formed the next year by John Duhig, Manuel Crespo, John J. Herrera, Juvencio Rodriguez, and Felix Tijerina. LAC became more political as it endorsed candidates and ambitiously tried to register the city's many Latin voters. Both groups held poll tax drives and sought to educate the community in their duties and responsibilities as American citizens while remaining advocates for Mexican-American rights. In 1939 LULAC and LAC combined into LULAC Council No. 60 and continued their efforts to make Mexican-Americans a more integral part of Houston society.

Another signal of local unrest was the hostility between working-class organizations and employers during the first quarter of the twentieth century. In this period of strong business growth, major strikes were called against the streetcar lines, building contractors, and shipping firms. The Houston Labor Council, which had been organized in 1889, became the focus of union activity. By 1914 fifty unions had been organized in the city. About one fifth of the white work force were members of the unions which were particularly strong in the building trades and transportation.

By contrast, unionization came slowly to the Gulf Coast petroleum industry. In 1916 a local union was formed in the Goose Creek oil field. Other locals were subsequently organized in neighboring fields. Producers, however, refused to recognize the oil field workers or to enter into negotiations with them. As a result, some ten thousand workers in the Gulf Coast fields, seeking a minimum wage of four dollars a day, went on strike on October 31, 1917. Federal mediators eventually settled the strike. Although there was no immediate improvement of wages and hours, the continued demand for oil and an increase in prices did indirectly benefit the oil field workers. As the unionization movement grew in Texas in the 1930s, oil companies vigorously resisted the demands of union members. Union sympathizers were often fired or harassed. By the late 1930s, however, the Oil Workers' Union of the Congress of Industrial Organizations (CIO) was representing employees of Gulf Coast refineries.

The port was another site of turmoil among the labor force. Work on the waterfront was hard, and in the mid-1920s laborers received only thirty-five cents an hour. At the onset of the Depression, workers outnumbered jobs, and, when the situation worsened, workers began organizing strikes against the steamship lines. The worst strike was threatened in 1935, finally erupting in October when longshoremen in Houston and other Gulf ports walked off their jobs. The strike lasted ten weeks, and by its conclusion fourteen men had died in the wake of strike-related violence in Texas and Louisiana. Another seamen's strike occurred at the port the next year. Although few issues were settled by these strikes, a representative of organized labor was added to the Port Commission, and labor relations on the waterfront were somewhat improved.

In 1930, the Chamber of Commerce magazine, Houston, made a brief list of the city's most influential leaders in the growth period of the previous decade. On the list were bankers John T. Scott and J. W. Neal; Humble

Oil executives W. S. Farish and Ross Sterling; attorney James A. Baker Sr.; and cotton magnate Will Clayton. At the top of the list was Jesse H. Jones, described in the article as a "master of men and money," who as a developer "decorated the city's towering skyline."

Jones had come to Houston in 1898 as general manager of his uncle's lumber company. His involvement in the lumber industry led to his career as a builder and developer. By the mid-1920s Jones had constructed thirty important commercial buildings in the city, retaining ownership of all of them. Real estate activities led to Jones's involvement in the newspaper industry. In 1908 he constructed a building for the publisher of the *Houston Chronicle* and received half-interest in the paper as a down payment on the building. After buying the other half-interest in 1926, Jones became sole owner of the *Chronicle*.

However, Jones's most significant business activities were in the area of finance. To fund his real estate projects, he borrowed heavily from banks in Dallas, New York, and Chicago, as well as those in Houston. Seeing the need for further development of local financial institutions, Jones entered banking himself. By 1915 he was a major owner of the National Bank of Commerce and a key player in Houston's financial arena.

Jones was a vigorous booster for his adopted hometown. In 1928 he brought a national political convention to the city. As the finance director of the Democratic National Committee, Jones attended the meeting at which the convention site was to be chosen. As cities across the country submitted their bids to host the convention, Jesse Jones decided that Houston was a viable choice, even though the Democrats had not met in the

South since 1872. He presented the committee with a personal check for two hundred thousand dollars and promised that a twenty-five-thousand-seat hall would be constructed for the June convention, just five months away. True to its "can-do" spirit, the city built Sam Houston Hall in just sixty-four days, raised $350,000 for the cost of the meeting, and hosted thousands of delegates for four days. The convention provided Houston its first national publicity and gave notice that this city on the bayou was destined to play a larger role in the affairs of the country.

As Houston approached its century mark, the future seemed bright and secure. Annual building permits were at an all-time high of more than $35 million. Local banks recorded $106 million in deposits. The Port of Houston ranked third in the United States in foreign exports, and the industrial complex along the channel had grown tremendously. Then, almost without warning, hard times hit the city.

In May 1929, Buffalo Bayou flooded, inundating a large section of the city and causing damage estimated at more than $1 million. Five months later on "Black Tuesday," October 29, Wall Street experienced its worst day in history as sixteen million shares of stock exchanged hands, and the New York Times industrial average plunged nearly forty points. Over the next few weeks, as stocks on the New York exchange continued to fall, the country began to feel the effects of a growing economic depression.

Houstonians initially remained optimistic and temporarily ignored the harsh realities of a collapsing economy. In March 1930, the *Post Dispatch* announced that "Houston is comparatively free of discontent due to economic conditions." Admittedly, Houston was unique among American cities during the Depression in that none of its banks failed. However, in 1931, two were in trouble. To forestall closure, Jesse Jones called a group of Houston bankers and other business leaders to his office. After a two-day meeting, which included all-night vigils, conferences, bank examina-

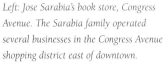

Above: Jesse Holman Jones. Involved in both business and civic affairs, Jones was often referred to as "Mr. Houston."
COURTESY HOUSTON ENDOWMENT, INC. ARCHIVES.

Right: Tickets, Democratic National Convention, June 26-29, 1928. Persons who were unable to gain admittance to the convention hall—pictured on the reverse side of the tickets—listened to the proceedings over outdoor loudspeakers.
COURTESY HOUSTON ENDOWMENT, INC. ARCHIVES.

Below: Houston skyline, 1927. The rising framework of the Niels Esperson Building exemplified the construction explosion occurring in Houston in the late 1920s.
COURTESY HOUSTON METROPOLITAN RESEARCH CENTER, HOUSTON PUBLIC LIBRARY.

tions, plans, and counterplans, a solution was reached. The $1,250,000 needed to save the failing banks was raised by assessing the stronger banks in the city in proportion to their deposits and by soliciting funds from local businesses. The two weak institutions received new ownership, and the crisis was averted.

While Houston may have been less affected by the Great Depression than most other cities, there was nevertheless a downturn in the economy. Building permits dropped, and unemployment skyrocketed. Throughout the city the deepening crisis brought insecurity and hardship to thousands of families as large numbers of workers were forced to go on relief. A Houston movie house sponsored "jobathons" in which donors, instead of pledging money, promised to hire unemployed men to do odd jobs in return for food, clothing, or money. The cities of Houston, Pasadena, and Galveston pooled their resources and formed the Tri-City Relief Association, creating soup kitchens. In response to the dire conditions, a voluntary repatriation movement developed in Houston among its Mexican population. During the early years of the Depression, at least two thousand Mexican residents returned to their native land to escape the conditions in Houston.

Fortunately, in the latter half of 1932, emergency relief money began to flow from the Reconstruction Finance Corporation (RFC), a federal government agency headed by Houstonian Jesse Jones. These funds, along with allocations from the Public Works Administration (PWA) and the Works Progress Administration (WPA), were used for county road repair, slum clearance, civic art, and public buildings. A new City Hall, the Sam Houston Coliseum and Music Hall, Mirabeau B. Lamar and Stephen F. Austin high schools, a new Jefferson Davis Hospital, and the San Jacinto Monument were built with this funding. Works of local artists Emma Richardson Cherry, Angela McDonnell, Ruth Uhler, Grace Spaulding John, and William McVey adorned several public buildings.

The San Jacinto Monument represented

Harris County's role in the Texas Centennial observance. Although Dallas was chosen as the site of the Centennial Exposition, federal funds were allocated for improvements to the historic San Jacinto battlefield and for construction of a monument to commemorate the victory of April 21, 1836, which brought independence to Texas. Houston architect Alfred Finn designed a 570-foot-high masonry structure, which at that time was the largest monument ever attempted and the first to be anchored to its own man-made bedrock. The towering shaft, topped by a symbolic Lone Star, was dedicated on April 21, 1939, as a beacon for freedom.

Houston became known as "the city the depression missed" largely because the oil industry remained strong as the demand for petroleum continued to rise. Between January 1932 and March 1933, hundreds of companies, including dozens of oil-related firms, opened for business in the city. Shell Petroleum Corporation and Tidewater Oil

Company transferred their headquarters to Houston, bringing the number of oil companies based in the city to thirty-eight. By the mid-1930s Houstonians were proudly labeling their city "the oil capital of the world." There was some justification for this boastful assertion in that, following the discovery of the world's largest oil field in East Texas in 1931, half of the world's oil production was located within six hundred miles of Houston. In addition, forty-two hundred miles of pipelines linked the city to hundreds of oil fields, and nearly half of all Texas oil was shipped through the Port of Houston. During the 1930s, a series of technological innovations in refining facilitated an increase in the quantity and quality of gasoline extracted from crude oil. By 1940 the Gulf Coast was a leading refining region with Humble Oil's Baytown refinery as one of the largest in the world.

Despite the Depression, transportation facilities continued to improve. The Port of Houston had emerged as a tremendously successful operation during the 1920s. By 1930 its rank in foreign exports from the United States was surpassed only by New York and Los Angeles. Almost eighty shipping lines called regularly at the Port that year, carrying cargo valued at $500 million.

To dramatize the progress made during the 1920s, Port officials invited the cruiser *Houston* to visit the city for Navy Day, October 27, 1930. Congress had named the ship for the city a year earlier after an intensive letter-writing campaign by Houstonians of all ages, from the mayor to schoolchildren. The six hundred-foot-long *Houston* was the largest vessel ever to navigate the Ship Channel. A full week of celebration was planned, and Houstonians collected fifteen thousand dollars to buy a silver service to present to the cruiser. During its week in port, approximately a quarter of a million persons visited the ship.

In the 1930s, however, flood-related problems threatened the continued success of the Port of Houston. As the city had grown, more and more drainage water had been channeled into Buffalo Bayou. Although the 1929 flood had caused major damage, a much worse flood in December 1935 turned the entire city into a disaster area. Twenty-five blocks of the

downtown district and a hundred blocks of the residential area were flooded to depths ranging from four to twelve feet. Eight people died, and property damage ran into millions of dollars. The 1935 flood proved to Houstonians that the Ship Channel could no longer serve as a drainage ditch for the city. Aided by newly elected Congressman Albert Thomas, a committee of influential citizens joined port officials and the United States Army Corps of Engineers to formulate a plan to protect both the city and the channel from further disasters. In 1937 the state legislature created the Harris County Flood Control District, and eventually the army engineers completed the Addicks and Barker dams west of the city.

By 1937, the Port of Houston was ranked second only to New York in tonnage and importance. A writer for *Fortune* magazine expressed amazement that the waterway was man-made. He called the Port a "channel parvenu" that was challenging the "river aristocrat," New Orleans, for Gulf trade. The article continued: "For twenty-five miles, you will negotiate a man-deepened channel through Galveston Bay. And then for another twenty-five you will poke your way through a meandering, landlocked, man-dredged bayou in which you can't turn around until you reach the

Above: City Hall by Thera Case, oil on canvas. City Hall was placed in a park-like setting when it was relocated from its Market Square site in 1939. Joseph Finger designed the structure in a modern style to represent, in his words, "the masses."

PHOTOGRAPH BY STORY J. SLOANE III.
COURTESY THE HERITAGE SOCIETY, HOUSTON.

Below: Pipeline construction under Houston Ship Channel. This Shell Oil Co. pipeline was constructed in 1931 to connect facilities on both sides of the channel.

COURTESY HOUSTON METROPOLITAN RESEARCH CENTER, HOUSTON PUBLIC LIBRARY.

Turning Basin, heart of Houston's waterfront.... And you will have realized how all the dredging, the thirty-odd wharves, the nineteen new-fangled locomotive cranes, the $4 million grain elevator, and other developments can represent an investment of federal, county and private funds amounting to $250,000,000."

The most dramatic development in transportation, however, occurred in the field of air travel. The first airplane flight in Houston occurred in 1910 when twenty-five hundred curious Houstonians watched a French pilot demonstrate his biplane over a field south of the city. However, no attempt was made to establish air service until an airmail route was considered in 1926. Two years later a group of businessmen formed the Houston Airport Corporation and inaugurated airmail service between Houston and Dallas. In 1937 the city administration, spurred by the fact that Dallas and Fort Worth were already promoting commercial aviation, purchased the Houston Airport Corporation's private facilities and instituted regularly scheduled flights by Braniff and Eastern airlines. In 1940 the city expanded the facilities and began planning how Houston could become an international air carrier.

Local newspapers continued to inform Houston's citizens. During the nineteenth century numerous publications had educated Houstonians, publicized the city's progress, and impelled it to new achievements. In the 1920s, three daily newspapers were being published: the *Houston Post*, the *Houston Chronicle*, and the *Houston Press*. Several weekly publications, the *Houston Informer*, the *Texas Freeman*, and the *Houston Sentinel*, were directed to the black community within the city. By 1930 the *Houston Defender* had been founded by C. F. Richardson, a leading advocate of black business expansion in Houston. As the Mexican *colonia* grew, Spanish-language publications appeared, including at least four newspapers, *La Tribuna*, *El Anunciador*, *El Tecolote*, and *La Prensa*.

Radio Station WEV began broadcasting music and impromptu speeches for three hundred receiving sets in 1922, and other stations—WCAK, WEAV, and WPAN—soon began operating. The first station to endure was KPRC, which started in 1925 with call letters that stood for "Port, Railroads, and Cotton" and the greeting, "Hello folks, everywhere." Broadcasts of sporting events became popular programs; one such event was the Gene Tunney-Jack Dempsey boxing rematch in 1927, heard by fifteen thousand listeners at Miller Theater in Hermann Park.

Local athletic activities provided a variety of entertainment for Houstonians. Horse racing, horse shows, boxing, wrestling, handball, auto racing, basketball, golf, dog racing, and roller skating were all popular. Baseball, however, became the most widely attended sports event. Houston had been a center of baseball activity since 1888, when it became a member of the Texas League. By 1921 the Houston Buffaloes team, popularly known as the Buffs, had won a number of league championships and had forged colorful rivalries with other cities in Texas. The next year the team was sold to the St. Louis Cardinals of the National League. As the Cardinals' farm team, the Buffs gave Houstonians years of pleasure at Buff Stadium, which was built on the east side of the city in 1928. Major league baseball, however, was still a dream for the future.

Houston's annual livestock show and rodeo started as a purely commercial venture. Although there were about two million head of cattle in the sixteen counties that comprised the Houston metropolitan area in

Above: Presidential visit to Houston, June 11, 1936. President and Mrs. Franklin Roosevelt visited Houston during the Texas Centennial celebration. The president took a yacht down the Ship Channel and spoke to a crowd of 28,000 at the San Jacinto Battlefield. Pictured with the Roosevelts are Jesse Jones, Governor James Allred, and Mayor Oscar Holcombe.

Below: The Pipe of Peace by Grace Spaulding John, fresco, Sidney Lanier School, 1934. Mrs. John is shown producing a piece of public art, which remains intact today. Most of the WPA artwork created in Houston in the 1930s has vanished—the victim of building demolitions.

1931, Houston ranked only thirty-seventh among the livestock markets in the United States. Most ranchers in the area still shipped their cattle to Kansas City and Chicago for processing. To promote the potential for a local cattle market, a group of business leaders organized the Houston Fat Stock Show and Livestock Exposition. In 1938 a rodeo was added to the annual event, and the Chamber of Commerce encouraged Houstonians to "grow beards, wear big hats, boots and spurs… and put a little touch of the Wild West into this thing." Little did the business community know that it had instituted a tradition that in the future would attract two million people each year.

For the general public, however, the most popular form of entertainment was the motion picture. As talking pictures replaced silent films, elaborate movie houses were built in downtown Houston. The Majestic replicated an Italian garden, while the Metropolitan placed movie-goers in an Egyptian temple and the Loew's State transported them to classical Greece. By the mid-1930s smaller theaters— the Tower, the River Oaks, the Heights, the Azteca, and the Juarez—were in outlying neighborhoods to serve a growing interest in the silver screen.

Suburban development, spurred by increased automobile ownership, continued at

an accelerated pace. Small shopping centers, including the River Oaks Community Center, the Tower Community Center, and the Village, sprang up around new residential subdivisions. In the South End, the Montrose area expanded into several smaller neighborhoods, including Fairview, Hyde Park, Cherryhurst, and Broadacres. Riverside Terrace and Braeswood were developed along Bray's Bayou, while to the north Independence Heights was laid out. Eastwood, Idylwood, and Garden Villas were developments to the southeast. Several enclaves—West University Place, Bellaire, Southside Place, Pasadena, South Houston, and Galena Park—became incorporated towns. The towns of Harrisburg and Houston Heights were annexed to the city. By 1940 Houston encompassed almost seventy-four square miles, more than double its 1920 area.

The central business district had also grown. The 1920s were years of expansive construction. In 1921, the Humble Oil and Refining Company received the city's first million dollar building permit for its corporate headquarters. Other skyscrapers built during this period included a new Cotton Exchange, the Commerce and Petroleum buildings, Houston National Bank, the Post-Dispatch building, the Niels Esperson building, and the Gulf building. The Esperson and Gulf buildings would dominate Houston's skyline for the next three decades.

In 1940, in the midst of this progress, Houston, along with the rest of the nation, began anxiously to eye events in Europe. As it became increasingly apparent that the United States might be drawn into the war there, improvements were made at Ellington Field and Camp Wallace, both situated just outside the city limits. Several industrial plants, including Humble Oil and Refining, Sheffield Steel, and Cameron Iron Works, were awarded contracts to furnish war materials. In September 1940 more than seventy-five thousand Harris County men registered for the first peacetime draft in American history.

Six months later the federal government announced that an ordinance depot would be built opposite the San Jacinto battlefield. Slips and docks were to be constructed along

❧

Top, left: Metropolitan Theater, 1926. Aware of the public's fascination with the 1922 opening of Tutankhamen's tomb, Alfred Finn designed this opulent interior reminiscent of ancient Egypt.

COURTESY HOUSTON ENDOWMENT, INC., ARCHIVES.

Top: San Jacinto Monument. In spite of an admonition that it should not top the Washington Monument in height, the Texas structure is actually fifteen feet taller.

COURTESY HOUSTON METROPOLITAN RESEARCH CENTER, HOUSTON PUBLIC LIBRARY.

Above: Initiation of air traffic into Houston. Flight time between Houston and New York in 1938 was more than 11 hours, while it took 9 hours to fly from Houston to Chicago.

COURTESY HOUSTON METROPOLITAN RESEARCH CENTER, HOUSTON PUBLIC LIBRARY.

Below, left: Flood waters in downtown Houston, 1935.

COURTESY HOUSTON METROPOLITAN RESEARCH CENTER, HOUSTON PUBLIC LIBRARY.

a lengthy frontage of the Ship Channel so the depot could serve as a storage and distribution point for all Gulf Coast military bases. The large amount of scrap iron stored at the Port of Houston took on new significance as it was shipped abroad. The federal government also awarded the Hughes Tool Company a contract to manufacture bomber parts for the Army and Navy, and the first contingent of airmen arrived for training at Ellington Field.

After Japan's attack on Pearl Harbor on December 7, 1941, and President Roosevelt's "Day of Infamy" address the next day, Congress de-clared war against Japan. World War II would have a profound effect upon the city of Houston.

YEARS OF TRIUMPH AND TURMOIL

World War II provided the momentum that propelled Houston toward becoming a metropolis. As Houston Post columnist George Fuermann noted, "Before the war Houston was an ambitious small city. A few years afterward… the city was altered in character, aspirations, and appearance." The war years and the decades immediately following were unquestionably a time of dramatic change for Houston.

As war became a reality to Houstonians, they found themselves sacrificing in many ways. On the home front rationing became a way of life, and books of stamps were issued for purchasing meat, sugar, coffee, shoes, rubber, auto parts, and eventually gasoline. Adults bought war bonds and school children purchased savings stamps to paste into bond books. The community held frequent drives to collect scrap iron, and many families planted "victory gardens" to conserve food for the war effort.

Many Houstonians responded to the call to defend their country. Perhaps the greatest single display of patriotism occurred on May 31, 1942, when a thousand volunteers gathered on Main

Street to be sworn into the armed services. This was only two months after the cruiser *Houston*, still remembered for a 1930 visit to its namesake city, had been sunk in the Sunda Strait. Houstonians responded to this loss not only by furnishing new recruits but also by purchasing $85 million in war bonds to build a new *Houston*.

For the first time women served in large numbers as members of the armed forces. A Houstonian, Oveta Culp Hobby, was named first director of the Women's Army Corps (WAC) and was the first woman in the nation to hold the rank of colonel. In the fall of 1942, Ellington Field began training female pilots to become Women Airforce Service Pilots (WASPs). These women would contribute significantly to the war effort ferrying aircraft, towing targets for gunnery practice, and transporting military personnel and cargo.

Civilians also found many ways to serve. The local American Red Cross chapter provided nurses' aides, ambulance drivers, and bandage rollers. A United Service Organization (USO) chapter was opened to serve the growing number of military personnel in the area. Other volunteers stood watch on around-the-clock shifts to report any unusual aircraft activity in the Houston area, the information then being relayed to a tracking center in the Houston Club Building.

While the war years were a time of loss and sacrifice for many Houstonians, the city nevertheless experienced tremendous industrial growth during this time. The Texas Gulf Coast had the ingredients—oil and gas, sulfur, and fresh water—to develop a petrochemical industry, and the Houston Ship Channel was

a highly desirable location for this development. The oil refineries expanded to meet the demand for wartime products. Some facilities turned to the production of high-grade aviation gasoline, while others produced toluene, a basic ingredient for explosives.

The most revolutionary development in the petroleum field, and one that held great significance for the Houston area, was the development of a synthetic rubber. Early in the war, the Japanese took the Malay Peninsula, the United States' primary source of natural rubber. An urgent need for a substitute resulted in the development of Buna-S rubber, which would become the main ingredient in tires, lifeboats, and balloons. By 1943 it was being manufactured at two Baytown plants by utilizing butadiene, a petroleum by-product.

Investment in the local chemical complex totaled $600 million during World War II and generated a regional boom in the petrochemical industry. This boom continued after the war and attracted to the Houston area many of the country's major chemical companies including DuPont, Monsanto, Dow, and Union Carbide.

The protected harbor of the Houston Ship Channel made Houston an ideal location for defense industries. Sheffield Steel Corporation built its plant on the waterway and utilized iron ore from East Texas. Following the war, Sheffield became the only steel company in the central United Sates to produce finished pieces from raw material.

Shipbuilding also flourished along the channel. Using assembly-line techniques and specialized teams, Houston Shipbuilding Corporation turned out 208 cargo vessels and fourteen tankers during the war. Brown Shipbuilding, started by local engineers George and Herman Brown, produced more than three hundred submarine chasers, destroyer escorts, and landing craft by April 1, 1945. The Houston shipyards employed forty thousand people and had a $2 million weekly payroll.

Other Houston companies also responded to the war effort. By April 1943 forty-five local industries held prime contracts, with the federal government having spent about $265 million in Houston. In 1944 *Houston* magazine recognized the city's tremendous industrial growth by noting that nineteen of the nation's twenty basic industries were represented within the city.

Left: The launching of the Mirabeau B. Lamar, *Houston Shipbuilding Yards, June 1942.*

COURTESY HOUSTON ENDOWMENT, INC., ARCHIVES.

Below: Women employees of Hughes Tool Company machining rock bit cones during World War II.

COURTESY HOUSTON METROPOLITAN RESEARCH CENTER, HOUSTON PUBLIC LIBRARY.

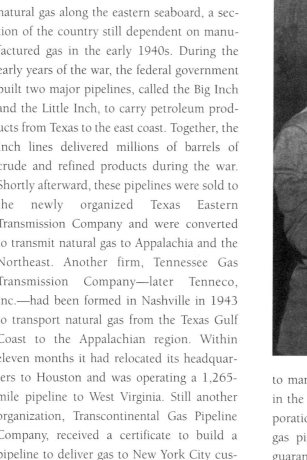

Right: Sergeant Macario Garcia receiving the Congressional Medal of Honor from President Harry Truman, 1945. Garcia, a Sugar Land resident, was cited for heroism in Germany.

COURTESY HOUSTON METROPOLITAN RESEARCH CENTER, HOUSTON PUBLIC LIBRARY.

Below: Brothers George and Herman Brown. Their company, Brown & Root, Inc., completed numerous federal war projects. After the war the Browns, along with other investors, purchased the Big Inch and Little Inch pipelines from the government and organized a new company, Texas Eastern Transmission Company, to transmit natural gas to the eastern United States.

COURTESY HOUSTON METROPOLITAN RESEARCH CENTER, HOUSTON PUBLIC LIBRARY.

Wartime conditions created a demand for natural gas along the eastern seaboard, a section of the country still dependent on manufactured gas in the early 1940s. During the early years of the war, the federal government built two major pipelines, called the Big Inch and the Little Inch, to carry petroleum products from Texas to the east coast. Together, the Inch lines delivered millions of barrels of crude and refined products during the war. Shortly afterward, these pipelines were sold to the newly organized Texas Eastern Transmission Company and were converted to transmit natural gas to Appalachia and the Northeast. Another firm, Tennessee Gas Transmission Company—later Tenneco, Inc.—had been formed in Nashville in 1943 to transport natural gas from the Texas Gulf Coast to the Appalachian region. Within eleven months it had relocated its headquarters to Houston and was operating a 1,265-mile pipeline to West Virginia. Still another organization, Transcontinental Gas Pipeline Company, received a certificate to build a pipeline to deliver gas to New York City customers. Moving its headquarters from Austin to Houston, Transcontinental—later renamed Transco Energy Company—captured the lucrative New York market, which put an end

to manufactured gas as a significant industry in the United States. These locally based corporations became major components of the gas pipeline business in the United States, guaranteeing that Houston would play an important role in the national marketing of natural gas.

Although the war ended in 1945, Houston's boom continued to escalate. In the three years immediately following the war, Harris County ranked first in the United States in the value of construction, giving Houston the distinction of being called "the fastest growing city in the country" in 1948. Building permits that year totaled more than $300 million.

The price of real estate soared during this period. Newspaper headlines announced the sale of land on Main Street for two thousand dollars per front inch. Retail establishments experienced tremendous growth in the downtown area, as reflected by Foley Bros.' construction of a $6 million store, described by *Newsweek* as "the most radical and practical store in America" with an almost windowless facade and conveyor belts to move merchandise from storeroom to showroom. New office buildings altered the downtown skyline.

In the midst of this building boom, the city administration approved the annexation of

83.74 square miles, primarily on the city's south side. This action more than doubled the area of Houston, from seventy-six to nearly 160 square miles, and increased the population by more than a hundred thousand people. This growth-by-annexation process would be repeated many times in the years ahead.

As the city limits expanded, Houstonians began moving to the suburbs. Large neighborhood shopping centers were built to serve the growing population, and in 1949 oil magnate Glen McCarthy's resplendent Shamrock Hotel was opened with great fanfare. Located at the end of South Main Street, the Shamrock was the first major hotel located outside the downtown business district.

A new concept in residential planning appeared in Meyerland, Tanglewood, Braes Heights and other new subdivisions constructed to meet suburban housing demands of post-war Houston. Oak Forest, begun in 1946 by developer Frank Sharp in the northwest section of the city, typified these large-scale developments on single plots of land. During the next two years Sharp teamed up with thirteen other builders to provide five thousand homes, all priced between seven and ten thousand dollars.

In 1954, Sharp expanded his vision and acquired ten square miles of land on the southwestern fringe of Houston for a totally

planned community. In Sharpstown he not only constructed thousands of new homes, but also set aside land for institutional buildings and for the construction of Houston's first air-conditioned shopping mall.

The move of so many Houstonians to the sprawling suburbs stimulated the development of a new road system. As early as 1930, a superhighway had been proposed for the Houston area, but planning at the time had been highly speculative and no funding

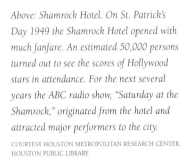

Above: Shamrock Hotel. On St. Patrick's Day 1949 the Shamrock Hotel opened with much fanfare. An estimated 50,000 persons turned out to see the scores of Hollywood stars in attendance. For the next several years the ABC radio show, "Saturday at the Shamrock," originated from the hotel and attracted major performers to the city.

COURTESY HOUSTON METROPOLITAN RESEARCH CENTER, HOUSTON PUBLIC LIBRARY.

Left: Oak Forest Subdivision. Home construction in Oak Forest introduced innovative features: concrete slab foundations, large picture windows, and carports. All became standard components of houses in the years ahead.

COURTESY HOUSTON METROPOLITAN RESEARCH CENTER, HOUSTON PUBLIC LIBRARY.

sources had been identified. While local and state authorities agreed that a new route between Houston and Galveston was needed, they could not agree on a precise location for the route. In the late 1930s the city had acquired ownership of the right-of-way of the interurban railway and had tenaciously continued to support using the interurban route for locating the new road. Finally the state concurred, and construction began in late 1946. The state and federal governments shared the major cost of $24 million under the first nationwide program to improve urban roadways.

The four-lane Gulf Freeway—named through a local contest—formally opened in August 1952 when the halfway point was reached. Newspaper headlines proclaimed it to be the "longest toll-free superhighway in the United States constructed since World War II." Almost immediately the widely acclaimed freeway was carrying more automobiles than traffic planners had anticipated. By 1960 it was woefully inadequate in moving traffic, but it had provided the impetus for the development of new subdivisions along the route and had also given rise to a new concept in retailing, the shopping center mall. Gulfgate, opened in 1956, would become a prototype for regional retail centers in the decades to follow.

A state survey in 1952 had indicated that all major Houston highways should be four lanes wide. The next year the Texas Highway Department announced plans for a system to encircle downtown Houston. By 1957, eighty-five miles of the 237-mile system had been completed. Houstonians' long infatuation with the automobile, and the absence of adequate public transportation, would continue to place a heavy burden on road development in the greater Houston area.

Air transportation improved dramatically during the post-war years. In 1946, the Civil Aeronautics Board designated Houston an international terminal and certified Braniff, Southern, and Pan American airlines for flights to Central America, South America, and the Caribbean area. Despite the difficulty in obtaining east-west routes, air traffic increased as new airlines entered Houston. In 1950, six national companies, two local ones, and an air freight line utilized the terminal, which despite improvements, was already inadequate.

In 1951, construction began on a new facility. Houston International Airport was completed three years later. Through the efforts of the Houston Chamber of Commerce, an east-west flow of traffic had finally been established. Furthermore, a French airline had introduced the city to jet travel. By 1957, the airport was handling 111,000 people each month, and the need for larger facilities was obvious.

Foreseeing this need, a group of seventeen businessmen—operating as Jet Era Ranch Corporation—in the 1950s purchased 3,126 acres on the northeastern edge of the city for a new airport. They held the property until 1960 when they sold it to the city at cost. Work started on the new $100 million Houston

WAUGH

MEMORIAL

Intercontinental Airport two years later. The construction featured two major terminals and utilized a concept of stacking the facilities vertically and connecting them by escalators, ramps, and elevators. Boarding areas extended fingerlike from the terminals, thereby eliminating the necessity for passengers to walk long distances. The innovative facility was opened to air traffic on June 8, 1969.

Houston's other major transportation artery, the Houston Ship Channel, also experienced tremendous growth in the post-war years. As the United States government acted to rebuild the war-shattered economy of the world, large quantities of cotton, grain, petroleum products, and other goods flowed through the Port of Houston on ships from Great Britain, France, Belgium, Holland, Italy, Spain, India, Scandinavia, Greece, Australia, and China, as well as from Latin American countries. In 1948 the Port ranked second in the country in tonnage.

An increase in traffic necessitated further improvements to the waterway. Once again Congress approved widening the channel, and at the suggestion of the army engineers the depth was increased to thirty-six feet. In addition, two tunnels were built underneath the channel to enable automobiles to cross without the need for ferry boats. The Washburn Tunnel, between Pasadena and the north side of the channel, was opened to traffic on May 25, 1950. The Baytown-LaPorte Tunnel was completed three years later.

Although the rapidly growing petrochemical industry resulted in the establishment of many new facilities along the channel, the Port in 1955 slipped to fourth place in tonnage surpassed not only by New York City but also by Philadelphia and New Orleans. Port officials were forced to recognize that their facilities had once again become inadequate. Houstonians faced a major decision: should they renew their quest for primacy in international trade or remain content with the status quo?

Exemplifying the visionary attitude by now so characteristic in Houston history, Port officials decided in 1956 to move forward and asked the taxpayers to approve a bond issue. City leaders united behind this effort and reminded the electorate that the destinies of

the Port and the city had always been interwoven. A writer for the Houston Post emphasized that "This is no ordinary election. It is a bread-and-butter matter affecting the future of the community."

Voters overwhelmingly approved the bond issue, and construction began almost immediately on new wharves and transit sheds. In 1958 the army engineers recommended increasing the depth of the entire channel to forty feet. Upon completion of this work, the Port became accessible to the largest oceangoing vessels.

In 1964, the Port of Houston celebrated its fiftieth anniversary. In ceremonies reminiscent of those in 1914 when President Wilson had pressed a button in Washington to fire a cannon at the Turning Basin, President Lyndon B. Johnson—a native Texan who had taught school in Houston earlier in his career—pressed a button in the Texas White House at Johnson City. This time the button set off a charge that broke ground for three new docks on the waterfront.

The private sector, still mindful of the city's needs, continued in its efforts to meet those needs. Monroe D. Anderson, a partner in Anderson, Clayton and Company, had established a foundation in 1936 for "charitable, scientific or educational purposes in Texas…

Houston International Airport, 1950s. After several years of inactivity during the 1970s, this facility—renamed William P. Hobby Airport in 1967—is once again a busy hub for air transportation.

Above: Monroe Dunaway Anderson.

COURTESY HOUSTON ACADEMY OF MEDICINE,
TEXAS MEDICAL CENTER LIBRARY, HOUSTON

Below: James Abercrombie,
Hugh Roy Cullen, and Leopold Meyer.
These civic-minded citizens were strong
supporters of hospital expansion in
Houston. Abercrombie and Meyer
assisted in founding Texas Children's
Hospital; Cullen was a generous benefactor
of many medical facilities in the city.

COURTESY HOUSTON METROPOLITAN RESEARCH CENTER,
HOUSTON PUBLIC LIBRARY.

the benefit of mankind and... the advancement of human welfare," but its charter did not designate specific plans for the funds. After Anderson's death in 1939, the trustees of the M. D. Anderson Foundation—John H. Freeman, W. B. Bates, and Horace Wilkins—decided that medical institutions and scientific research would be the top priorities for the $20 million willed to the foundation by Anderson.

In 1941 these trustees succeeded in having the University of Texas place its new cancer research hospital in Houston, with the Anderson Foundation furnishing a building and operating funds. Then the trustees decided to think big and planned an entire medical complex. They convinced Baylor University's School of Medicine to move from Dallas to Houston and secured an agreement from the University of Texas School of Dentistry to join in the venture. They continued to attract other medical institutions by promising them sites and money to stimulate their own fundraising. By late 1945 the Anderson Foundation had acquired a large tract of land near Hermann Park and had made commitments not only to the University of Texas and Baylor but also to The Methodist Hospital, St. Luke's (a proposed Episcopal hospital), the Shriners Hospital for Children, Hermann Hospital, and a medical library. Each nonprofit institution would remain autonomous, but agreed to use its facility for medical care, teaching, or research.

At this point, the Anderson trustees realized they had created an entity too large for any one private foundation. As a consequence the Texas Medical Center was established, and the Anderson Foundation transferred the land and its previous commitments to the new corporation. The new center was dedicated on February 28, 1946, with Dr. E. W. Bertner becoming its president. The groundwork had been laid for what would become one of the world's preeminent medical centers.

The private sector had always been a major participant in Houston's development. This involvement was most apparent among the leaders of the business community. From the late 1930s to the 1960s this leadership was primarily centered in a loose coalition of businessmen named for their meeting place in the Lamar Hotel. The Suite 8F group exercised great influence in the development of modern Houston. Their power base was threefold: substantial wealth founded on corporate development, general support of the local business community, and intimate ties to major officials in local and national politics. While no formal membership list existed and the participants varied from time to time, the core of the Suite 8F group included Jesse H. Jones, brothers Herman and George Brown, Gus Wortham, and James A. Elkins, Sr.

The 8F group made decisions that greatly affected the city's development. Their influence in the economic arena was matched only by their political power. 8F's political position usually reflected that of the business community. Their endorsement of—or opposition to—a candidate could easily determine the outcome of a local election.

On a national level, members of 8F had strong ties to Texan John Nance Garner, a longtime congressman who became vice president under Franklin D. Roosevelt, and to Speaker of the House Sam Rayburn, another Texan. Perhaps the most important politician associated with 8F was Lyndon B. Johnson. These associations were frequently responsible for federally funded projects in the city.

Perhaps the most dramatic evidence of this interplay of power occurred on September 19, 1961, when the National Aeronautics and Space Administration (NASA) announced that the city had been designated as the site of a new center that would serve as the hub of the

nation's space exploration program. Houston was chosen over some twenty other cities because, according to the announcement, it had an inland water network, a skilled work force, prominent universities, a mild climate, and adequate land for NASA projects. More importantly perhaps, the city had strong connections to individuals who wielded great decision-making power. Vice President Lyndon B. Johnson headed the National Aeronautics and Space Council, and the chairman of the House subcommittee responsible for approving NASA appropriations was Representative Albert Thomas, one of Houston's two congressmen.

Site availability played a critical role in the process. Humble Oil and Refining Company gave two tracts of land from the company's Clear Lake Ranch, twenty-two miles southeast of Houston, to Rice University with the stipulation that Rice give the larger tract of one thousand acres to NASA for the Manned Spacecraft Center. A member of the 8F group, George Brown, who was a key player in this process, served as chairman of Rice's Board of Trustees, and his ties to the business community placed him in a strong position to influence Humble, Rice, and NASA. Obvious benefits accrued to both Humble and Rice, as well as to NASA. Humble acquired the prestigious presence of the space facilities near its Clear Lake holdings, where commercial and residential development was planned. Rice University received funding for studies in the physical sciences, and an additional million dollars for the smaller tract, which was sold to the federal government.

Houston's economy quickly benefited from the presence of the new space facility. The number of manufacturing firms in the Houston metropolitan area shot up almost instantly. In 1962 alone, twenty-nine space-related companies established plants in the Houston vicinity. New corporate headquarters began moving to the city, now considered a technological center.

On July 4, 1962, the Chamber of Commerce staged a parade to welcome NASA to the city. Honored guests were the first seven astronauts. Houston soon became known as "Space City USA." This new appel-

lation reflected the vision, determination, and shrewd planning displayed by Houstonians on behalf of their city.

The war years brought changes to local government. In an effort to dilute the strength of the mayor's office, which had become a powerful center of authority under the reins of Oscar Holcombe, reformers instituted a city-manager system of municipal government in 1942. Under this plan the city manager had direct authority over municipal departments. However, after voters reelected Holcombe in 1947, the position of city manager was abolished and the authority to appoint department heads reverted to the

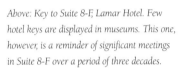

Above: Key to Suite 8-F, Lamar Hotel. Few hotel keys are displayed in museums. This one, however, is a reminder of significant meetings in Suite 8-F over a period of three decades.

PHOTO BY AUTHOR. EXHIBIT: THE HERITAGE SOCIETY MUSEUM, HOUSTON.

Below: Congressmen Bob Casey and Albert Thomas, Rice University Board of Trustees Chairman George Brown, and Vice President Lyndon Johnson. Through the efforts of these influential men, Houston succeeded in securing the Manned Spacecraft Center, later named the Lyndon B. Johnson Space Center.

COURTESY HOUSTON METROPOLITAN RESEARCH CENTER, HOUSTON PUBLIC LIBRARY.

ers or ranchers from the Southwest... many are distant arrivals from New York or California... all have come here for the same reason: to seek their fortune." Indeed, opportunities seemed limitless.

Progress, however, was not welcome in all quarters. To some, change was a frightening experience, and to counteract it, some groups coalesced around efforts to maintain conformity and the status quo. This contradiction of attitudes of progressivism versus conservatism fostered a local version of what became known throughout the United States as the Red Scare. Fueled by fears arising out of the so-called Cold War with the Soviet Union and the virulent rhetoric of Senator Joseph McCarthy, many Houstonians joined the militant anti-communist campaign. While Houston's Red Scare affected many aspects of the city's life, its greatest manifestation was in the public schools.

One faction of citizens supported the anti-communist crusade by protesting federal aid to education, racial integration, and any manifestation of progressive education. The opposing side vigorously denounced the scare tactics used by this group. The Houston School Board became the battleground for these warring factions. The initial issues were federal funding for a lunch program and the ideological content of textbooks and curricula. The bitterly waged 1952 school board election set the stage for widespread witch hunts within the school system. The deputy superintendent of the school district and numerous teachers were fired amidst innuendos and allegations of communistic affiliations or sympathies. Tension remained high in the community for the next several years.

By 1961, international tensions had eased, national and state political environments were relatively calm, and the local press had become more outspoken in opposition to Red Scare tactics. As a result, the explosive Red Scare era began to fade away, only to be replaced by the equally volatile issue of racial segregation.

Racial segregation had been rigidly enforced in Houston since the turn of the century. Blacks were restricted to rear seats in public transportation and to separate bal-

mayor's office, which emerged more powerful than ever. The strong-mayor form of government became a lasting feature of Houston's municipal structure.

From 1947 to the early 1970s, Houston had only four mayors: Oscar Holcombe, Roy Hofheinz, Lewis Cutrer, and Louie Welch. Each had strong ties to the Houston business community and continued to promote Houston as a partnership between the local government and the private sector.

The decades following the war were a time of explosive growth for the city, and population continued to climb. A 1954 report noted that "most of the new city people are... farm-

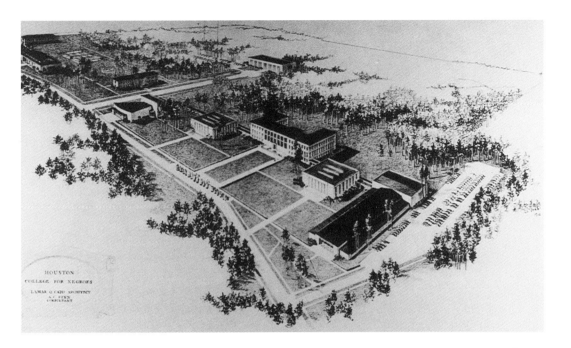

conies in entertainment centers. The black population had access only to those libraries and parks established specifically for them. Public schools were totally separate.

During World War II, the campaign for equal treatment of minority groups in Houston intensified. Black citizens adopted the slogan, "Win a Double Victory," referring both to the war being fought abroad and to the struggle to obtain civil rights at home. The struggle for civil rights had actually begun before the war when the NAACP in Texas confronted racial discrimination, especially in voting rights, employment, jury service, and education. The major objective of the civil rights struggle was to gain the right to vote in Democratic primaries, at the time the only significant elections in Texas, which was virtually a one-party state.

In March 1940, black leaders from all over the state met in Houston to strategize. Their goal was the reversal of the United States Supreme Court's 1935 decision in *Grovey v. Townsend*, a case that had been filed after Houston barber R. R. Grovey was denied an absentee ballot in the 1934 Democratic primary. In its decision the Court had found the Democratic party to be a private organization free to set its own rules for membership and for participation in the primary.

Dr. Lonnie E. Smith, a Houston dentist and activist who had been denied a vote in the 1940 primary, was the plaintiff in a new case

filed in 1942. When the lower courts found against Smith, NAACP lawyers filed appeals that ultimately reached the Supreme Court. On April 3, 1944, the Court ruled that the primary was an integral part of the election process and that the white primary violated the Fifteenth Amendment to the Constitution of the United States. Lulu B. White of the Houston NAACP chapter spoke of the decision as the "second emancipation of the Negro," and on election day in July 1944 more than twenty-six hundred registered black voters cast their ballots in the Harris County Democratic primary.

The struggle of black Houstonians to gain access to educational facilities also expanded after World War II. Just as Houston had been the geographic focus of the legal cases challenging the white primary, so would it be in education. In 1946 Heman Sweatt, who was a Houston postal employee, World War II veteran, and honor graduate of Wiley College, was denied admission on the basis of his color to the University of Texas School of Law. As a result of a lawsuit filed by Sweatt, the state in February 1947 opened in Houston, as a so-called "separate but equal" school, the School of Law of the Texas State University for Negroes.

Left: Architectural rendering, Houston College for Negroes. This proposal was incorporated into the plan for Texas State University for Negroes, which opened in 1947 after acquiring the campus of Houston College for Negroes. In 1951 the name of the school was changed to Texas Southern University.

COURTESY HOUSTON METROPOLITAN RESEARCH CENTER, HOUSTON PUBLIC LIBRARY.

Below: Heman Sweatt, working as a mail carrier while awaiting his admission to law school. Although Sweatt did not acquire a law degree, the racial barriers at the University of Texas had fallen, and, in 1952, the university awarded its first degree to a black student.

COURTESY HOUSTON METROPOLITAN RESEARCH CENTER, HOUSTON PUBLIC LIBRARY.

Sweatt, however, continued to pursue his case until it finally reached the United States Supreme Court, which held in June 1950 that Sweatt had a constitutional right to attend the University of Texas School of Law. The Sweatt case helped lay the basis for the 1954 decision in *Brown v. Board of Education* that "separate but equal" policies were unconstitutional.

Segregation nevertheless continued in Houston's public schools even after the 1954 decision. The school board consistently appropriated more money per student at white schools than at black ones, and physical plants tended to be superior and better maintained at white schools. In 1955 a biracial committee suggested immediate desegregation of Houston schools. When the school board took no action to implement integration, United States District Judge Ben C. Connally ordered desegregation to commence in all first grades in September 1960 and to advance one grade per year thereafter. The plan went into effect, but only twelve black pupils in the entire district met the strict enrollment requirements of the school board. In 1962 the district plan was overturned, and under an accelerated program the schools completed desegregation in 1966-67.

The wall of segregation also crumbled in other places. In the spring of 1960 students from Texas Southern University began a series of sit-ins to force equal service at local lunch counters. After the failure of several such sit-ins in downtown stores, several businesses quietly began serving the students. The scant publicity surrounding this development was the result of an agreement among black organizations, business owners and the local media. Within a few months the City Hall cafeteria began to serve persons of all races,

GOVERNOR
BARBARA JORDAN
JUNE 10, 1972

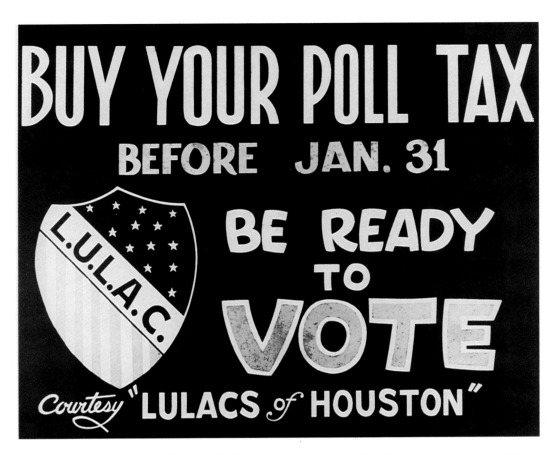

and in 1962 Mayor Lewis Cutrer ended discrimination in all city-owned buildings.

The 1966 election of Barbara Jordan to the state legislature illustrated the effectiveness of the civil rights movement in Houston. The first black elected to the Texas Senate since Reconstruction, Jordan would six years later again make history as the first black woman elected to the United States Congress by a southern state.

Segregation targeted not only blacks but also Mexican-Americans, who in 1950 numbered about forty thousand in Houston. They, too, were refused service at restaurants and seating in movie theaters. Most Mexican-American children attended less than adequate schools in their own neighborhoods. Discrimination was particularly strong in the workplace, where many employers refused to hire people of Mexican descent. Those able to secure employment usually earned less than their Anglo coworkers.

Realizing that these inequities could best be resolved through political action, leaders of the Mexican community in the late 1950s launched a systematic poll tax drive to increase the number of voters. Increasingly aware that an active electorate could effect change, a local chapter of the Political Association of Spanish-speaking Organizations (PASO) was formed in October 1961. Working with the LULAC Councils, PASO members focused on such issues as increasing the minimum wage, ending school segregation, and developing anti-poverty programs. By the late 1960s the Mexican-American community numbered 150,000, or twelve percent of Houston's total population. An indication of the community's growing presence was the 1966 election to the Texas legislature of Lauro Cruz, the first Mexican-American from Harris County to hold a state-level office.

During the post-World War II years, advanced technology played an important role in Houston's development. The first words spoken on Houston television, at 9:30 p.m. on January 1, 1949, were: "There's been trouble, plenty of trouble." This communication came from an engineer explaining that equipment problems had delayed transmission of the initial broadcast from KLEE-TV, a station owned by local businessman W. Albert Lee. Soon, televi-

claimed a hundred thousand television sets. Coaxial cables reached Houston in 1952, and a year later KGUL-TV began broadcasts from Galveston. This station became KHOU-TV after moving to Houston in 1959. A third station entered the local scene in 1954 when KTRK-TV began its operations. That same year KPRC-TV became Houston's first station to broadcast in color.

When KPRC-TV moved into new quarters in 1952, the Hobbys gave the old facilities jointly to the University of Houston and the Houston Independent School District. In May of the next year, KUHT-TV began operating as the nation's first educational television station, a noteworthy accomplishment for the university, which eventually assumed full control of the station.

Improved construction technology produced the Harris County Domed Stadium in 1965. The plan for a covered, air-conditioned sports arena was conceived by Roy Hofheinz, who attributed his idea to the Roman Colosseum, which featured awnings to protect spectators from the weather. Hofheinz's

sion sets appeared in homes throughout the city. In 1950 Lee sold the station to William P. and Oveta Culp Hobby. The Hobbys, who had owned KPRC Radio since 1925, changed the television station's call letters to match those of their radio station. Within a year Houston

reputation had already been established by his election as Harris County Judge at the age of twenty-four and a later term as the city's mayor. From his respected position as a successful businessman, he promoted the innovative Astrodome, as he called it. Acting as the majority stockholders of the Houston Sports Association, Hofheinz and R. E. "Bob" Smith acquired a National League baseball franchise and immediately bought the Houston Buffaloes. Changing the name of the team first to Colt .45s, and later to Astros, Hofheinz began planning his spectacular new arena, which would be used for both baseball and football.

A site was chosen seven miles southwest of downtown. Many Houstonians protested that Harris County would be saddled with a tremendous debt if the project failed, but the stadium was endorsed by powerful factions throughout the city. In a brilliant promotion, Hofheinz proclaimed, "This stadium will take its place alongside the Eiffel Tower and the great wonders of the world in construction."

The Astrodome opened on April 9, 1965, with an exhibition game between the Astros and the New York Yankees. Governor John Connally threw out the first ball, and President Lyndon Johnson was among the crowd of 47,900 who cheered Houston to a twelfth-inning 2 to 1 victory. A local sportswriter exulted the next day that "baseball moved this side of paradise." Houston sports fans proudly claimed the "Eighth Wonder of the World" as their own.

Other professional sports franchises took up residency in the city, joining the Astros and the Houston Oilers football team, which K. S. "Bud" Adams had established in 1959-60. In the early 1970s, the Houston Rockets brought professional basketball to the city and the Aeros introduced ice hockey. In 1975 the Summit arena was built for the hockey and basketball teams.

As in the past, Houstonians remained strongly committed to the arts. During the post-war years the Houston Symphony increased the number of concerts from ten to forty per season and inaugurated free summer evening concerts in Hermann Park. Under the batons of such noted conductors as Efrem

Kurtz, Leopold Stokowski, and Sir John Barbirolli, the orchestra matured as a symphonic ensemble and began receiving national recognition.

In 1955 two new arts groups, the Houston Grand Opera and the Houston Ballet, were established. Operatic music had long been a favorite with Houston audiences. When German-born conductor Walter Hebert contacted cultural leaders in Houston about organizing a professional opera company, they responded enthusiastically. On August 9, 1955, a group of citizens met informally, hired Hebert as general director, and adopted a forty thousand dollar budget. The first two works performed were Richard Strauss's *Salome* and Puccini's *Madame Butterfly*. In 1972 David Gockley would succeed Hebert and lead Houston Grand Opera to a highly respected prominence among opera fans throughout the world.

Houstonians had been entranced by ballet since Anna Pavlova's appearance in the city in 1917 and the Ballet Russe de Monte Carlo's visits through the years. When the Ballet Russe was disbanded, a group of local balletomanes established the Houston Ballet Foundation to form a local training academy and a performing company. Under the guidance of former Ballet Russe dancers Tatiana Semenova and Nina Popova, the company began giving public performances. Their successor, Ben Stevenson, would take the Houston Ballet to new heights.

In 1966, the Jesse H. Jones Hall for the Performing Arts was constructed on the site of the old City Auditorium. The new twenty-nine hundred seat facility, which occupied a full city block, became home to the Houston Symphony, the Houston Grand Opera, and the Houston Ballet Foundation. It also served as the performance hall for the Society for the Performing Arts, established in 1966 as a non-profit organization to bring outstanding touring groups to Houston.

The dramatic arts continued to be a popular form of entertainment for Houstonians. In 1947 a young drama

Above: Rudy Tomjanovich. A player for the Houston Rockets from 1970 to 1981, Tomjanovich coached the Rockets to consecutive NBA championships in 1994 and 1995.
COURTESY HOUSTON METROPOLITAN RESEARCH CENTER, HOUSTON PUBLIC LIBRARY.

Bottom, left: Nina Vance on the stage of the Alley Theater.
COURTESY HOUSTON METROPOLITAN RESEARCH CENTER, HOUSTON PUBLIC LIBRARY.

teacher, Nina Vance, gathered support for an intimate theater in which serious drama could be performed. Operating in a dance studio off an alley and utilizing volunteer help, the new venture was an instantaneous success. In 1960 the Alley Theater became a repertory theater using professional actors, and in 1968 opened a state-of-the-art facility near Jones Hall.

Houston's Museum of Fine Arts also participated in this cultural growth. Its collections grew with gifts from the Hogg family, the Robert E. Blaffer family, and Percy Straus. Wings were added to the museum through the generosity of the Blaffers, Nina Cullinan, and the Brown Foundation. In 1957 Ima Hogg gave the museum her home, Bayou Bend, and its furnishings—an extraordinary collection of American furniture, porcelain, brass, silver, and art—with the understanding that it would become a public museum upon her death.

To provide diversity in the city's art venues, another group of art patrons established the Contemporary Arts Museum in 1948. Additionally, numerous small art galleries opened as Houston began producing its own artists of note, including Dorothy Hood, John Biggers, Frank Freed, and Margaret Dreyer.

John and Dominique de Menil, both originally from France, became leading patrons of art in their adopted hometown. John reflected a deep concern for the city's cultural welfare, saying, "you must not go to London, Paris, or New York to be cosmopolitan. Just open your ears and your eyes and here you have it, right in Houston."

In 1961, Houston attained a population of one million, making it the nation's sixth largest city. The metropolitan area had been redefined to include Harris County and parts of Brazoria, Fort Bend, Liberty, and Montgomery Counties. Not only had it expanded physically, but its reputation had been firmly established as an important national and international city. Although the decades ahead would continue to bring achievements for Houston, they would also present to the bayou city economic problems of unparalleled magnitude and complexity.

SPACE CITY USA

First steps on the moon, July 20, 1969. Astronauts Armstrong and Aldrin were the first humans to set foot on an extraterrestrial body when they landed on the moon. The event, controlled from Houston's Johnson Space Center, was watched by millions of Americans on television.

COURTESY NATIONAL AERONAUTICS AND SPACE ADMINISTRATION.

On July 20, 1969, at 3:17 p.m. the words, "Houston, Eagle has landed," were heard around the world as astronauts Neil Armstrong and Edwin E. Aldrin landed on the moon. The Apollo flight followed the successful Mercury and Gemini projects, which paved the way for the historic moon landing. The Manned Spacecraft Center at Clear Lake had been completed in 1964, and while space launches continued to be made from Cape Kennedy (formerly Cape Canaveral) in Florida, all missions upon becoming airborne were directed from Houston. One Mission Control Center technician noted, "We work in a place where 13,000 men can feel like Columbus."

The space industry not only focused attention on Houston as the center of advances in space exploration but also significantly diversified the city's economy. New capital was directed to aerospace and electronic enterprises. Such well-known companies as McDonnell, Grumann, Lockheed, Boeing, General Electric, and International Business Machines established Houston offices. Predictions were made in 1965 that the spacecraft industry would attract two hundred thousand new residents within twenty years.

Houston did indeed grow rapidly during the next two decades, almost doubling in population. By 1980, it was the nation's fifth largest city, numbering more than 1.5 million residents, with the surrounding metropolitan area including another million. Through a series of annexations

Metropolitan Houston viewed from space.
A crew member aboard the earth-orbiting
Atlantis spacecraft recorded this image.
COURTESY NATIONAL AERONAUTICS
AND SPACE ADMINISTRATION.

Houston's area expanded as well. The Municipal Annexation Act, passed by the Texas legislature in 1963, allowed the city to reserve all lands within five miles of its limits for future expansion. A 1978 issue of *U. S. News and World Report* noted that Houston "is not a city. It's a phenomenon—an explosive, roaring juggernaut that's shattering tradition as it expands outward and upward with an energy that stuns even its residents." In 1980 the city contained more than 521 square miles, seven times its size at the end of World War II.

As the city expanded, large business centers began to be built outside the central business district. Greenway Plaza was begun in 1967 by developer Kenneth Schnitzer on 127 acres four miles southwest of downtown.

Designed to be a mixed complex of office and commercial buildings, it eventually housed forty-one thousand employees and contained a luxury hotel, high-rise apartments, a heliport, and the Summit sports arena.

One mile west of Greenway Plaza, the Galleria complex was developed by Gerald D. Hines, who declared when the first section opened in 1969, "A shopping center it is not. It will be a new downtown." Modeled after the Galleria Vittorio Emmanuele in Milan, Houston's Galleria featured a three-level retail mall, an ice-skating rink, two hotels, multistory office buildings, and, astonishingly, 11,263 parking spaces. The opening of the Galleria spurred construction of other office buildings in the Post Oak Boulevard area. Numerous corporate, divisional, and regional headquarters for oil, gas, computer, and real estate companies located in this corridor. Considered a suburban minicity, the Galleria-Post Oak area in 1986 became officially known as Uptown Houston.

A third concentrated business district was expanding rapidly at the Texas Medical Center where pioneering achievements in healing, teaching, and research were recorded. America's first successful heart transplant was performed there in 1968, and a year later the world's first artificial heart was implanted— both achievements of Dr. Denton Cooley of the Texas Heart Institute. A television program watched simultaneously by surgeons on six continents—another first for the medical field—originated in an operating theater at The Methodist Hospital with Baylor College of Medicine's Dr. Michael DeBakey performing surgery.

Only fifty years since it was founded, the Texas Medical Center has become the world's largest facility of its kind and is internationally acclaimed for its work. Each day there are under way in the Center more than fifteen hundred research projects that have resulted in such vital discoveries as those made in the field of brain hormones by Dr. Roger Guillemin, the first Nobel laureate from Texas. The Center's fourteen hospitals attract patients from all over the world, while more than ten thousand students attend its educational institutions, which offer instruction

ranging from high school level through post-doctoral studies.

Neighborhoods also began to develop far beyond the central city as Houston's growth continued unabated. During the 1970s developers built several hundred suburban subdivisions with such names as Kingwood, Kings Forest, Pecan Grove Plantation, Golf Villas, and Whispering Pines. Suburban living was further advanced through the concept of a satellite city, devised by oilman George P. Mitchell as he planned The Woodlands, a project twenty-seven miles north of downtown. Designed as a totally self-contained community, The Woodlands master plan included not only residential housing of all types, but it also provided for office buildings, schools, shopping centers, churches, recreational facilities, and transportation lines. While The Woodlands did not grow as quickly as Mitchell had envisioned, it nevertheless was the most successful example of planned development since River Oaks was laid out in the 1920s.

Comprehensive planning continued to be sporadically addressed by the city, and the related issue of zoning periodically resurfaced. Unique among major cities in the United States, Houston has never utilized zoning laws to control patterns of land use. Several attempts have been made to persuade City Council and Houston voters to accept zoning ordinances, but all have been defeated. As a result, the only significant regulation over land use has been accomplished primarily through deed covenants imposed and enforced by the private sector.

The city's public transportation has been another matter of widespread concern and divided opinion. When streetcars ceased to function in 1940, they were replaced by busses. By 1948 the privately owned Houston Transit Co. was operating a fleet of 610 vehicles.

Above: Port of Houston, 1996. The Houston
Ship Channel, a 52-mile inland waterway,
connects Houston with the sea lanes of the
world.

COURTESY GREATER HOUSTON PARTNERSHIP

Below: Downtown, ca. 1970. The oil
industry expanded Houston's skyline with
such buildings as the Tennessee Building and
the Humble Building, which—at forty-four
stories—was the tallest building west of the
Mississippi River when it was constructed.
The weather ball on top of Conoco's
headquarters provided Houstonians with a
favorite pastime—watching the changing
colors forecast the weather.

COURTESY HOUSTON METROPOLITAN RESEARCH CENTER,
HOUSTON PUBLIC LIBRARY.

Houston's bus service remained in private
hands until 1974 when the city purchased it,
renamed it HouTran, and hired a private operator to run it.

As bus ridership declined and automobile
traffic increased, monorail was considered as
a possible transit solution. On February 18,
1956, a 970-foot pilot line, the Trailblazer,
was installed at Arrowhead Park on Old
Spanish Trail. Since it was the American prototype of an elevated monorail, the first run of
the Trailblazer was accompanied by much
fanfare and national media coverage. Despite
the public interest generated by this unique

transit system, however, it received little
interest from city officials because of its construction cost of five hundred thousand dollars per mile and its slow speed of ten miles
per hour. Less than a year later, the line was
dismantled and moved to Dallas, where it
operated at the Texas State Fair for several
years. A second small monorail system was
installed in far southwest Houston in 1958,
but it too was soon abandoned.

The idea of monorail transportation as a
possible solution to Houston's transportation
problems, however, was not abandoned. In
1988, voters gave approval to the Houston
Metropolitan Transit Authority (METRO),
which had been created in 1978 to oversee
mass transit in Harris county and the surrounding areas, to develop a $1 billion, twen-
ty-mile rail transit system. METRO proposed
the use of monorail over light rail for the new
system technology. However, two years of
highly charged debate among city officials,
the public, and the press effectively killed the
issue. Even today, private automobiles and
METRO busses running on an ever-expanding
though perpetually overcrowded freeway system remain the primary means of moving
people about the city.

Houston rode a crest of prosperity and
progress in the 1970s. The Port of Houston
ranked fourth in the nation in value of manufactured products shipped and led the nation
in foreign tonnage. In 1979 Houston became
the first city in the United States to issue more
than $1 billion in building permits.
Nationally known architects created a stunning new downtown skyline through their
designs of the twin trapezoids of Pennzoil
Place, the neo-Gothic style of the
RepublicBank Building, and the soaring shaft
of Texas Commerce Tower.

Texas continued to lead the nation in oil
and gas production. In the early 1980s about
thirty-five percent of the jobs in the Houston
area were directly connected to the oil and gas
industry while another twenty percent were
greatly dependent on the industry. Most
downtown office space was occupied by energy-related corporations, including hundreds
of oil and gas companies, geological firms,
drilling contractors, supply companies, and

other oil-related businesses. Houston had evolved into a major center for the world's oil industry, and the city's economy was considered "depression-proof."

However the 1982 plummet in oil prices resulted in severe reductions in oil production. The number of active drilling rigs in Texas decreased significantly, in turn bringing hard times to Houston's oil production companies as well as to its tool and supply companies. As a result, unemployment rose sharply. In all the nation, Houston was the metropolitan area most directly affected by production shifts in the world oil market.

Many sectors of the Houston economy were affected by the 1980s crisis in the oil industry. Shipments at the Port of Houston dropped sharply. Building permits also fell dramatically, and record numbers of property foreclosures were reported. The number of annual business bankruptcy filings increased to sixteen hundred by 1986. Eleven banks were closed in Houston during the first nine months of 1987. Recovery from the 1980s economic downturn became one of the city's greatest challenges.

To lead the recovery, the Chamber of Commerce formed the Houston Economic Development Council (HEDC) in 1984. Realizing that a greater diversity of businesses was needed in order to broaden the economic

base, the HEDC began strengthening research and graduate training in local universities and research laboratories. It targeted not only energy but also biotechnology, space enterprises, international business, and tourism as areas for reinvigorated economic development.

Although recovery was gradual, the economy eventually began to stabilize as the city became a major center of applied technology. NASA and the Texas Medical Center joined Houston's network of professionals in engineering, computer science, and technical administration to achieve this new status.

Above: Downtown Houston, 1996.
COURTESY GREATER HOUSTON PARTNERSHIP.

Bottom, left: Rendevouz Houston: A City in Concert, *April 1986. In observance of the city's sesquicentennial, French composer Jean-Michael Jarre produced a dazzling music and laser show against a background of downtown skyscrapers. A crowd estimated at one million persons witnessed the extravaganza.*
COURTESY GREATER HOUSTON PARTNERSHIP.

Below: George Bush, 41st President of the United States and a long-time resident of Houston.
COURTESY OFFICE OF GEORGE BUSH.

Above: Texas Medical Center, looking southeast, 1996.

PHOTO BY STATE AERIAL COMMERCIAL PHOTOGRAPHY.
COURTESY TEXAS MEDICAL CENTER, HOUSTON

Below: International Festival. Each spring a two-week-long festival features the cultural and social life of a selected country.

COURTESY GREATER HOUSTON PARTNERSHIP.

Vietnamese. One Chinese language television station and three Spanish language stations broadcast in Houston while local cable channels regularly feature programs in Arabic, Chinese, Hindi, Persian, Russian, Spanish, and Vietnamese.

In an educational system where sixty languages—from Urdu to German—are spoken, the Houston Independent School District has instituted an extensive English as a Second Language program that helps students convert learning in their own languages to learning in English. At the same time, the district is promoting expanded language development by offering Arabic, Mandarin Chinese, French, German, Italian, Hebrew, Hindi, Latin, Russian, and Spanish through its language magnet program.

During these recent years of "boom to bust and back again," there have been changes in municipal government. In 1979, Houstonians voted to expand City Council from eight members, all elected at large, to a total of fourteen members with five elected at large and nine by districts. The November, 1979, election was a landmark one in that women and an Hispanic were elected to the council for the first time, the first African-American council member having been elected in 1971.

Four mayors—Fred Hofheinz, Jim McConn, Kathy Whitmire, and Bob Lanier—have led Houston during the last two decades. As annual budgets have risen to more than $1 billion, the city's leaders continue to struggle with the century-old dilemma of providing a favorable business climate as well as adequate public services and a healthy environment for all Houstonians.

In a city with a population approaching two million and an area that covers more than six hundred square miles, these problems will continue to exist. Undaunted, however, Houstonians face the new century with their traditional initiative and "can-do" spirit.

Houston also gained new recognition as a major international city, becoming not only the base of operation for the international oil and gas exploration and production industry, but also headquarters for many of the world's largest international engineering and construction firms. In addition, the Port of Houston continued to rank high among United States ports in foreign tonnage, which accounts for more than half of the Port's total volume. By 1996, sixty-six consular offices were located in Houston. Only New York, Los Angeles, and San Francisco had more.

Houston is also international in the composition of its population, with more than a hundred nationalities represented in its makeup. The 1990 census revealed that twelve percent of Harris County's residents were foreign born. According to Dr. Stephen L. Klineberg of Rice University, "This region is rapidly becoming one of the most ethnically and culturally diverse in America."

This cultural diversity is manifested by the publication of three Chinese daily newspapers, several Latin American weeklies, and periodicals in German, Italian, Korean, and

Sam Houston Statue, Hermann Park. Legend says that Sam Houston, sculpted by Enrico Cerrachio in 1925, is pointing toward the San Jacinto Battleground, where he experienced a momentous victory. Perhaps, instead, he is pointing with pride to this dynamic city bearing his name.
COURTESY GREATER HOUSTON PARTNERSHIP.

EPILOGUE

On a very warm day in July 1990, the world's attention turned to Houston. The Economic Summit of Industrialized Nations, hosted by the President of the United States, Houstonian George Bush, convened at Rice University. Hundreds of camera lenses focused on the leaders of the Western world as they walked through the Sallyport of Lovett Hall. The event was broadcast live from the Rice University campus to television sets around the globe, and within an hour the image of this moment was transmitted to newspapers from Mexico City to Moscow. It was fitting that a gathering of such importance to the entire world was held in a place that had evolved from modest beginnings, had confronted many adversities during a century and a half of life, and had emerged as a shining example of what people with a vision and a strong dedication to that vision can accomplish.

PRESERVING HOUSTON'S HERITAGE...
A RESOURCE GUIDE

Houston has a rich history. People and events from the past have shaped the city we know today, and an understanding of that past provides us with a deeper appreciation of who we are as a community. Our understanding is enhanced when we experience history through some tangible evidence of it.

Through the preservation of our city's historical sites and structures, we are given an opportunity to view history in this vital way.

Perhaps the most visible reminder of Houston's early history is Buffalo Bayou. The spot chosen by the Allen brothers for their new town on the bayou became the principal

dock for boats throughout the nineteenth century. Known today as Allen's Landing, this site—after years of neglect and deterioration—is currently slated for extensive rehabilitation. In another project, the stretch of bayou east of downtown is being redeveloped as Houston's Heritage Corridor, which will include a green belt for recreational activities and renovated industrial sites as reminders of the historical significance of Buffalo Bayou. In the opposite direction, in the heart of the Theater District, the bayou has been incorporated into Sesquicentennial Park. When

Clockwise, from top, left:

Brashear Building, 1882, 910 Prairie Avenue

Sweeney, Coombs & Fredericks Building, 1889, 301 Main Street

Market Square Park, (1904 Market House Clock), Corner, Travis and Congress

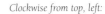

completed the park will include an amphitheater for outdoor performances and a setting for selected artwork. Further upstream the bayou retains much of its primitive beauty, reminiscent of earlier times. The renewed attention to Buffalo Bayou encourages recognition of the stream as significant in Houston's history.

The block designated on the original plan for Houston as Congress Square became the center of the city's commercial and governmental activities. Simple utilitarian structures facing the square housed a variety of businesses, while a succession of market houses stood on the square itself. The oldest surviv-

ing structure in the area is the Kennedy Building erected in 1861, while a few late nineteenth century structures remain facing the east side of the square. Today Market Square Park occupies the historic block, recalling much of the city's history through artwork, building fragments, and photographs.

The square is included in a larger area which was designated as the Main Street-Market Square Historic District by the United States Department of the Interior in 1983. The district's more than fifty historic structures—dating from the 1860s until World War II—reflect not only Houston's commercial and industrial roots but also the evolution of the city's architectural styles and tastes.

Among the historic structures are Houston's first steel-framed skyscraper, the first building containing an electric elevator, the only remaining iron-fronted structure, Houston's first cotton exchange, and the only surviving downtown theater building.

Commercial buildings outside the downtown historic district also reflect Houston's history, especially during the early twentieth century when the city began growing into a metropolis. The Texas Commerce Bank Building, known as the Gulf Building in its early years, dominated Houston's skyline for more than three decades, and its banking lobby is one of the most impressive spaces in our city today. The Texas Company Building, designed on a monumental scale by a New York architectural firm, characterizes the oil industry which contributed so significantly to the city's development. Another important contributor to Houston's emergence as a major city were the railroads, which are represented today by Union Station. Houston's tremendous industrial growth is reflected in the Peden Iron & Steel Company Building in what has become known as the warehouse district.

Older buildings are frequently renovated for adaptive reuse—a process which retains the historic integrity of the structure while giving it new purpose and increased value in

today's economic climate. A revival of interest in downtown Houston has prompted conversion of numerous buildings to residential housing, the largest project being the 1913 Rice Hotel. As the number of downtown residents grows, the entire area will undoubtedly experience an increased demand for services and goods, thus resulting in the establishment of new businesses. This broadly-based revitalization of a section of the city is one of the obvious economic benefits realized from historic preservation. There are many commercial structures—not only downtown, but also in outlying areas—which reflect important aspects of Houston's development. Preserving and using these buildings is vital to an understanding of how our city has grown and matured since its founding.

Neighborhoods are at the heart of a city's very being. Houston neighborhoods now listed in the National Register of Historic Places include: Old Sixth Ward, Courtlandt Place, Houston Heights, Freedmen's Town,

Clockwise from top, left

Christ Church Cathedral, 1893, 1117 Texas Avenue

Eastwood Elementary School, 1916, (now Dora Lantrip Elementary School), 100 Telephone Road

Bethel Baptist Church, 1923, 801 Andrews Street

Top, left: Peden Co. Building, 1930, 610 N. San Jacinto Street

Middle, right: St. Peter United Church of Christ, 1864, 9022 Long Point Road

Bottom, right: Old Sixth Ward

Broadacres, Westmoreland, Independence Heights, and West 11th Place. They reflect Houston's history from the emancipation of the slaves after the Civil War through the boom years of the early 1920s and the Depression which followed. Historic neighborhoods have the ability to combine the best of the past with contemporary lifestyles, creating unique havens for their residents. Older neighborhoods, however, are seriously in danger of disappearing. They face the ever-present possibility of being engulfed by encroaching development and, at the same time, being decimated by deteriorating infrastructure and services. It is critical to the fabric of our city that these pockets of tradition, stability, and culture survive.

Public buildings—schools, libraries, museums, courthouses, and the like—represent the collective life of a community. They are the places where people of all ages engage in a wide range of activities reflecting their lives from day to day. History is made in these structures, and they too have a story to tell.

Houston's religious properties serve not only as spiritual anchors but also as places that reveal the area's history and identity. In Houston these range from a simple frame church erected by German farmers

to cathedral-like edifices with elegant interiors. Each reflects how people of faith have witnessed to that faith through their houses of worship.

Cemeteries, too, are a constant reminder of our roots, providing physical links to the past and helping to chart a social and cultural history of the city. The locations and sizes of Houston's historic cemeteries tell us much about how the city has grown and changed. Glendale, the oldest, documents the first Anglo settlers in this area, while burial grounds like Evergreen Negro Cemetery and Olivewood contain the graves of the earliest black residents, and Magnolia preserves the heritage of the city's Hispanic population. Others like Glenwood and Forest Park Lawndale provide a visible record of how the park-like cemetery was created in Houston to provide not only beautiful resting-places for the dead but also places of meditation

and relaxation for the living. Although cemeteries are protected by law from being destroyed, they frequently suffer from neglect and vandalism. Individual and collective initiative is often the most effective means for the preservation of these older burial grounds.

The importance of green space to a city cannot be overestimated. Parks create calm oases in the midst of urban life. Trees provide a natural canopy which shelters those beneath. Gardens delight us with their ever-changing wonders. Conservation of our nat-

Top, left: Independence Heights

Right: Glendale Cemetery, est. 1831, Lavaca Street

Below, right: Broadacres

ural surroundings is essential in maintaining our historic identity.

Historic buildings have a language of their own. They speak of the dreams and achievements of those who have come before us. They also tell us about overcoming hard times and adversity. They have the ability to be the threads which bind past to present and point toward the future. Historic areas have the same potential. They are a vital component in developing a sense of place and well-being in a community. A city's character is fully defined only when both old and new threads are woven into the tapestry which reveals its life.

Creating a tapestry reflective of Houston's unique history will not just happen. This task demands vigilance, advocacy, and action on the part of all Houstonians who care about this city in which we live. Each of us must become aware of our historic resources, understand their importance, and join forces to protect them. The Greater Houston

Preservation Alliance has been committed to this task since 1978. Working together we can ensure that Houston's heritage survives for future generations—not just on paper, but in reality.

Top: 300-year-old tree, 2615 Augusta Street

Below: Gardens in Hermann Park

Sharing the Heritage

historic profiles
of businesses and organizations
that have contributed
to the development and economic base
of Houston

120	*banking & professions*
128	*the marketplace*
146	*industry & energy*
182	*quality of life*
194	*service & networks*

FRIENDS OF HISTORIC HOUSTON

Fayez Sarofim
Company

Houston Distributing
Company

Mesa Southwest
Construction Company

Pennzoil

Reading & Bates
Corporation

Humble oil field, 1930.
COURTESY HOUSTON METROPOLITAN RESEARCH CENTER,
HOUSTON PUBLIC LIBRARY

BANKING & PROFESSIONS

*banking and professional corporations
provide the foundation for a host
of Houston enterprises*

122   *Sanders Morris Mundy*

123   *Houston Trust Company*

124   *Baker & Botts, L.L.P.*

125   *MetroBank*

126   *Southern National Bank*

127   *Mohle, Adams, Till,
          Guidry & Wallace, L.L.P.*

Merchants National Bank, 1908.

SANDERS
MORRIS
MUNDY

Top: Don A. Sanders

Middle: Ben T. Morris

Bottom: George L. Ball

It required an uncommon amount of courage to launch a new investment banking enterprise in Houston in 1987. The city was reeling in the aftermath of the regional energy and real estate bear markets of the mid-80s and the financial community was regrouping, taking no risks, after the national banking crisis that accompanied the regional collapse.

But Don Sanders, Ben Morris and John Mundy, looking beyond the devastation, saw the enormous potential for renewal and growth and decided to put their faith in Houston's future.

"What motivated the founders of Sanders Morris Mundy was the enormous opportunity," explains George Ball, now one of the principals of the flourishing decade-old firm. "Small and medium-sized companies throughout the region were crying out for capital. Many of these companies had proven their viability during the crash, had learned the lessons hard times teach, and were ready to make huge leaps in productivity and earnings. The climate was right for a company that understood the opportunities and knew how to manage the risks."

Together the founders had an abundance of the required expertise, bringing with them resumes that include senior positions in some of America's foremost investment firms and corporations, as well as such high-profile community involvements as Don Sander's ownership in the Houston Astros.

They brought, too, the respect of Houston's investment community and a rich network of personal relationships that made it possible for Sanders Morris Mundy to find money in highly difficult markets.

"Most of the investment clients had known Don for years and trusted him enormously," Ball, a former governor of the American Stock Exchange and of the Chicago Board Options Exchange, notes. "We built on those relationships by establishing and adhering to three very firm, unbreakable policies, forming a covenant of trust among the firm, our investors and our client companies."

The first of those policies, Ben Morris explains, is a commitment to an extremely rigorous investment evaluation process — the firm reviews several hundred potential investments for every one in which it decides to invest. The second is a policy of investing 'in common' with

clients: either the firm or its individual principals buy between 25 and 35 percent of each of its offerings.

"And, the third cornerstone of our business is a belief in investing for the long-run," says Sanders. "When we make a financial commitment to a company, we're in — doing whatever it takes, for as long as it takes, to try to assure the company's success. This means our clients have actively monitored holdings and our companies get a partner in growth, an arrangement that works to the benefit of everyone."

Taken together, these policies have propelled Sanders Morris Mundy, in just ten years, from start-up to star status. In 1987, the company had six employees — the three principals and their support staff. Today, the company's 80 professional and administrative staff members occupy two floors of the Texas Commerce Tower in Houston and another floor on New York City's Park Avenue. Even more importantly, the firm has developed an outstanding reputation among investors, corporations and other investment bankers who have witnessed its achievements.

"I think we can tell Houston exactly what we tell the companies we represent," says Ball. "Sanders Morris Mundy is with them for the long pull."

The shareholders and officers of the Houston Trust Company see their firm as a bridge between the city's past and its future, providing highly personalized, client centered services which guarantee that the financial legacies of the past will pass intact to coming generations.

"Our goal when we formed the company in 1993 was to fill a gap left by the consolidation of financial services the city had just experienced," says third generation Houstonian James A. Elkins, III, chairman. "Those mergers shifted most of the city's financial leadership to large out-of-state institutions, making it difficult for people to find the kind of personal service they need when making important decisions about the financial security of their families."

With William C. McCain Jr., president, Elkins developed a plan for a locally owned and managed independent trust company that emphasizes superior personal service and competitive investment performance for individuals and families. To this carefully-crafted package, they added their own credentials and expertise. Elkins, whose grandfather founded Houston's Guaranty Trust Company (predecessor of First City National Bank) in 1924, contributed more than 21 years experience in trust, banking and financial management. McCain added more than a quarter century's experience in banking and finance, including tenure with banking and Big-Six accounting firms. David R. Lummis, a fourth-generation Houstonian with 16 years of business experience with Wall Street investment banking and Big Six accounting firms, joined the team in 1994.

"We shared our plan with the city's top professionals in accounting, law, estate and tax planning, and money management," McCain recalls. "Their response was overwhelmingly positive. The city needs what we have to offer."

Within a few months, representatives of seven of Houston's oldest, most established families joined the management team as shareholders, providing a solid, local financial underpinning for the long-term effort of creating a Houston based financial services organization.

"We are building the Houston Trust Company one client at a time, marketing the only way that works — by reputation, a reputation we earn by providing the highest quality services to each family and foundation who entrusts their assets to us," Elkins says.

At the Houston Trust Company, quality service begins with a low professional-client ratio, one that encourages continuing communication.

"We hire only experienced, credentialed account administrators, never talented youngsters who are still 'in training,'" Elkins says. "We want even our smallest account holders to feel comfortable calling any time, with any question. And, we want their calls to result in immediate, satisfactory responses."

The company also emphasizes focus, specialization and flexibility.

"We rely on independent, professional investment firms to advise us on portfolio decisions, freeing us to focus strictly on service and administration," says McCain. "We choose these advisors carefully, after an in-depth study of each firm's personnel and independent research and analysis capacity. The resulting network of alliances allows us access to a full array of financial products and services, enabling our clients to choose the investment teams that best suit their needs and styles."

Perhaps the company's most important distinguishing characteristic, however, is its determination to build relationships that transcend time and history.

"With every new client, we begin building a relationship that will endure long after we are gone," says Elkins. "Our job is to make sure our clients' grand- and great-grandchildren have the assets they will need to continue inventing this city. To do this well, we must focus on the future, on building a company that will last for many generations. Our corporate descendants will be here, filling the roles we fill today, in the years 2100 and beyond."

Below: (Left to right) David Lummis, Jim Elkins, Melinda Myers, Bill McCain

BAKER & BOTTS, L.L.P.

Baker & Botts, L.L.P., Houston's oldest law firm, traces its origins to the 1840 law practice of Peter W. Gray.

Peter Gray followed his father, William Fairfax Gray, into the practice of law in early Houston. William Fairfax Gray, a leader in the community, led the formation of Christ Church, Houston's first organized church and now Christ Church Cathedral, in 1839 and held the office of District Attorney.

Peter Gray, who served as District Attorney, District Judge, member of the Texas Supreme Court, and as the first president of the Houston Bar Association, was joined in his law office in 1865 by Walter Browne Botts, a cousin from Virginia, to form Gray & Botts. In 1872, Judge James A. Baker of Huntsville moved to Houston to join them under the name Gray, Botts & Baker with offices in Gray's Opera House, fronting Court House Square. In the early twentieth century, Judge Baker's son, Capt. James A. Baker, led the firm's efforts in New York City to protect from fraudulent and murderous claimants the endowment promised by William Marsh Rice's will to establish the educational institution that became Rice University. Capt. Baker, a highly regarded trial lawyer, served two terms as President of the Houston Bar Association and actively participated in real estate development and banking interests in early Houston.

The roster of early partners of Baker & Botts, L.L.P., also included Rober S. Lovett, who was later General Counsel and Chairman of the Board for the Union Pacific and Southern Pacific Railroad systems; Edwin B. Parker, who served as chairman of the Houston Board of Park Commissioners and subsequently was Chairman of the United States Liquidation Commission following World War I and General Counsel of The Texas Company (later Texaco, Inc.); and Hiram M Garwood, who was a former judge and member of the Texas Legislature. Partners in the firm playing active roles in the early years of Houston's cultural institutions, in addition to Capt. Baker as Chairman of the Board of Rice Institute, included Walter H. Walne as President of the Houston Symphony for six terms in the 1920s and John P. Bullington as an early President of The Museum of Fine Arts.

The firm's Houston clients in the early 20th century included The Commercial National Bank and The South Texas National Bank, predecessors to Texas Commerce Bank, Houston General Electric Company and Houston Electric Street Railway Company, Houston Lighting & Power Company, Houston Gas Company (a predecessor of Entex), Imperial Sugar Company, and Foley Brothers Dry Goods Company. Representative clients of the firm with substantial Houston ties in the second half of the twentieth century have included Exxon USA, Gerald D. Hines Interests, Houston Industries Incoporated, Pennzoil Company, Schlumberger Ltd., Shell Oil Company, Tenneco Inc., Texas Commerce Bank, United Gas Pipeline Company and Zapata Corporation.

Baker & Botts, L.L.P., has grown with Houston. With additional offices in Austin, Dallas, New York, Washington, London and Moscow, its 500-plus lawyers practice in almost all areas of civil law, representing many of Houston's major companies as they respond to the increasing globalization of the nation's economy.

SOURCES:

FREEMAN, J.H., THE PEOPLE OF BAKER BOTTS (1992).

HOUGHTON, D., SCARDINO, B., BLACKBURN, S. AND HOWE, K.,
    HOUSTON'S FORGOTTEN HERITAGE (1991).

JOHNSTON, M., A HAPPY WORDLY ABODE-CHRIST CHURCH CATHEDRAL 1839/1964 (1964).

JOHNSTON, M., HOUSTON - THE UNKNOWN CITY - 1836-1946 (1991).

LIPARTITO, K. J., AND PRATT, J.A., BAKER & BOTTS IN THE DEVELOPMENT OF
    MODERN HOUSTON (1991)

The obstacles that faced MetroBank in its formative days would have sunk some other financial institutions. It opened in 1987, in the midst of a major recession. It started with $3 million in capital—a shoestring budget for a bank. And its target market comprised only a small percentage of Houston's population.

Yet, MetroBank has thrived. Today, it's the city's seventh-largest independent bank with almost $500 million in assets and about 220 employees. Its loan portfolio and deposits, which totaled $261 million and $367 million, respectively, in 1996, continue to grow at double-digit rates.

What's the secret to MetroBank's success? Its commitment to customer service and to meeting the unique banking needs of Houston's multicultural community.

"We were founded to serve southwest Houston's growing Asian population," Don Wang, chairman and chief executive officer of the bank, recalls. "Asian immigrants who were moving here and opening small businesses were having problems dealing with the big banks. There were language barriers, and because Asians are reluctant to share financial information, they were seen as credit risks."

From the start, customers streamed into the bank not only from Houston but also from around the state. Within a year, MetroBank's assets had soared to $16 million. Then in March 1989, it acquired Industrial Bank, boosting its assets to $100 million and establishing a presence in Houston's predominantly Hispanic east side.

Expanding its boundaries, MetroBank opened eight more branches in Houston and one in Dallas. It established lending offices in New Orleans and San Antonio to provide financing alternatives for minority communities there. And it began working with the Department of Agriculture to offer loans to businesses in rural areas.

MetroBank also opened a Small Business Administration (SBA) Lending Department and became certified by the Business Consortium Fund, which loans working capital to minority businesses. It initiated an Overseas Chinese Credit Guaranty Fund. In addition, it established financing with banks in Mexico, Latin America and Asia through the Export-Import Bank (Eximbank), which facilitates lending for commerce between the United States and other countries.

MetroBank was named an SBA preferred lender and was awarded priority lender status by Eximbank, allowing it to authorize loans without prior SBA or Eximbank approval. And it was designated by the Federal National Mortgage Association (FNMA) as a Community Development Financial Institution, enabling it to expand the availability of mortgage funds to traditionally underserved markets.

"We're more committed than ever to providing personal service to customers," Wang reports. "We want people to feel at home here—and they do. We offer coffee or tea in our reception areas, and customers come in to visit." They might meet Wang or other bank executives who drop by the branches to greet customers.

A truly multicultural institution, MetroBank has personnel on staff who can communicate with customers in all Asian dialects, French, Spanish, Portuguese, and Dutch. It participates actively in the communities it serves through sponsorship of such events as Asian New Year celebrations and Cinco de Mayo festivities.

"Our ability to understand and address the unique banking needs of Houston's diverse populations has consistently earned us 'outstanding' ratings from the Community Reinvestment Act regulators as well as awards and honors from non-profit and government agencies," Wang concludes. "We're proud of our achievement of becoming Houston's premier multicultural bank."

Top, left: MetroBank's management team.

Below: MetroBank Sugar Land, serving the growing communities of Fort Bend County.

SOUTHERN NATIONAL BANK

Thomas Jefferson, the most qualified person to be elected president of the United States, served in the Continental Congress, formed a political party and served as governor of Virginia, ambassador to France, secretary of state and vice president before becoming leader of his country. He wanted to be remembered as the author of the Declaration of Independence, founder of the University of Virginia and, author of the Statute of Virginia for Religious Freedom.

Jefferson was a farmer, lawyer, diplomat, inventor, scientist, musician, political philosopher and architect of the University of Virginia and numerous beautiful homes. He also was the architect and builder of Monticello, his Virginia home, which today attracts more than a half-million visitors annually.

It's no surprise that the man and his monument inspired officials of Southern National Bank of Texas. They designed their headquarters with Monticello in mind.

"But our building reflects more than Jefferson's architectural style," Bank Chairman Lisa Clements maintains. "It's a symbol of the bank's commitment to quality, to Southern hospitality, to treating customers as family members, and earning their loyalty and trust."

Founding director Harvey Zinn is president and chief executive officer and has created a strong infrastructure for the enterprise. It is named Southern National Bank to reflect its focus on friendly, customer-oriented service.

To serve Southwest Houston and Fort Bend County, Southern National Bank has its headquarters in Sugar Land, a full-service branch on Bellfort Boulevard with a motor bank on the Southwest Freeway and a full-service branch in the Professional Building II at Memorial Hospital Southwest. The bank installed automatic teller machines at Memorial Hospital Southwest, on the Houston Baptist University campus, and at the Stewart Title Building near the Galleria.

Clements began planning the new headquarters when she joined the bank in 1993. Opened in 1995, the red brick, colonnaded structure bears a strong resemblance to Jefferson's home. Such features as Louisiana plantation pecan floors, a century-old steel and brass automatic vault door, presidential draperies that are Jefferson's own design, floor coverings made in England on the same looms as the carpets of Dolly Madison and a community meeting room with a three-story-high domed ceiling — a replica of the dome at Monticello — reflect the architectural style of Jefferson's day.

"We're a community bank in every sense of the word," she adds. Clements, for example, serves on the boards of numerous nonprofit organizations. In addition, the bank sponsored publication of a book on the region which is sold to support local charities.

Civic associations frequently hold meetings in the bank's community rooms. Another room will become available in 1998 when the Southern National Bank Office Building completes construction of its new home next door. Housed in the office building will be the Museum of Southern History, with Joella Morris serving as the museum's president emeritus.

"This is a locally owned institution and will stay that way," says Clements. "That gives it stability and helps ensure continuity of service and philosophy. It also means bank decisions will be made by community members, not outsiders.

"Southern National Bank will remain committed to this community well into the future," she concludes. The consummate contributor to his community and the world, Thomas Jefferson would have been proud.

Top, right: An exact footprint of Jefferson's Monticello, Southern National Bank is "Monticello West."

Below: The Jefferson Room is a 35 foot domed community meeting room.

MOHLE, ADAMS, TILL, GUIDRY & WALLACE, L.L.P.

In the early 1930's, Mr. Theodore "Ted" Mohle, a native Texan was working for the national CPA firm, Lybrand, Ross Brothers & Montgomery, at their New York headquarters. However, when it was decided to open a new office in Houston, Mr. Mohle seized the opportunity to move back to his home state! Mr. Mohle was a leader in the accounting profession and became active in the local and regional professional organizations. He served as president of the Texas Society of Certified Public Accountants from 1937 to 1938.

After establishing the Houston office for the national firm, he decided to "hang out his own shingle" and established T. W. Mohle & Co. Mr. Mohle, a man known for his vision and integrity, quickly assembled a staff of hardworking professionals with construction, petrochemical, and real estate expertise.

In the mid 1950's, the firm broadened its practice and began helping individuals, fiduciaries, and nonprofit organizations. This expansion, in turn, led to his adding associates. In 1957, Robert A. Till and Thomas C. Adams became partners. Subsequently, David P. Guidry and Richard E. Wallace reached partnership status nine years later.

When Mr. Mohle retired in 1971, the firm adopted its present name, Mohle, Adams, Till, Guidry & Wallace. Concomitantly, Robert Till became the managing partner. He aggressively expanded the firm's administra-tive, compliance, financial reporting, management consulting, and tax planning services.

As Houston's economy boomed throughout the 1970's and early 1980's, Mohle, Adams, Till, Guidry & Wallace added both clients and employees. In 1986, Robert Till decided it was time to retire. Therefore, he "passed the baton" to Mr. Adams, who managed the firm until his semi-retirement in 1992. At this juncture, Mr. Wallace assumed the leadership position. The firm celebrated its fiftieth anniversary in 1996.

Presently, this premiere CPA firm has five partners and eleven associates. Together, they focus on three major segments. These are (1) individuals, (2) businesses and nonprofit organizations, and (3) estates and trusts. According to Mr. Mike Till, whose father is Robert, "a CPA can provide better assistance by first listening to the individual client's needs and then applying appropriate technical expertise." Similarly, businesses expect "competent, highly-trained, well-educated, professionals, who can offer personalized attention to their financial reporting, consulting and compliance requirements." Finally, this younger partner notes that "nonprofits want a CPA firm with considerable strength, stability, consistency, and integrity."

Mohle, Adams, Till, Guidry & Wallace recently installed technically-advanced computer systems at its 3900 Essex Lane headquarters. These, in turn, allow it to do instantly tasks which took Mr. Mohle weeks to do. Nevertheless, its current management team serves many of Mr. Mohle's original clients! Likewise, it remains committed to Mr. Mohle's value-added principles of "honesty, fairness, and client satisfaction." With this creed and a double digit annual growth rate, Mohle, Adams, Till, Guidry & Wallace is well positioned for the next fifty years.

THE MARKETPLACE

*Houston's retail and commercial establishments
offer an impressive variety of choices for Houstonians.*

130   *Landry's Seafood Restaurants, Inc.*

132   *Visible Changes*

134   *MHI*

136   *Nils Sefeldt Volvo*

137   *Continental Airlines*

138   *Lancaster Hotel*

139   *United Business Machines, Inc.*

140   *Computer Station Corporation*

141   *Southwest Airlines*

142   *Fiesta Mart*

143   *Molina's Restaurants*

144   *RELO.net*

145   *Randall Davis Properties, Inc.*

David Helberg's grocery store, 1911.
COURTESY HOUSTON METROPOLITAN RESEARCH CENTER,
HOUSTON PUBLIC LIBRARY

LANDRY'S SEAFOOD RESTAURANTS, INC.

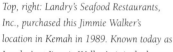

A GROWING OPERATION

As a young boy, Tilman Fertitta knew a thing or two about the seafood business, having grown up peeling shrimp at his father's surfside eatery at Pier 23 in Galveston. Like the vast majority of full-service restaurants at the time, Pier 23 was one of a kind, owned and managed by a single family.

Fertitta graduated from high school, leaving Galveston to attend the University of Houston. But his love for seafood and the business was always with him.

During his college career, Fertitta started his own sales and marketing firm to pay his way through school. Quite the young entrepreneur, he started his own construction and development company after college, while still continuing to operate his sales and marketing firm. He built and developed residential housing, restaurants and hotels. Yet he continued to maintain an interest in the seafood business, longing to create his own enterprise in the industry.

In 1986, Fertitta believed the time was ripe for a national chain of Gulf-flavored seafood restaurants featuring a casual, festive atmosphere, providing fun for the entire family. He purchased from two partners sole interest in Landry's Seafood House, opened in Katy, Texas in 1980, and the slightly more upscale Willie G's Seafood & Steak House a year later.

At a time when steakhouses and Italian restaurants were popular, Fertitta felt the seafood restaurant business was untapped and decided to expand, envisioning his high energy, full-service, casual dining concept throughout the United States. He looked for faltering independent restaurants located on waterfronts. In 1988, he acquired sole ownership of the company and developed it into a recognized seafood company with four distinct concepts.

Fertitta opened his first restaurant in his hometown of Galveston, and in five years, the company grew from two to 11 restaurants, including locations in San Antonio, Corpus Christi, Austin and Dallas. In 1993, he took the company public, a decision many would consider risky since 95 percent of restaurant startups fail. However, Fertitta parlayed his cash flow from one restaurant into more, with all earnings invested into company development. He subsequently raised nearly $300 million in four stock offerings, and Landry's Seafood Restaurants, Inc., continues to be one of the best performing restaurant stocks on Wall Street.

Fertitta, 40, is chairman, president and chief executive officer and largest shareholder of Landry's Seafood Restaurants, Inc., one of the fastest growing restaurant companies in the industry, and the second largest casual dining, full-service seafood restaurant company, employing more than 15,000 nationwide. Through acquisitions and new construction, the company owns and operates more than 100 restaurants, with four distinct concepts: Landry's Seafood House, Joe's Crab Shack, The Crab House and Willie G's Seafood & Steak House. By developing this four-concept approach, Landry's seeks to appeal to patrons of all ages, backgrounds, income brackets and interests, and to set the standard for the industry, not follow it.

Fertitta also is president of Fertitta Hospitality, Inc., a development, hotel and entertainment company which owns and operates the 22-acre beachfront resort consisting of The San Luis Resort and Conference Center, the Galveston Island Hilton, restaurants, specialty shops and other properties and projects.

In 1997, Landry's acquired the Kemah Waterfront in Kemah, Texas. The company plans to develop the area into one of the most exciting showplace boardwalks in the United States — an entertainment complex of attractions, restaurants and retail shops that he hopes will triple the number of visitors to the area to more than three million.

In its innovative marketing approach to make his concept unique, Fertitta has styled all Landry's Seafood House restaurants with neon movie-style marquees, with many located on waterfront sites. The company continues to expand, with plans for 250 new restaurants over the next five years.

Fertitta devotes a significant amount of time to numerous charitable organizations, serving on the boards of the Greater Houston Convention & Visitor's Bureau, the Crohn's & Colitis Foundation of America, The Childress Foundation, The Children's Museum, Houston Children's Charity, Space Center Houston, Better Business Bureau, the University of Houston Alumni Organization and the Houston Livestock Show and Rodeo. He also pledges his time to Chuck Norris' Kick Drugs Out of America Foundation.

Also active in the national and state political scene, Fertitta and his wife, Paige, have hosted two private receptions at their home for President Bill Clinton, as well as many receptions for other national and international government leaders.

In addition to opening their home for political fundraisers, the Fertittas have hosted numerous charitable organizations, as well as contributed funds, resources and ideas to bring awareness and assistance to many important causes.

Above: Many of the restaurants are located on the waterfront, so that diners can enjoy a relaxing atmosphere, watching ships sail by and suns set.

VISIBLE CHANGES

John and Maryanne McCormack, CEO and president, respectively, of the Visible Changes chain of beauty salons, have grown rich by helping their staff members earn big money.

"After only two or three years on the floor, our average hairdresser earns more than $30,000," says Maryanne, who was selected one of Houston's Women on the Move in 1986. "That's about three times what the average hairdresser in the United States earns. Sounds like magic, doesn't it?"

But, it's not magic, Maryanne insists - it's focus. At Visible Changes, the focus is on empowering team members — teaching them everything they need to be successful and supporting them with personal attention and continuing education as they progress along the company's carefully-defined career and benefit paths.

"When John and I hire a hairdresser for one of our 17 salons in Houston, Austin, Dallas or San Antonio, we start from the beginning, giving the newcomer a total professional education," she explains. "New team members do not step foot onto our salon floors to work as stylists until we're convinced they are ready to be a winner."

Formal training to be a winner at Visible Changes can take from several months to a full year, with the student-trainees coming two or three days a week to the company's Spring Branch headquarters to absorb techniques it took the McCormacks years to perfect.

"Before we married, Maryanne told me she was determined to be the best hairdresser she could be," says John, the former New York City policeman who was named Entrepreneur of the Year by *Inc. Magazine* in 1988. "We invested more than $65,000 in her training, working during the day to pay for her to study at night with some of the world's greatest stylists."

From her studies, Maryanne refined a whole new haircutting technique — one she says guarantees perfect results every time, on every type of hair. "Our new staff training begins with that technique, which removes any guesswork," she says. "With the technique under their belts, they are ready for

our continuing education program, which encourages all employees interested in advancement to learn a new style at least once every six weeks."

Visible Changes trainees and haircutters, however, learn more than how to make a pair of scissors sing. They also learn winning professional skills, attending continuing education seminars and classes on everything from self-esteem, to time management, to how teach a customer to use professional hair care products.

"Our hairdressers are encouraged to think of themselves as teachers, charged with providing customers the skills and products they need to take care of their hair at home," Maryanne explains. "We believe making a customer look good when she leaves the salon is only half the job. The other half is making sure she can duplicate the look at home, on an every-day, on-going basis."

Goal-setting is another basic of the Visible Changes management philosophy. The McCormacks and the Visible Changes management team coach all staff members every year in making and reviewing decisions about where they want to go in their careers.

"We encourage our 750 team members to set goals that force them to stretch, to grow, to go beyond where they think they can," Maryanne says. "John and I can see what they are capable of and we support them while they learn to see it, themselves. The fun is sharing with them the wonderful experience of becoming everything they have always wanted to be."

The McCormacks back their philosophy of empowerment with their pocketbooks, financing an incentive plan that includes profit sharing, generous year-end bonuses for team members who meet their goals, and an almost-infinite variety of awards. In their view, the company's on-going investment in its staff works like a kind of fertilizer, assuring a rich harvest of human potential and growth.

"My feeling about money is that it's like horse manure. If you pile it in a corner, it's going to start to stink," John says. "But, if you spread it around, it makes things grow. At Visible Changes, we spread the money

around, putting more than $20 million in our profit sharing plan. For a company that does $30 million in sales, that's unheard of, but we figure we can't afford not to return 40 percent of our profits to our team members — it makes them grow. And, when they grow, we grow."

Another expensive program which the McCormacks consider too valuable to discontinue is the company's annual meeting, a festive event culminating in the presentation of more than 300 awards, each of them earned by staff who have progressed in some way in technical or professional skills.

"Our first meeting, when we were only five years old, cost something like $300,000," John recalls. "I was horrified, telling Maryanne that we could not afford to hold another for at least five years. But, when I read the staffs' evaluations and saw how excited they were, how much motivation they derived from watching their colleagues walk across the stage to accept their awards, I changed my mind. The company meeting is an annual event, even though its

now costing us more than $700,000 a year now."

A few years back, the McCormacks extended their empowerment program to embrace the children of their employees, establishing a foundation to finance their needs in education. The foundation is funded by contributions from the business and by proceeds from John's book, *Self-Made in America, Plain Talk for Plain People About the Meaning of Success*, as well as the motivational engagements he does for other companies and professional organizations.

"The foundation is our way of backing something Maryanne and I said a few years ago at an annual meeting," John recalls. "We told our team members, we would not consider ourselves successful until the majority of our staff member's children graduate from college. Only then will we know we've achieved our mission — to teach people they can achieve whatever they want if they're willing to go for it. When people believe in their own potential, then act on what they believe, dreams do come true."

MHI

The way Frank B. McGuyer saw it in 1988 when he became a casualty of Houston's real estate recession, downsized from his management position with one of the nation's largest home builders, he had two options.

"I could sell my services as an expert in dealing with a consolidating real estate market in another part of the country, or I could bet on the people and resiliency of Houston," says McGuyer, chairman and CEO of MHI, the 1996 Greater Houston Builder's Association "Builder of the Year."

It would not have been difficult, McGuyer recalls, to find a new job. "Builders all over the country were preparing for the problems Houston faced," he says. "But, I decided to stay in Houston, convinced that the economy was basically strong. The city had already begun to diversify. From there on, it was just a matter of gaining momentum."

McGuyer persuaded another veteran of the Houston housing slump, Michael K. Love (now MHI's president and chief operating officer) to join him, forming an expertise-packed building partnership guaranteed to impress lenders. For working capital, McGuyer and Love turned to David F. Chapman, Clive Runnells and Ralph O'Connor, three savvy Houstonians who believed it was time to invest in Houston again. "These three investors were able to see what I saw — that recovery was not just around the corner, but actually already underway," McGuyer says.

With the financial support of these "anchors," the new partnership was able to secure bank financing to finish and sell one hundred homes in 1989, producing revenues of more than $10 million. MHI more than tripled that respectable performance the next year. By the end of 1992, the company had taken a quantum leap, closing on more than 1000 units, for revenues greater than $100 million.

In 1996, MHI closed nearly 2000 homes, generating revenues of more than $200 million, earning the status of largest builder in the city, according to the American Metro Study that year.

"No one buys a house for investment reasons any more," McGuyer says. "Whether you're courting first-time buyers or people ready to move up, you've got to offer products that enhance their lifestyles and you've got to accompany those products with lots of personal service."

McGuyer and Love took time to define their markets carefully, catering to each niche

with specially-designed products merchandised under distinct "signatures."

Pioneer Homes is the MHI signature division, creating homes priced from $80,000 to $100,000 for first-time buyers. Plantation Homes (which has built the Channel 8 auction home each year since 1991) caters to buyers in the $100,000 to $200,000 range. Coventry Homes addresses the tastes and needs of the semi-custom market, with homes costing between $200,000 and $500,000; and Carmel Builders specializes in custom homes costing over $500,000.

Careful attention to detail and "an almost obsessive responsiveness" to customer needs has earned the company an impressive array of local, state and national design and merchandising awards and has brought them warm welcomes in such new markets as Austin, Dallas, San Antonio and Tampa, Florida. In 1996, the company ranked 27th among single family detached home builders in the Annual Giant 100 listing compiled by *Professional Builder Magazine.*

McGuyer won't predict what the future holds except to say, "We've come this far this fast by listening to our customers, designing new homes responsive to their tastes and building them to accommodate individual needs. We're not going to change a strategy that works as well as ours does."

Above: Today's family showhome, built by Coventry Homes, as featured in Better Homes and Gardens® Special Interest Publications.

Below: The Columbus model showcases the innovative architecture and attention to detail built into every Pioneer Home.

NILS SEFELDT VOLVO

Bob Heckeroth, president of Nils Sefeldt Volvo, believes Volvos will become one of the most popular vehicles in Houston. Their reputation for safety and durability already has made them top-selling cars and trucks in Europe, and Heckeroth has seen how these attributes are contributing to Volvo's growing acceptance here as well.

More than 1.2 million Volvos have been sold in the U.S. since 1955, when Nils Sefeldt introduced the first model to this country. He had visited American aircraft plants and had imported U.S.-made cars into Sweden, and he was convinced that Volvos would appeal to American motorists.

Both the Volvo factory in Sweden and the Swedish government considered it a foolhardy mission. But Sefeldt wasn't afraid to take risks. As a pilot in the Swedish Air Force, he had flown over 100 types of aircraft and had survived an airplane crash. He also had become Europe's first licensed helicopter pilot and instructor and had established its first helicopter training school.

So with $3,000 in cash, one Volvo sedan and $10 worth of spare parts, he immigrated to Fort Worth, Texas, in 1955 to start a Volvo distributorship. He soon relocated to Houston to be closer to the port.

That first year, Sefeldt sold five Volvos to new dealers around Texas. By 1962, annual sales had jumped to 20,000. Eventually, his company expanded into a 16-state distributorship with more than 70 dealers.

In 1967, Sefeldt sold his distributorship to AB Volvo, which had established factory-owned distributorships on the East and West coasts. But he continued operating a dealership in Houston. Nils Sefeldt died in 1993. In 1995, Houston attorney Bob Friedman of Friedman & Associates and Bob Heckeroth acquired the business.

Today, Nils Sefeldt Volvo is Houston's only exclusive Volvo dealership. It sells about 800 new cars annually—more than any other dealership in Texas—and has one of the largest stocks of used Volvos in the state. It also boasts the world's largest Volvo parts inventory.

In 1996, Nils Sefeldt Volvo moved into a new 35,000-square-foot facility in west Houston. "We added space to accommodate Volvo's new line of sporty and luxury vehicles," Heckeroth says. "A coupe and convertible are in production, with safety a Number One concern."

Volvo's new look enhances the value of the brand that sets standards for safety and durability. "Volvo consistently has led the industry in safety innovations," Heckeroth reports. "For instance, it began installing laminated windshields in its vehicles in 1944, and more recently it was the first with side-impact air bags. That's why it is insurance companies' car of choice for safety.

"As for durability, it's not unusual to see Volvos with 150,000 to 200,000 miles. One car traded into us had 400,000 miles."

The facility also enabled the dealership to expand its service department. "We pride ourselves on service," Heckeroth says. "Volvo conducts an annual customer survey, and most employees' pay is based partly on the results."

The dealership also prides itself on its employees, who contribute to its reputation for exceptional service. "Our salespeople undergo 10 days of training annually so they can answer customers' questions. Our mechanics are Volvo-certified, so their training is focused on one vehicle. And since our service and parts managers have been here for years and have served generations of Volvo owners, they know many customers on a first-name basis.

"Nils Sefeldt was a personable man who took care of his customers," Heckeroth says. "We're continuing his tradition. We're committed to fulfilling his vision of making Houston—and America—a big market for Volvos."

Below: New state-of-the-art facility built in 1996.

Bottom: Nils Sefeldt standing next to a 1958 PV544 in his showroom.

In 1995, employees of Houston-based Continental Airlines purchased the chief executive officer a Harley-Davidson for Christmas. That's how they expressed their gratitude for the leadership Gordon Bethune had exhibited since taking the company's helm late in 1994.

The gift reflected the fact that Continental, whose history had been characterized by two bankruptcies and years of financial losses, had reported a record $224 million profit for Bethune's first year, sending its stock prices soaring from $6.50 to $47.50 per share. Furthermore, it had managed to move from dead-last in its industry to at or near the top in several critical success factors. In 1996, Continental was rated first by frequent fliers in the J. D. Power & Associates survey for best airline on long flights. Continental was again rated first by frequent fliers in the 1997 J.D. Power and Associates survey, becoming the only airline to do so in consecutive years.

Continental's rise from the ashes can be credited, in part, to the Go Forward Plan, a program instituted by Bethune and chief operating officer Greg Brenneman in early 1995. Its first component, Fly to Win, focused on enhancing assets and activities that boost profits and eliminating those that don't. To contain costs, for example,

Continental began withdrawing from unprofitable routes and hubs and unpopular services, replacing big jets with smaller ones to eliminate empty seats and reducing staff. To enhance travel agent allegiance, it restored competitive commissions.

The second component, Fund the Future, was designed to improve Continental's financial picture. Steps were taken to reduce debt and interest payments, build cash reserves and invest in technology and other aspects of its business.

Until early 1995, the Department of Transportation (DOT) reports, Continental placed last among major U.S. airlines in two key success factors—on-time performance and baggage handling—and it led the list in customer complaints. The plan's third component, Make Reliability a Reality, awarded bonuses to every employee for improvements in these statistics. It also called for such enhancements as a unified look for the jet fleet and telephones at every seat. As a result, Continental has become an industry leader in all three of the DOT Consumer Report categories.

The fourth element, Working Together, focused on improving work force satisfaction by rewarding cooperation, enhancing communication, minimizing management interference and encouraging employees to treat each other with dignity and respect. Successful implementation of this program component has led to reduced absenteeism and attrition rates, improved morale and labor relations and an increase in the number of job applications.

Today, Continental is more secure, operationally and financially, than it has been for many years. It's well on its way to becoming the best airline anywhere, as measured by its employees, its customers and its shareholders around the world.

CONTINENTAL AIRLINES

PHOTOS BY PATRICK CURREY

LANCASTER
HOTEL

Top, right: Lobby setting evokes distinguished English manor.

Below: Guest rooms convey a relaxed and timeless elegance

In the heart of Houston's cultural and business district, almost hidden among the skyscrapers downtown, stands a small luxury hotel that Conde Nast Traveler magazine calls "one of the best places to stay in the world." For more than six decades, guests have come to the Lancaster Hotel to enjoy the comfort, elegance and personal service that only this four-star hotel can provide.

Built in 1926, the Auditorium Hotel, as it was known then, was a favorite stopover for noted entertainers in the 1930s. After its basement — now the wine cellar for Charley's 517 Restaurant next door — was converted into a USO entertainment center during World War II, it attracted such celebrities as Helen Hayes, Fay Bainter and Gene Autry.

The hotel, though, had fallen into disrepair by 1981, when it was acquired by Bill Sharman and a group of investors. During an $18 million renovation, they gutted the interior of the 12-story structure, converting its 200 rooms into 96, including 10 suites, and creating one of the most distinctive hotels in Houston. The Lancaster was designated a national landmark in 1984.

An ever-present doorman greets guests as they arrive at the burgundy canopy-covered entrance of the hotel, just across from the Alley Theater and Jones Hall. As General Manager Sergio Ortiz explains, "We want them to feel pampered from the moment they walk in the door."

That pampering, he says, extends to the amenities, from padded hangers and potpourri bags in every closet to baskets of toiletries and terrycloth robes to fresh flowers, that guests find in every room. And it includes such personal touches as overnight shoe shines, valet service, 24-hour room service, daily newspapers at the door and complimentary limousine service within the central business district.

The decor—the overstuffed chairs, antiques and 18th-century English oil paintings in the lobby and the fine reproduction antiques, imported wallpapers, imported fabrics on windows and beds and marble bathrooms with brass fixtures in each guest's quarters—remind visitors of the timeless elegance of an English manor. But they also enjoy conveniences that were unheard of during the Auditorium Hotel's heyday: remote control, cable-equipped TVs, video cassette players, hi-fi stereo systems with CD players and mini-bars, all housed in armoires, as well as digital phone systems, in-room fax machines, computer data ports, two-line speaker phones with conference call capabilities and cellular phones on request.

The Bistro Lancaster features cuisine from Texas, Louisiana and the Florida Panhandle. In addition, the hotel features three elegant meeting rooms and function space for corporate and social gatherings of six to two hundred guests.

"Since we're within walking distance of the financial district and the federal and county courthouses, many of our guests during the week are lawyers, bankers and other members of the business community," Ortiz explains. "And on weekends, we cater to theater-goers, performing arts enthusiasts and, of course, performers because of our location in the Theater District."

Not surprisingly, about half the people who stay at the Lancaster are repeat guests, Ortiz points out. "That's why we keep records on each visitor," he explains. "For example, we'll note if someone likes extra towels or prefers cheesecake with strawberries or doesn't like to be disturbed before noon.

"We pride ourselves on our high standards and our attention to detail," he concludes, "and beyond providing great service, we delight in creating a bond with our guests. We want each guest to feel like a long-awaited houseguest—and to want to come back to the Lancaster, again and again."

The Lancaster Hotel is owned and managed by Houston-based Lancaster Hotels and Resorts.

UNITED BUSINESS MACHINES, INC.

While employed at Texas Instruments, Mr. A. A. Jamal saw the need for reliable, durable, IBM compatible personal computers. Similarly, the University of Houston graduate envisioned that the individuals and organizations buying these machines wanted fairly-priced accessories, peripherals, and software. Therefore, in April 1984, the engineer founded United Business Machines, Inc.

Using his industry knowledge, the Who's Who business leader purchased large quantities of motherboards, and other components, from reputable, name brand manufacturers. Likewise, the man who helps feed the homeless hired A+ industry certified technicians to design and manufacture superior-performance products. In such a manner, United Business Machines (UBM) produced exceptionally dependable, upgradable computers at extremely low cost.

With a winning combination of high quality and consistently lower prices, the field hockey player's business thrived! However, to help it grow faster he employed "experienced, knowledgeable sales representatives." This led to the Novell and FCC certified business opening a second facility in January 1986. At this site, Mr. Jamal's professionals built NT and PC compatible units.

As the need for computers grew during the late 1980's and early 1990's so did UBM. In fact, this company prospered during that period for three reasons. The first was that persons were reluctant to spend much money on a "name brand" whose technology would be obsolete within two years. Second, Houston's economy went through a recession where corporations strived to lower costs. Third, clients wanted a partnership with an organization that would be around for years to come. Thus, to keep up with demand Mr. Jamal expanded to his third facility.

This awe-inspiring "Computer SuperCenter," visible from Beltway 8, opened in September 1991. It houses the company's warehouse, manufacturing facility, service department, and more than 20,000 square feet of space! Moreover, this corporate headquarters is where UBM provides warranty repair work, software training, Inter/Intranet solutions, and networking support. Furthermore, the SuperCenter is where UBM's specialists write algorithms to span millenniums, and where they serve accounting, energy, legal, manufacturing, and medical clients.

Because of Mr. Jamal's motto of "service for years to come," UBM's helpful staff works with its clients to develop systems solutions. In other words, they first analyze a customer's current and future needs. This, in turn, lets them determine the best combination of hardware and software, for a given budget. UBM then manufactures specialized units, and loads them with the appropriate software. Finally, it tests each machine and all accessories before delivering them to clients.

Additionally, UBM's highly-educated programmers write tailored code, in every major PC-based language! They do this at either their 10290 Westheimer headquarters or a customer's site. Thus, Mr. Jamal's team can often help his clients achieve maximum productivity from their current investment, rather than forcing them to buy an entirely new system. In fact, UBM even helps clients with their Acad, data processing, desktop publishing, mapping, and Web page design work.

UBM recently posted its product information on the Internet. As a result, the rapidly growing business is now serving customers throughout the United States, and in several other countries! Even so, Mr. Jamal remains committed to his value-added principles of "integrity, pride in construction, and flexibility to help customers better." With this regal attitude, and multimillion annual revenues, the premiere service-oriented UBM will continue to be a sparkling Houston gem!

Top, left: UBM Supercenter at 10290 Westheimer

Below: UBM's new facility, opening in the summer of 1998.

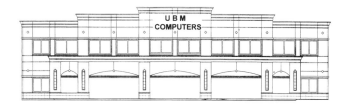

COMPUTER STATION CORPORATION

Just a few years after the first personal computers were introduced to the market, Jeff Jow made a prediction: In 10 years, he prophesied, PCs will be as essential to the business world as telephones. That conviction convinced him to quit his job in the Texas Medical Center and start his own company, Computer Station Corp., in 1983.

The move was a major step for Jow, who had come to this country from Taiwan to study at the University of Houston. After earning his master's degree in electrical engineering, he had accepted a job designing, installing and servicing computers for physicians.

"I was in my early 20s, didn't speak good English and didn't have a financial background," he recalls. Despite these challenges, his company grew quickly as many of the doctors who had worked with him in the Medical Center became his clients. He boasted $100,000 in sales his first year in business. By 1987, his annual revenues had reached $6 million.

"At that point, I considered taking my company public," he recalls. "But I didn't want to grow too fast too soon and lose control. I chose to take a more conservative route."

The decision, he says, was a wise one. "I've been in business fourteen years, and I don't know of any other company like this that has been here as long without merging with someone else or going out of business. One reason is that many of them grew too fast for their own good.

"Longevity is one of our selling points," he adds. "Our clients want to know we'll still be in business down the road."

In the mid-1980s, Jow began focusing his efforts on gaining corporate clients. In 1987-1988, he spent $250,000 on newspaper advertising, a strategy that helped him build a client list comprising about 1,000 companies and organiza-

tions, including NASA, the Houston Independent School District, the City of Houston, the University of Texas Health Science Center, Baylor College of Medicine, Krug Life and United Space Alliance, a major NASA-area contractor.

Clients come to Computer Station Corp. for PCs, notebooks, printers, printer supplies, accessories, peripherals, software and networks. As Jow explains, "Almost everything we offer is name brand, like IBM, Compaq, Hewlett-Packard, Epson, Okidata, Toshiba, Brother, Microsoft, Novell, NEC, Digital, 3COM, Panasonic and much more, because we're committed to quality."

An authorized service center for Compaq, IBM, Okidata, Epson, Panasonic and Hewlett Packard, Jow's company also provides carry-in and on-site repairs and upgrades.

"One of our primary benefits to clients is the knowledge we provide," he continues. "Our industry is constantly changing, and it's hard for them to keep up with the latest technology. We read constantly and attend seminars, and we get frequent updates from vendors, so corporations can count on us to keep them up to date.

"They also know we're honest," he adds. "We won't sell them products they don't need. We find out what they really need and sell them the right tools for their needs and their budget. That saves them money and aggravation in the long run."

Jow's prediction about PCs' future was right on target, and his decision to build a business based on that prediction has paid off. Fourteen years of success with Computer Station Corp. also have given him the experience he needs for his next major steps: to acquire other companies in his industry, to expand into other markets around the country to take his company public at last.

Above: Jeff Jow and his family in front of his old house in Taiwan, as he was leaving his home town to study in America in 1979.

Top, right: Computer Station's showroom

Below: Computer Station trade show booth.

The history of Southwest Airlines is legendary in Texas. What started out as an idea for intrastate air travel, scribbled on a napkin, has grown into a major force within the airline industry.

Southwest Airlines began operating in Texas 26 years ago with service to Houston, Dallas and San Antonio. Now, it flies to 51 cities in 25 states. But Southwest is not one to forget its roots. The city of Houston played a major role in the early development of Southwest Airlines and continues to be one of its biggest and most profitable markets.

Just as Houston has helped Southwest Airlines, Southwest Airlines has helped Houston. Southwest's original service to Houston, which began June 18, 1971, was to Intercontinental Airport. But during the first couple of months of operation, it became apparent that service to the outlying airport was dying. It was suggested that Southwest serve close-in Hobby Airport instead. The switch was made, revitalizing Hobby Airport and doubling Southwest's load factors in Houston.

On May 14, 1972, Southwest transferred all Houston service to Hobby. The move proved very profitable. But that profitability was threatened in February 1973. That was when Braniff, which was still flying out of Hobby, announced a three-month "get acquainted" sale which was flying Braniff passengers from Dallas to Houston for $13—half of Braniff's and Southwest's regular fare. This was a small market for Braniff, but a major one for Southwest, and Braniff thought the scheme would put Southwest out of business.

But Lamar Muse, Southwest's president in 1973, came up with a counter strategy that became the most successful advertisement in Southwest's history. Running double-page advertisements in both the Houston and Dallas papers, the ad read: "Nobody's going to shoot Southwest Airlines out of the sky for a lousy $13." The next line announced that Southwest would match Braniff's $13 fare. Southwest's customers were given their choice of a $13 fare or a free bottle of premium liquor with each full price ticket. Southwest won the fare war and became the largest distributor in Texas of Chivas, Crown Royal, and Smirnoff for two months in 1973.

Competition for the Houston market helped turn the tide for Southwest Airlines. The first quarterly profit in the company's history was made, and 1973 became Southwest's first profitable year. Each year since then has been in the profit column.

Houston helped Southwest Airlines make headlines again in 1979. On January 25 of that year, Southwest began service from Houston Hobby to New Orleans with one round-trip weekdays. This was the first scheduled interstate flight for Southwest.

On September 8, 1980, Southwest Airlines reinstated service between Dallas Love Field and Houston Intercontinental, now known as George Bush Intercontinental.

Another landmark day for Houston and Southwest Airlines came on June 1, 1984. That was when Southwest opened its pilot base in Houston, the airline's first crew base outside of Dallas. Southwest's Houston reservations center soon followed, opening on August 9, 1987. It is now one of nine Southwest Airlines reservations centers across the country. A year later, on November 29, 1988, Southwest opened a $5.7 million maintenance base at Houston Hobby.

Houston continues to be a major force in Southwest Airlines' operations. Currently, the airline operates 137 daily nonstop departures out of Houston Hobby Airport, with additional direct or connecting service to 29 cities. And Southwest operates seven daily nonstop departures out of George Bush Intercontinental, with additional direct or connecting service to eight cities. The airline has 2,656 employees in Houston—further proof that Southwest's relationship with Houston will continue to prosper.

SOUTHWEST AIRLINES

Top: Houston Hobby 10th Anniversary, 1981.

Middle: Herb and Houston Rockets head coach Rudy Tomjanovich at the dedication of the Houston Rockets gate at Houston Hobby.

Bottom: The latest specialty plane, Triple Crown One, honoring Southwest Airlines employees, was unveiled on June 7, 1996.

FIESTA MART

Donald Bonham and O. C. Mendenhall, co-founders of Fiesta Mart, Inc., opened their first Houston supermarket in 1972, combining their experience to meet the needs of the rapidly growing Hispanic community on the city's near north side.

Bonham had worked with the Chilean government, building a chain of supermarkets and improving food distribution in that country. He had also operated a chain of stores in his home town of Corpus Christi and built a chain that served the entire region of South Texas. Mendenhall was an equally experienced grocery man from Oklahoma.

Together the two men introduced one-stop shopping, a concept that was new to the supermarket industry at that time, allowing customers easy access to a broad range of services. Bonham and Mendenhall borrowed a time-proven pattern — that of the traditional outdoor markets which have been thriving for centuries in towns and cities throughout the world. The atmosphere of these markets, where customers come to socialize while selecting and purchasing a variety of goods for daily consumption, was exactly the atmosphere the founders wanted for their stores.

In the almost three decades since Fiesta's first opening, many stores have adopted the idea of providing customers access to many services under one roof. But, few have done it with Fiesta's distinctive multi-cultural marketing flair.

The first Fiesta supermarket had fewer than 100 employees. Within ten years, the company added five more stores, increasing employment to almost 1000. With the opening of its seventh store, at Bellaire and Hillcroft in southwest Houston, Fiesta was established as a store which attracted customers eager to "discover the difference," individuals who wanted to combine grocery shopping with an opportunity to explore a variety of tastes and cultures. Opened in August, 1982, this 110,000 square-foot supermarket was the largest store in the city at the time. It was also the first truly international supermarket, displaying products from dozens of countries to serve a sector of the city that continues to be known for its ethnic diversity.

This unique approach to marketing gained national publicity for Fiesta and provided the momentum to expand the chain, which nearly doubled in size during the next two years. By 1989, Fiesta Mart had distinguished itself as one of the most creative and innovative retailers in the country, gaining further national recognition when it opened a 235,000 square-foot hypermarket on NASA Road One in the Clear Lake area. Among its many unique attractions, the Clear Lake store featured a glassed-in hydroponic garden which produced pesticide-free vegetables in the midst of the shopping environment.

Fiesta Mart now serves the international communities of Houston, Dallas, Fort Worth, Austin and Galveston, with 35 store locations in these major Texas cities. The work force numbers more than 6000 employees, all trained to work in accordance with the company's guiding principal of providing consumers with purchasing experiences that enhance their quality of life.

Top, right: Fiesta's unique store front.

Above: The produce department stocks over 300 items.

Bottom: Fiesta Mart's International Foods Department features products from around the world.

For members of one family, mi familia, "my family," embraces not only relatives, but employees and customers who walk through a door to come home to Molina's. "My father just wanted a little business, where people could come in and feel like they were wanted," says Raul Molina, Jr. "I don't think he expected it to grow the way it has!" Today, Raul, Jr. and his children run a restaurant company in its third generation of service.

Raul Molina, Sr. came from Mexico to seek a better life in Houston in the late 1920s. He began as a dishwasher and busboy in the restaurant of a Houston hotel. By 1940, he opened his own Old Monterey Restaurant near downtown, and when his first "little business" boomed, he opened Molina's Mexico City Restaurant on South Main. Raul, Jr. worked in the restaurants as a teenager, then took off for college and later the Army. While he and brother George were both in the service, his father made them partners in the business.

"It was just for tax purposes, we thought," Raul, Jr. laughs. "When we came home, though, there it was. We were partners!"

Over the next decades, they opened and relocated restaurants at various sites to take advantage of Houston's growth and changing demographics. Each time he opened new doors, Raul, Jr. carried on his father's commitment to make everyone feel wanted. The philosophy extended to employees. A senior chef, Santo Gonzalez, stayed with the Molinas for 50 years. A waiter, Gilbert Miranda, worked at the restaurants for 40 years and "Leonora, well, she's been here 27 years," muses Raul, Jr.

Yet when Raul, Jr. acquired full interest in the business in 1977, he did not plan for his own children to join him. "I wanted them to choose for themselves," he says. Four of his five children chose the business. Today Raul III serves as chief financial officer, Ricardo as general manager of the chain, Rosanna is catering director, and Roberto manages the Highway 6 location and public relations. The younger Molinas continue the tradition of generations: customers are also family.

Before he moved to Washington, D.C., George Bush used to treat his family to dinner at Molina's Mexico City Restaurant on Houston's west side. "One day he mentioned he would be gone for awhile," says Raul, Jr. "I asked him 'where to?' and he said 'China,' and then said he was an ambassador. He had never said a word about that before."

After Bush became president, he maintained the family ties. When he decided to serve Mexican food at a feast for foreign dignitaries, he ordered it from Raul Molina, Jr. There was only one glitch.

The day of the event, Raul Jr. received a frantic call from the White House chef. "They didn't know how to serve tamales," he explains. "They didn't know what to do with the shucks!"

≈

Newspaper copy announcing the formal opening of the Old Monterey Cafe, 1919 W. Gray, in 1940. Pictured are Raul Molina, Sr., Mrs. Molina, and the restaurant's lone waiter, Tony Chavez.

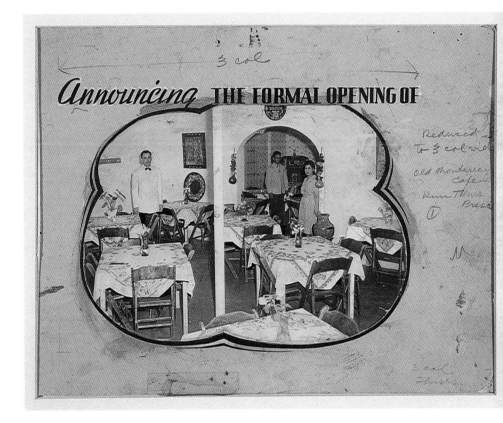

Although Molina enjoys his famous customers, he insists that all of his customers are part of his success. The other day he visited the Westheimer location and saw an attorney who has been eating at Molina's for 35 years. "It felt so good to stop and say 'hi' to him," Raul, Jr. says.

Like all families, this extended family of the famous and the not-so-famous, the wealthy and the ordinary, is bound by corazon, the "heart" of Molina's.

RELO.NET

There's excitement in Dana Pierson's voice when she talks about RELO.net, her Houston-based corporate and temporary housing company.

"We have a talented, experienced staff. Our list of clients includes such corporations as Union Carbide, NASA, Siemans, Exxon, Computer Services Corporation, Stewart & Stevenson, GE, Allied Signal, Marathon Oil, Prudential Relocation and Raytheon. We have a solid foundation, including financial stability .The momentum at which our company is moving excites our team, and that excitement is passed on to our clients. As one indicator of our success, our sales are projected to exceed $8 million in 1998.

"We continue to excel in our ability to provide temporary and corporate housing throughout Houston," she adds. "The economy is on a definite upswing, international business is increasing and as companies reorganize to be more efficient and competitive, they've discovered that focusing on their core products or services increases their profits. That's why human resource departments are outsourcing specialized services such as corporate housing and relocation."

With one phone call, RELO.net's clients are offered a full array of relocation services, including corporate housing, rental assistance for unfurnished apartments, townhomes, condos and single-family homes; and permanent home buying through RELO.net's partnership with over 500 area realtors.

That's an impressive picture for a company that was founded just a few years ago. Pierson spent years preparing the groundwork that has contributed to RELO.net's growth.

After earning an interior design degree, she joined the nation's top architecture firm. From there, she was recruited by Dow Chemical's architecture department,where she handled projects worldwide. Later, she started her own company, which became a division of one of Houston's top architectural firms, Hermes & Reed Architects.

In 1993, Pierson entered the corporate housing field and formed Temporary Furnishings, Inc. Temporary Furnishings quickly became an industry leader and set the standards for rental furnishings, housewares and maid service for hundreds of corporate and model apartments. RELO.net, which was founded in 1996, was a natural extension of that service.

Instead of a small, impersonal hotel room, RELO.net's clients live in comfortable, spacious apartments, condos, townhomes or single-family homes of their choice. The accommodations come complete with all utilities, phone service, furniture, housewares and linens. Other available items are color TVs, VCRs, cable, microwave ovens, washer and dryers, maid service, stereo/CD players, fax machines, computers, additional phone lines for modems, office packages, cribs, high chairs and mobile phones, to mention a few. Along with all the amenities, welcome baskets complete with groceries, toiletries and area information await each RELO.net guest. All RELO.net clients need is to bring their suitcase and any personal belongings.

RELO.net offers corporate housing at over 250 apartment communities throughout the Houston area. Some of the property amenities include state-of-the-art fitness centers, 24-hour business centers, on-site dry cleaners, sparkling pools with jacuzzis, tennis courts, garages, concierges and controlled access gates. A RELO.net representative often meets clients at their office and visits selected properties while giving area tours to help them choose their temporary housing.

RELO.net provides these services at almost half the cost of a hotel room. "And RELO.net clients can move into their corporate units as soon as 24 hours. Corporate, individual and direct billing on one monthly invoice are available to be paid by check or any major credit card.

Pierson concludes, "Our customer-oriented service and quality has fueled RELO.net's expansion as satisfied clients with offices in other cities and states have requested our services nationwide. In just a short time, RELO.net has become recognized as one of the service leaders in our industry."

Spacious and comfortable interiors complete with designer furnishings and housewares.

After his graduation from the University of Texas, Mr. Randall J. Davis accepted a job with Harry Reed & Company. Two years later, the man with a personnel management degree was president! In this capacity, he managed 12,000 apartments and developed 6,000 residential units.

During 1986, Mr. Davis started his own diversified real estate services firm. For the next few years, he renovated properties owned by Coastal Banc, First Gibraltar, and Merrill Lynch. Concurrently, he was a broker for residential complexes valued at more than $100 million!

However, the native Texan, whose childhood memories include visiting Houston's Shamrock Hotel, became disillusioned. The reason was that contractors were demolishing structurally-sound, older buildings. Construction workers would then build new "plain-vanilla" buildings, much to the dismay of local residents.

Therefore, Mr. Davis decided that he would "cultivate our rich heritage." This led to his visiting historical districts throughout the United States. He did this to learn how he could restore crime-ridden, drug-infested neighborhoods to their original vibrant status!

Mr. Davis, in September 1991, bought the old James Bute Company's paint factory, at 711 Williams Street. He then converted the neglected eighty one year old facility into 53 lofts! The units ranged from 800 to 1700 square feet. Mr. Davis rented them for $600 to $1400 per month. He called them Dakota Lofts, since the development was similar to one in New York. Within three weeks of his June 1, 1993 opening, the man from Beaumont had 90% occupancy!

While completing this $2.5 million project, Mr. Davis purchased the former Clarke and Courts Printing Plant on West Clay. By year's end, he finished this 25-loft complex, which he named the TriBeca Lofts, after a

borough in Manhattan. The luxury living spaces had skylights, fireplaces, whirlpools, double-size slate showers, and large kitchens. Residents willingly leased these 1,300 to 2,600 square foot dwellings for $1,000 to $2,100 per month!

Building on his Houston successes, the urban preservationist bought a Galveston Island building in January 1994. In fact, it was another Clarke and Courts Printing Plant. However, within twelve months, the warehouse wizard had again worked his charm, and out popped the 37 unit Strand Lofts!

Next came the former Hogg Building on Louisiana built by William C. Hogg, Governor Jim Hogg's son. He paid $1.5 million, in 1994, for the 1921 red brick structure. With a few exceptions, the 80 units rented for $725 to $2,100 per month. In return, the residents received rooftop terrace gardens, a theater, and a fitness centre.

Recently, the University of Texas tycoon raised $30 million to renovate the Rice Hotel. As his 312 delectable dwellings develop, Mr. Davis, the "Adonis of ambient lofts," will emerge as "lord of the luxury lofts!"

RANDALL DAVIS PROPERTIES, INC.

Original exposed brick and concrete walls and ceilings in large living area of two-story loft.

INDUSTRY & ENERGY

*Houston's industrial and energy companies
provide technology-based solutions
to global problems and energy for the world*

148	Schlumberger Oilfield Services
152	Torch Energy Advisors, Incorporated
154	The Way Companies
156	Waukeshaw Pearce Industries, Inc.
157	TIW Corporation
158	The Westlake Group of Companies
160	El Paso Energy Corporation
162	H & W Petroleum
164	UTEX Industries
166	American Exploration Company/ Louis Dreyfus Natural Gas
168	Global Marine
170	ICO
172	Aramco Services Company
173	Saudi Refining, Inc.
174	Philip Service Corporation
175	Warren Electric Company
176	Tideland Signal
177	Petroleum Information/ Dwight's, L.L.C.
178	Rose Metal Recycling, Inc.
179	Browning-Ferris Industries, Inc.
180	Merex Corporation
181	Walter Oil & Gas Corporation

Hughes Tool Co., c. 1920

SCHLUMBERGER OILFIELD SERVICES

The Schlumberger engineering and manufacturing facility at the Gulf Freeway was in operation from 1953 through 1995.

For the greater part of this century, the Houston area and Schlumberger have enjoyed a symbiotic relationship that shows every sign of continuing through the next century. The city and the company have grown together, both in size and in mutual support, and have benefited from each other economically and culturally. The cooperation and encouragement of local governments and institutions have been determining factors in the success of Schlumberger, and Schlumberger has reciprocated by contributing to the success of Houston.

Like many enterprises, Schlumberger began as a family business. Prior to World War I, Conrad Schlumberger, a professor of physics at the National School of Mines in Paris, developed the theory that various kinds of rocks—sandstone, shale and limestone—would react differently to electrical charges. By recording the differences, he could learn more about what lay hidden under the surface of the earth. After the war, Conrad was joined in this research by his brother Marcel, who shared his belief that electrical prospecting could be used to find oil or minerals. Later, Conrad's son-in-law, Henri Doll, who was also an inventor, joined the team.

The first Schlumberger connection with Houston was made in the mid-1920s. Following the success of surface prospecting in locating an oil-bearing structure in Romania, the Royal Dutch Shell Company's American affiliates decided to test the method in the United States.

In June 1925, Marcel Schlumberger came to the Texas Gulf Coast to test the application of surface prospecting in the oil and mining industries. From Houston he proceeded to the nearby oil fields of Pierce Junction, Blue Ridge, Goose Creek and Humble, and then on to Beaumont and Spindletop. In each field, Marcel and his crew planted electrodes, ran profiles and measured the electrical conductivity of the terrain.

In October 1926, Eugène G. Léonardon, who had become Conrad Schlumberger's assistant after graduating from the Ecole Polytechnique, opened an office in Houston to oversee surface prospecting surveys in the United States. By 1927, Léonardon was conducting surface surveys in the San Joaquin Valley in California, and six of the eight prospecting crews at work throughout the world were in the United States.

Oil and gas exploration changed forever on September 5, 1927, when the Schlumbergers ran the first electric log down an oil well in France using a wooden winch operated by hand on a bicycle chain. For the first time, geologists could use the accurate record obtained by logging to correlate the strata of one well with those of other wells nearby and gain a clear picture of the location of faults and other structural information.

In August 1929, the first electric log in the United States was run in a Shell Oil Company well in California. The Humble Company also tried logging, but had to cancel the trial in 1930 because of the depression. However, in 1933, Schlumberger crews sent to the Texas Gulf Coast at the request of Shell were spectacularly successful, leading to the discovery of more than a dozen fields. From then on, the destinies of Houston and Schlumberger became ever more closely intertwined.

In 1934, Conrad Schlumberger came to Houston to work out a charter and bylaws for an American company. On September 4, Schlumberger Well Surveying Corporation (SWSC) was incorporated and established its headquarters in the Esperson Building. The new company, headed by Léonardon, started out with 12 engineers, 40 other employees and 11 trucks.

SWSC was an economic boon to a city that, like the rest of the country, was in the middle of the depression. For the next six decades, the company's expansion and diversification mirrored the petroleum industry's growth as Schlumberger transformed itself from a wireline logging company to an oilfield services company offering a full slate of oilfield services.

The first major challenge SWSC faced was hiring and training technicians to meet the growing demand for logging services. Conrad Schlumberger, who had lectured at the Royal Academy of Mines in England, approached that school about hiring one of its petroleum geologists. William J. Gillingham, who was frustrated with the "inexactness" of geology, jumped at the chance to become an engineer. In January 1934, he was dispatched to Houston.

Almost immediately, Léonardon sent Gillingham to conduct field work in Houma,

Louisiana. Gillingham rose rapidly through the ranks at SWSC. By the end of his career, he was executive vice president of Schlumberger Limited, in charge of wireline operations throughout the world.

In late 1936, Schlumberger put up the first of many buildings that have poured millions of construction dollars into the Houston area economy over the years. Located at 2720 Leeland Avenue, this first building was a garage where trucks were assembled and field equipment was built. By 1938, shops and lab-

Above: Conrad Schlumberger makes a surface electrical measurement over a known iron ore deposit in Normandy, France, in 1912. Surface prospecting would eventually lead to the discovery of wireline logging in 1927.

Below: Standing on a logging truck in Big Creek, Texas, William Gillingham logs a well in 1936. Gillingham was the first native-English-speaking Schlumberger engineer in the United States.

Schlumberger Anadrill technicians check out a logging-while-drilling tool at the Sugar Land Product Center.

oratories had been added and a new administration building opened. This complex was the main office for North and South American operations until 1953, when Schlumberger moved to a location on the Gulf Freeway.

Over the years, Houston's intellectual and cultural life have also been greatly enriched by the Schlumberger family. World War II led to the relocation to Houston of a young French couple who, over the next 40 years, would heighten the city's appreciation of art and significantly enhance Houston's reputation as a cultural center.

By the time they arrived in Houston, Jean and Dominique de Menil, both in their early thirties, had experienced their share of wartime adventures. Jean de Menil, who had been able to travel across Europe on his business credentials as a Schlumberger executive, had also been on covert assignment for the French resistance to sabotage oil shipments from Romania to Nazi Germany.

Dominique de Menil, who was the daughter of Conrad Schlumberger, began a long and prolific career in Houston collecting the artwork that forms the core of the Menil Collection. Exhibited in a museum building designed by architect Renzo Piano, the renowned eclectic collection is one of Houston's cultural highlights.

When she spoke at the opening of the Menil Collection, Dominique de Menil credited her grandfather, Paul Schlumberger, with making

the gift of the museum to Houston possible. If he had not been willing to finance the research of his son, Conrad, there would have been no Schlumberger company and no reason for members of the Schlumberger family to live in Houston.

Schlumberger also supported the Allied effort in World War II by organizing the nonprofit Electro-Mechanical Research, Inc., for the U.S. Army and giving army engineers the first prototype of a vehicular-mounted mine detector. As the war continued, the company developed mine detection equipment for the army, navy and air force and designed a detector that recovered the 240-ton treasure of gold and silver that the Bank of the Philippines had shoved over the cliff into the ocean at Corregidor.

Henri Doll, who had also moved to Houston after the Germans occupied France, was deeply involved in the mine detector research. He was awarded a Certificate of Appreciation by the U.S. government and the Legion of Honor medal by the French government.

Doll, who became Chairman of the Board of Directors of Schlumberger in the 1960s, firmly believed that research and technology development were key to the success of Schlumberger. He held more than 70 patents and was author or coauthor of more than 30 publications. He also oversaw the public offering of Schlumberger during that decade.

Another Schlumberger executive who made a noteworthy contribution to the war effort was Roger Henquet, the Schlumberger general manager in Houston. Henquet was trained by the OSS to parachute into France before D day to organize the French resistance forces. He was made an American citizen the night before his jump and a second lieutenant the next day—both by overseas radio. Henquet was awarded the Distinguished Service Cross for his months of work with the French underground.

In 1952, Schlumberger purchased a 190-acre test site near Rosharon to use for the development of shaped charges. These explosives are used to perforate oil and gas wells, allowing hydrocarbons to flow from the underground formations into the tubing that carries them to the surface.

Starting with one engineer and five technicians who worked from a small office at the Rosharon site, Schlumberger eventually established a strong leadership position in perforating. The mass production of shaped charges began at Rosharon in 1980. Today, it is known as the Schlumberger Perforating & Testing Center. In addition to shaped charges and perforating gun systems, intelligent downhole testing tools and coiled tubing services for oil and gas exploration and production are also developed there.

On May 4, 1953, Schlumberger celebrated the opening of its complex on the Gulf Freeway. Newspaper accounts heralded it as "a major factor in Houston's industrial growth." Built on 36 acres of land, the Gulf Freeway plant started with seven buildings totaling 241,000 square feet that cost $6 million. It remained the North American center for wireline operations, engineering and manufacturing until 1993, when another major move was made, this time to Sugar Land.

Marcel Schlumberger's son, Pierre, who had moved to Houston from France to succeed Eugène Léonardon as president of the company, bought the Sugar Land site in 1956. The unimproved land cost $2250 per acre, and the transaction was signed by William Gillingham.

The move to the Sugar Land campus reflected the transformation of Schlumberger to a global integrated service provider to the oil and gas industry. This 200-acre complex of 17 buildings and 650,000 square feet of office space is the workplace for 1200 employees of Anadrill, Dowell, IPM and Wireline & Testing operations, as well as the Sugar Land Product Center and Vector Cable. The Sugar Land campus is the foremost center for oilfield product development and technical innovation in North America. Along with facilities in Austin, Tokyo and Clamart, France, the campus supplies the Schlumberger oilfield service companies worldwide with new technology for more efficient oil and gas extraction.

Today, Schlumberger employees number 2,500 in the Houston area, 5,000 in Texas, and 13,000 in the United States. The spirit of enterprise passed down to them from the Schlumberger brothers prevails throughout

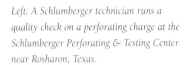

Left: A Schlumberger technician runs a quality check on a perforating charge at the Schlumberger Perforating & Testing Center near Rosharon, Texas.

Below: The Forum serves as the main entrance for the Sugar Land campus. More than 1200 Schlumberger employees work on campus to transform new technology into more efficient products and services for oil and gas extraction.

the company and is reflected in their determination to transform technology into high-quality, cost-effective products and services for their clients. As in the past, Schlumberger intends to be the leader in this transformation, and Houston will again be a beneficiary.

TORCH ENERGY ADVISORS INCORPORATED

In 1981, J. P. Bryan, a former E. F. Hutton & Co. investment banker, had an innovative idea: by focusing on their core activities and farming out essential but noncore functions ranging from accounting and financial services to asset acquisition and management, oil and gas companies could improve their efficiency and reduce their overhead costs. With these opportunities in mind, Bryan formed Torch Energy Advisors, Inc., using capital from the Birmingham, Alabama-based Torchmark Corporation. In addition to specialized outsourcing and asset management, Torch provides growth capital, in the form of mezzanine financing and equity capital, to independent oil and gas producers.

RAPID GROWTH

Although this concept, called outsourcing, is common today, it was almost unheard of in the energy industry back then. The downturn in the oil industry gave Torch a chance to demonstrate its value.

In the mid-1980s, Torch invested about $20 million in 23 troubled oil and gas properties. Its success in managing these assets on its clients' behalf enabled it to attract other investors into new investment programs. Its client roster grew to include a wide range of insurance companies, corporate and public pension funds, foundations, endowments, foreign investors, and public oil and gas companies. By 1985, it had successfully completed three joint ventures and had begun refining its specialized expertise.

"We grew during the tough times in the industry because we learned to operate efficiently," Robert J. Bensh, the company's director of investor relations, recalls. "Our clients knew we could improve the efficiency of their operations, too."

During this same downturn, Torch also launched the first of three publicly held companies. In 1987, it salvaged several poorly performing limited partnerships from a consortium of institutions in the United Kingdom. After consolidating and merging the properties, adding new ones and refinancing the package, it created a privately held corporation owned by the institutions and Torch.

The corporation was merged into a publicly held exploration and production company, called Bellwether Exploration Company, which has properties in Texas, Louisiana, offshore California and the Gulf of Mexico. Since the merger, Bellwether has experienced a twenty-fold increase in asset value.

In mid-1990, Torch merged several limited partnerships to form Nuevo Energy Company, an independent oil and gas company with initial assets of $151 million. Today, it's one of the top independent producers in the United States, with assets valued at approximately $1 billion and upstream oil and gas activities onshore and offshore California, East Texas and onshore Gulf Coast region and internationally offshore the Republic of Congo and Ghana in West Africa.

Then in 1993, the company formed Torch Energy Royalty Trust to take advantage of the Crude Oil Windfall Profits Tax Act enacted by the IRS. The Trust combined the assets of investors and enabled Torch's tax-exempt institutional clients to take advantage of tax credits for production from certain low-volume gas-sand reserves.

STRUCTURED FOR SUCCESS

Today, Torch Energy Advisors manages about $2 billion in energy-related assets, including its clients' assets and its own. With 750 employees based in Houston and California, it's structured to provide its clients with the support and capital they need to prosper.

Torch offers many services through its subsidiary companies. The largest, Torch Operating Company (TOC), operates properties in the major onshore and offshore producing areas of the U.S. TOC also manages properties for clients from exploration through depletion, providing experienced operational planning and execution, in addition to comprehensive evaluation of exploration and exploitation opportunities and the use of new technologies to discover oil and gas and implement enhanced recovery techniques. These services allow companies to acquire properties without adding staff.

Above: San Anastacio,
Oil on Canvas, c. 1800

Below: The Torchbearer Volunteer Program

To complement its outsourcing services, Torch formed Torch Energy Marketing, Inc. (TEMI), to market products and manage midstream asset for independent producers. TEMI markets an average of 450 million cubic feet of natural gas production daily for its clients along with more than 400 million cubic feet of third-party gas, which it purchases for resale to trading partners.

In addition, TEMI manages the scheduling and sale of more than 65,000 barrels of crude oil and about 15,000 barrels of natural gas liquids a day. It operates four natural gas processing plants, an intrastate gas pipeline and a low-pressure gas gathering system. The subsidiary's specialty products division markets solvents, mineral spirits, kerosene, gasoline blendstocks, cutterstocks, slack waxes, ethylene cracker and reformer feedstocks, carbon black oil and paraffins, and it places hydrocarbon intermediates, blendstocks and feedstocks into the chemical and petrochemical markets.

Using an innovative, sophisticated information infrastructure, another subsidiary, Torch Systems Advisors, provides strategic information technology and consulting to energy industry clients. Vital to corporate growth, the Torch Acquisitions Group manages all aspects of the acquisitions process from conception to completion and since 1989 has closed 96 transactions totaling almost $2 billion.

Recently, Torch established the Torch Energy Finance Fund which provides growth capital to small and mid-size oil and gas companies so they can quickly capitalize on acquisition and exploitation opportunities. Another fund, the Energy Fund, was created to seek investment opportunities across the upstream business.

PRESERVING THE PAST

Though Torch is at the forefront of the energy outsourcing industry, it also plays a significant part in preserving the past through The Torch Collection. The Torch Collection consists of Texas, western and Mexican art, artifacts and archives, and serves as the backdrop for Torch's corporate culture. The founder of Torch, J. P. Bryan, himself a relative of Stephen F. Austin, has

been a long-time supporter of Texas historical and preservation efforts. Beginning in 1969, Bryan collected antique books, documents and maps. In the mid-1980s, fine art spanning the century from 1850 to 1950 was added to the collection. Examples include works by artists such as Frederic Remington and Charles Russell. A collection of antique firearms, so important to the American settlement of Texas, is also on display as part of the Torch Collection.

As an extension of The Torch Collection, the Torchbearer Volunteer Program provides area schoolchildren and company visitors the opportunity to explore regional history, culture and art. This innovative, hands-on program is a designed experience that uses trained employee volunteers as Torchbearer guides to the art and artifacts displayed throughout Torch's corporate headquarters. The Torch Collection's community outreach also includes loans of its artworks to various regional museums and galleries.

LOOKING TO THE FUTURE

In 1996, Torch's management purchased the company from Torchmark in a transaction valued at more than $100 million, enabling its employees to own an equity stake in the enterprise. "That's only fitting, because our employees are the key to our success," Bensh believes. "There's an entrepreneurial spirit here, and there's no big bureaucracy to prevent our people from doing their jobs. Their focus is on adding value for our clients. If they can find a way to improve the way we work, they'll do it."

Concludes Bensh, "We'll continue to capitalize on our vast experience, knowledge, capabilities and reputation by providing clients with attractive energy-related investment opportunities, outsourcing and financial services and capital."

Above: The Torch Collection at the Harris County Heritage Society

Below: Factory-engraved Henry-marked Winchester Model 1866 rifle

Bottom: Texas Civil War guidon

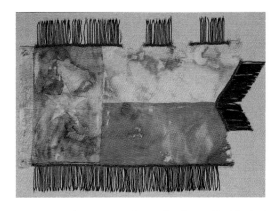

THE WAY COMPANIES

Without the technology underlying The Way Companies, Houston wouldn't be the city it is today — a city in which people routinely watch in cool, detached comfort while Weatherman Neil Frank explains exactly how HOT it is outside.

"My family's history in Houston pre-dates air conditioning, but only by a handful of years," explains Peter Way, president and CEO of Wehco, Inc., which manages four affiliated air conditioning, plumbing, and energy savings firms. "In 1918, Leo Way, my great-grandfather started a refrigeration and ventilation business. By the mid 1920s, he was installing primitive air conditioning systems in churches. The first systems were novelties, luxuries. But it wasn't long before they became necessities — a church without a cooling system was a church without a congregation."

The basic components of the early systems, Way says, were huge wooden boxes installed up around the organ area. Saturdays were devoted to hauling and storing ice in the bunkers. Sundays were cooled by fans blowing air over the ice onto the grateful congregants.

Technology evolved and, shortly before World War II, businesses began installing air conditioning systems. "It was often a situation

Above: Early commercial package air conditioning unit.

Top, right: L.C. Way, founder of Way Engineering Company, and a pioneer in air conditioning in Houston.

Right: Air conditioned and open for business.

of technology-culture clash," Way says. "My dad and grandfather used to reminisce about a customer who called every morning, complaining his system was broken again."

After several service calls, the Ways decided to investigate, stopping by in the early morning when the customer's troubles occurred. "People assumed you were closed if your door was shut. So, of course, the man's front door was open," Way reports. "The problem was, he had the back door open, too, to facilitate re-stocking and trash removal. The hot, humid outside air being pulled through the store was simply overwhelming the system."

The times, the technology, and The Way Companies' clients have grown much more sophisticated. Today, the firms offer highly technical services, specializing in HVAC and plumbing systems for hospitals and other large institutions.

"To insure sterile conditions, a hospital needs separate ventilation systems for each operating room and for each of the eight to ten different gases and fluids routinely piped throughout the building," Way explains. "To do quality work for modern institutions and industrial plants requires the latest computer design and monitoring equipment and skills. Our willingness to invest in that technology is one of the factors contributing to our consistent ranking among the top 100 largest contractors in the United States."

Another factor contributing to that status, Way says, was his decision during the dol-

drum-ridden 1980s, to "re-invent" the company.

"We cut back early, in 1982, and spent time researching new directions," he recalls. "One of the most important decisions we made was to form CES/WAY International, Inc. and become a leader in the emerging field of performance contracting."

Way Engineering Company, another Way affiliate, is currently completing the largest mechanical contract in Houston, a $47,000,000 contract for the newest addition to the M.D. Anderson hospital complex.

Way service companies work closely with their commercial and industrial clients, helping them save money through total maintenance contracts and energy saving measures. "We have more energy savings talent in our companies than any other firm we know of," Way says. "Our expertise helps our customers save money on their facility-operations side. We are continuing to prosper just as we've prospered throughout our 80-year history — by understanding our customers and working closely with them to meet their needs."

Top, left: Neighborhood gathering place to stay cool.

Below: Another "cool" place in Houston.

WAUKESHA-PEARCE
INDUSTRIES, INC.

Since it was founded more than seven decades ago, Waukesha-Pearce Industries, Inc., has grown into an organization whose reputation for responsiveness and quality is well-known throughout the industrial and energy markets it serves.

In 1924, Louis M. Pearce, Sr., formed Portable Rotary Rig Company to produce portable drilling rigs for the oil industry. It built the first wheel-mounted oilfield power unit — using a Waukesha engine — for Spindletop, the oilfield that had started the modern economic development of Texas.

In 1927, Pearce changed his company's name to Portable Rig Company. Convinced that the internal combustion engine would replace steam as the power source for oilwell drilling, he approached Waukesha Motor Company in 1933 and negotiated an agreement to distribute Waukesha engines in Texas. It was the beginning of a relationship that made Pearce's company the world's largest distributor of oilfield engines.

Louis M. Pearce, Jr., joined the company in 1934 and became its president in 1944. That year, its name was changed to Waukesha Sales and Service, Inc., signifying a focus in its role as the Waukesha distributor for the State of Texas. The company also acquired the distribution rights for the Kohler engine and generator lines in 1953.

The Construction Machinery Division was formed in 1955. Today it represents the Dresser, Komatsu, Haulpak, Galion and Gradall product lines from six locations in Texas as well as eight in Mexico.

Louis Pearce III joined the company in 1962. Five years later, the company's name was changed to Waukesha-Pearce Industries, Inc. In 1976, Pearce became its president, the position he holds today.

"With our acquisition of the Komatsu and Dresser product lines in the late 1980s, the Construction Machinery Division has established itself as one of the leading construction machinery distribution businesses in the country," Pearce explains.

Customer demand continues to grow for the company's Waukesha engines, particularly among clients involved in gas compression, power

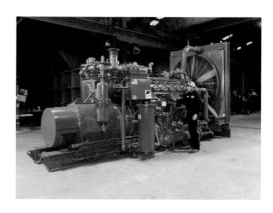

generation and crude oil pumping. The oil and gas industry comprises the majority of the Engine Division's customer base.

The world's largest natural gas engine distributor, Waukesha-Pearce serves clients from 13 locations in Texas, Oklahoma, Louisiana and Arkansas. In addition, its Engine Division recently became the Waukesha distributor for Mexico.

In 1994, the Packaged Power Systems Division was formed, and the company acquired a 164,000-square-foot facility in Houston to manufacture its packaged power system products. "In today's market, customers want more than just an engine," Pearce explains. "They want an engineered power system that includes the engine, the driven equipment, whether it be a generator, compressor or pump, and all the required piping, vessels and controls."

The common link between the company's divisions is customer demand for reliable, high-quality products, Pearce says. "We meet those expectations with our commitment to service from all of our locations in the Mid-Continent region as well as those in Mexico," he points out.

"The technical capabilities of our staff are exceptional," he adds. "They're well-trained individuals with many years of experience in supporting the products we sell."

Waukesha-Pearce is also proud of the relationships it has established with the manufacturers it represents as well as with its customer base. "We're not just selling products," Pearce concludes, "we're building relationships with these companies based on our commitment to provide world-class products to meet their performance expectations and to provide aftermarket support to those products throughout their useful lives."

TIW
CORPORATION

An oil company that's spending as much as $120,000 daily to drill a well can't wait long for equipment and the people to run it to arrive. And they can't afford for the equipment to be technologically behind the times.

That's why Steve Pearce, president of Houston-based TIW Corporation, is particularly proud of his company's ability to respond rapidly to its customers' demands. He boasts about the research and development capabilities that have made his company's products among the most technologically advanced in its industry.

TIW got its start when Steve's grandfather, Louis, and Louis' brothers-in-law launched a small oilfield repair shop in 1917. It wasn't long before they saw even more opportunities in designing and manufacturing equipment for the booming oil industry.

Today, the company they founded has become a leading provider of downhole drilling and production equipment—tools that are used inside the well bore—to oil industry customers around the world. Liner hangers are TIW's primary product line.

"Well bores are lined with steel casing to prevent cave-ins, cover lost circulation zones and high-pressure zones," Pearce explains. "Liner hangers are used to hang smaller pieces of casing inside larger ones, hence in many cases eliminating the need to run the casing all the way back to the surface."

TIW's Window Cutting Products Division designs and manufactures equipment used in window milling operations. Its Pac Solutions Division designs and manufactures downhole systems to keep sand out of the oil and gas flowing into the well bore. As Pearce points out, "These are both major growth areas for us."

The company also manufactures production packers, which are used to isolate different production areas in the well. In addition to these downhole products, it also makes Kelly and Safety Valves that are installed on the surface to seal the well in case a blowout occurs.

With a new Research and Development facility in place, TIW has strengthened its ability to continually develop new technology that will enhance the quality of its product lines. "When customers have difficult wells and need our help designing equipment to handle them, we're well-equipped to meet their demands," Pearce says. "We've developed a reputation for our technological innovation."

With manufacturing sites in Houston, Texas; Youngsville, Louisiana; and Nisku, Alberta, Canada; and service facilities spread across the eastern and western hemispheres, TIW has the infrastructure in place to respond quickly when customer orders come in. Pearce adds, "Because our manufacturing systems and processes are designed in a way to allow for short turnaround on actual manufacturing times, we have the ability to deliver equipment to our customers when they need it.

"We have personnel on standby 24 hours a day to respond when customers need them to operate equipment," Pearce says. "We hire people with oilfield experience, and we train them extensively on our equipment—and then retrain them as the technology changes—so that they can work as efficiently and expertly as possible."

Thanks to its commitment to technology and responsiveness, TIW has come a long way since its founders saw opportunities to prosper in the oil patch. "And as conditions in the oil industry continue to improve," Pearce concludes, "our future has become brighter than ever."

THE WESTLAKE GROUP OF COMPANIES

Packaging for baked goods. Plastic milk cartons. Toys. Bottles. Pipe and pipefittings. Blood bags and medical tubing. Vinyl siding. Floppy diskettes. Credit cards. Wall coverings. These and other products made from petrochemicals make a difference in our quality of life.

With 2,200 employees at 20 operating facilities in North America, the Westlake Group of Companies ranks among the major producers of petrochemicals, plastics and fabricated plastics products for the domestic and international markets. Established in 1986, it has continued the tradition of innovation and excellence established by T. T. Chao, a pioneer in the Asian petrochemical business.

A founder of Taiwan's plastics industry almost four decades ago, Chao built many "first of its kind" petrochemical facilities throughout Asia. He entered the American petrochemicals market when he acquired an idled polyethylene facility in Sulphur, Louisiana. Although he intended to dismantle it and move it to Asia, cyclical improvements in the polyethylene market convinced him to operate it in the U.S. instead.

"He liked doing business here because of America's abundant natural resources, skilled managerial and technical people, readily available land and sophisticated marketplace," Albert Chao, president of the Westlake Group and T. T. Chao's son, recalls. "He set up his U.S. headquarters in Houston because of the warmth of its weather and its people. Houston also is a large metropolitan city and the energy capital of the world. It has a major port that serves as a gateway to Central and South America, and it is located amid the Gulf Coast's concentration of petrochemical industries."

STRATEGY FOR GROWTH

Through acquisition and construction, the Westlake Group has grown rapidly into a world-scale participant in various petrochemical and plastics markets. "We've employed a strategy using vertical integration to enhance competitiveness and maximize the value we provide customers," Albert Chao explains. "This makes us a low-cost producer, ensures a steady feedstock supply, enhances our margins and promotes consistently high operating rates."

Through a series of expansions, the production capacity of the Westlake Group's polyethylene plant in Sulphur has almost quadrupled to 850 million pounds, making it the nation's fourth-largest producer of low-density polyethylene. In 1998, construction will be completed on another expansion: a state-of-the-art facility that can produce linear low- and high-density polyethylene. This expansion will substantially increase Westlake's polyethylene capacity and further broaden the company's product line.

Strengthening its presence in the Gulf Coast's petrochemical corridor, in 1991 the Westlake Group constructed a 1 billion-pound-per-year ethylene plant in Sulphur that provides feedstock to the polyethylene plant and other of the company's facilities. The next year, it began commercial production from a new styrene monomer plant in Sulphur: a 400-million-pound-per-year facility that also receives feedstock from the ethylene plant. In 1997, an expansion of the ethylene facility has boosted Westlake's total ethylene capacity at the Sulphur site to 2.3 billion pounds per year.

SERVING KEY MARKETS

Committed to serving other key polymer markets, in 1990 the Westlake Group acquired the first of several plants it now operates in Calvert City, Kentucky. The only inland vinyl chloride monomer (VCM) plant in the U.S., this 1.2 billion-pound-per-year facility produces feedstock for polyvinyl chloride (PVC) facilities in the Midwest and Northeast.

Expanding further, the next year the Westlake Group acquired PVC plants of its own in Calvert City and in Pace, Florida. These facilities use production from the Calvert City VCM plant as raw material to produce a total of 1.1 billion pounds of

Highly skilled personnel using comprehensive control equipment ensure product quality, safe operations, and compliance with environmental regulations.

PVC annually. Then in mid-1997 the company strengthened its feedstock position by acquiring the chlor-alkali and olefins plants that are adjacent to the Calvert City VCM plant.

Consistent with its strategy of vertical integration, the Westlake Group also manufactures and sells PVC and polyethylene pipe using feedstock from its PVC plants in Calvert City and Pace. With the acquisition of three PVC pipe manufacturing plants, it formed North American Pipe Corporation (NAPCO) in 1992. Now the company operates seven manufacturing plants serving the Sunbelt of the United States, where demand for these products remains strong. The Westlake Group is the second-largest PVC pipe manufacturer in North America.

The company also owns a vinyl window and door profile extrusion plant in Canada and produces PVC fence and siding through Westech Building Products; these products are distributed in North America and overseas. NAPCO's utility supply division in Birmingham, Alabama, sells pipes, fittings, valves and other pipeline construction products for piping systems contractors.

"Our strategy also includes creating synergy through international joint ventures and growth through globalization to better serve the worldwide marketplace," James Chao, vice chairman of Westlake, explains. With this in mind, the company has moved into the Pacific Rim, constructing numerous facilities and providing management and technical assistance to its affiliated petrochemical plants in Malaysia. It has launched several projects in China.

A DIFFERENT PERSPECTIVE

The Westlake Group has many attributes and strengths that distinguish it from competitors. "The blending of cultures in the way we do business makes us unique," Albert Chao explains. "We're truly an international company."

"Being privately held, we have a longer view than public companies do,"Chao adds. "We're not driven by pressures to report profits every quarter. That gives us a better perspective for responding to the cyclical nature of this industry."

"The Westlake Group is committed to maintaining the highest standards in all aspects of its business," Chao says. Evidence of this commitment is reflected in the results of a recent customer satisfaction survey conducted by Mastio & Company, a

marketing and management consulting firm specializing in analysis of chemical, plastics, packaging and natural gas markets. Survey respondents ranked Westlake's polyethylene business first among low-density polyethylene producers in weighted and mean performance for all attributes surveyed. In particular, the business earned top marks in such categories as attitude of continuous improvement, sales representatives who listen well, sales representatives' training,environmental issues assistance and statistical, quality and process control.

"We've built our company on long-term fundamental values, which include safety and citizenship, quality of service and product, care for the environment, accountability, ethics, fairness and teamwork," Chao notes. "We fully embrace the Chemical Manufacturers Association's Responsible Care Code of Management Practices."

That dedication to safety is reflected in the polyethylene plant's designation as a Star site by the Occupational Safety and Health Administration for its outstanding safety and health record. The company's commitment to community service can be seen in its support of numerous community organizations.

In Houston, Westlake is a contributor to United Way, Rice University, St. John's School and the Museum of Health & Medical Science, and it funded the T. T. Chao Scholarship Program at Baylor College of Medicine. Its executives serve on the boards of the Houston Ballet, Asia Society, Houston Grand Opera and Junior Achievement. In addition, the Westlake Group received the Diamond Patron Award for helping the Institute of Chinese Culture rebuild its school after a fire.

"The vision and courage of T. T. Chao led him to the United States, a country that is a world leader in the petrochemical industry," Chao concludes. "We're proud of the manufacturing and marketing base we've established here. We view it as our flagship for the 21st century."

Above: Numerous operating synergies have been created as Westlake has grown by acquisition and grassroots plant development.

Below: Westlake's customers and facilities benefit from the company's strategy of vertical integration.

EL PASO ENERGY CORPORATION

The 1920s were exciting times for the energy business in Texas. The discovery of oil in the Permian Basin of far west Texas and eastern New Mexico ushered in an era of growth and prosperity for the state and created instant millionaires out of daring entrepreneurs who were willing to gamble on high-risk oil field investing. A young Houston attorney, Paul Kayser, watched these developments with interest. By 1928 he was ready to risk the pitfalls of oil field speculation and headed for New York to gain backing for a new oil exploration company.

Rebuffed by bankers who could no longer back the stock of an oil exploration royalty company, Kayser was encouraged to establish a more-easily financed natural gas enterprise. Kayser's first challenge was to find customers for natural gas, and he soon determined that El Paso was the only major city in Texas not burning natural gas in its industrial plants. Next he had to find natural gas supplies to support a line into El Paso. After firming up supply from several gas wells near Jal, New Mexico, Kayser convinced El Paso's industrials to convert facilities from manufactured gas, coal and fuel oil to more cost-effective natural gas, and El Paso Natural Gas Company was in business.

Seventy years later, after it acquired Tenneco Energy in 1996, this small regional gas supplier has become one of the largest energy companies in the United States—

El Paso Energy Corporation. Led by William A. Wise, chairman, president and chief executive officer, the company has expanded into new markets and diversified its holdings into non-regulated areas. Today its reach extends to five continents, and its services cover key segments of the energy value chain, including natural gas transmission, field services, energy marketing, international project development and power generation.

El Paso Energy moved its corporate headquarters to downtown Houston in December 1996, following a move by its field services and energy marketing operations from El Paso. With the relocation of its headquarters, its management team and corporate level operations are now situated in the undisputed capital of the energy industry.

Several factors made Houston attractive to El Paso Energy, including the presence of other key energy industry players and the availability of a skilled employment pool. The Houston Chronicle recently ranked El Paso Energy 16th on a survey of Houston's top 100 companies. With over $8 billion in assets, 3,000 employees and almost 40,000 miles of natural gas transmission pipeline worldwide, El Paso Energy has the size, talent and experience to set the standard among Houston's energy service providers.

El Paso Energy's assets include the nation's only integrated, coast-to-coast natural gas pipeline. The regulated pipeline system spans over 26,000 miles and provides reliable, competitively priced transportation services into all major natural gas market areas.

El Paso Natural Gas Company manages two transmission networks on the western half of the system—El Paso Natural Gas and Mojave. These systems comprise over 10,000 miles of pipeline and offer long- and short-haul interstate gas transportation services from producing regions in New Mexico, Texas, Oklahoma and Colorado to markets in California, Nevada, Arizona, New Mexico, Texas and northern Mexico. Tennessee Gas Pipeline Company manages the system's eastern portion, including Tennessee Gas Pipeline, East Tennessee Natural Gas and Midwestern Gas Transmission. Over 16,000 miles of pipeline transport natural gas from

El Paso Energy's Chaco Crygenic Processing Plant in the San Juan Basin offers the latest in products extraction technology.

supply regions in Texas, Louisiana and the Gulf of Mexico to markets in 20 eastern and midwestern states as well as major metropolitan areas including New York City, Boston and Chicago.

El Paso Energy also maintains over $1 billion in gathering, intrastate transmission, processing and treating assets. Managed and operated by the company's field services business unit, these facilities are connected to gas producers throughout the southern United States and Gulf of Mexico. In 1997, the company was tied to over 11,000 wells and offered a full range of production services, including gas gathering, global compression, flow management, treating, processing and transmission.

El Paso Energy completed construction of one of the industry's largest cryogenic processing plants in 1997. The Chaco Cryogenic Processing Plant, located in the San Juan Basin, has a design capacity of 600 million cubic feet per day and produces over 50,000 barrels daily of natural gas liquids. The cryogenic process, which uses rapid cooling to separate liquids from the gas stream, represents the leading edge of liquids extraction technology. Compared to traditional lean oil recovery plants—which can recover only 50% of the propane from a typical gas stream, 95% of the butane and none of the ethane— the cryogenic process can recover 100% of the propane and butane from the gas stream and 95% of the ethane.

El Paso Energy's international business unit cultivates long-term partnerships to share in developing pipeline and power generation projects worldwide. The company has first-hand experience in developing, financing, owning and operating energy infrastructure assets in such locales as Australia, Argentina, the Czech Republic and Peru. By 1997, El Paso Energy was a co-owner and developer of 2,450 megawatts of power generation, 1,935 miles of pipeline, three gas fields with proven and probable reserves of 1.4 trillion cubic feet and two oil fields with reserves of 50.8 million barrels. El Paso Energy is committed to growing its international business and has projects underway in South America, Europe and the Pacific Rim.

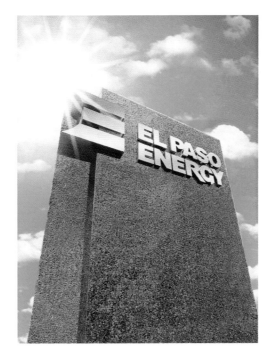

El Paso Energy's marketing company is one of the largest providers of wholesale energy marketing services in the natural gas industry. It provides short- and long-term market development, risk management and aggregation services to over 1,100 customers and is skilled in marketing all forms of energy and fuels including gas, crude oil, refined products, electricity and natural gas liquids.

The marketing unit is positioning itself to provide electricity marketing services in the wake of electric power deregulation. El Paso Energy is one of 30 natural gas companies certified by the Federal Energy Regulatory Commission to market electricity, and it's active in eight of North America's 10 National Electric Reliability Council regions. In 1996, El Paso Energy was the country's seventh-largest marketer of electricity.

By any measure, El Paso Energy is a dominant competitor in its industry. Its business units are designed to promote the core skills developed during many years in the gas industry, and it owns an enviable array of plant and pipeline assets. The management team comprises results-oriented men and women with a wealth of experience, and company employees are among the most highly skilled in the business. Sustained by the success of over seventy years in the energy business, El Paso Energy has the drive and commitment to remain a leader among energy providers.

H & W
PETROLEUM

One of Houston's greatest success stories began in 1946 when Mr. and Mrs. Bill Harkrider, Sr. founded Harkrider Distributing Company. At its onset, this corporation distributed Exxon's industrial solvents to dry cleaners throughout southeast Texas. However, in December 1973 Exxon approached Mr. Wayne Wetzel, an employee of Mr. Harkrider, about delivering gasoline and diesel fuel. The result was that the two men formed H & W Distributing Company.

During 1974, H & W delivered two million gallons of Exxon motor fuel. It did this by beginning the day at 5:30 a.m. so it could "have a load at the first customer when he opened the door." Similarly, according to Mr. Wetzel, H & W developed a policy that "if the customer will stay open long enough, we will make our next day deliveries... Guaranteed!" When their first year began, Wetzel and Harkrider were delivering 180,000 gallons per month. Yet, when it ended, they were doing more than one million gallons per month in southeast Texas!

To keep up with its demand, H & W purchased larger delivery trucks. Within five years, these vehicles were delivering 2.5 million gallons per month! However, Exxon in 1979 decided to "do away with" all agents. As part of the process, this nation's largest oil company turned H & W into a distributor, which meant it had to begin buying and inventorying products. Likewise, H & W had to bill customers, and it had to scramble to retain its larger clients.

To compensate for the lost fuel delivery revenues, Exxon awarded the two business partners its first Houston-area specialty lubricants' distributorship. This, in turn, led to H & W building a five thousand square foot warehouse in January 1980. It also changed its name from H & W Distributing to H & W Petroleum, and adopted its famous "right products, right time, right service" motto.

Because of his phenomenal success selling specialty lubricants, Mr. Wetzel joined Exxon's National Advisory Council, in 1984. Since then, H & W's president has served every year on the Council, and in 1987 H & W became Exxon's largest specialty products distributor in the United States!

At the start of the 1990's, Exxon selected H & W to market lubricants to Dow Chemical. This, in turn, resulted in H & W's purchasing Exxon's Freeport warehouse. Moreover, it fostered Mr. Wetzel's commitment to a "do-things-correctly-the-first-time, 'round-the-clock" service philosophy that has kept his partnership with Dow quite healthy.

President Wetzel reached his next major milestone in 1992, when Exxon selected his company to be a "Branded Wholesaler." Explained differently, H & W became along with forty-nine others a strategically-located, Exxon distributor. As a result, Mr. Wetzel obtained a "primary marketing area," ranging from Central Texas to the Oklahoma and Louisiana borders.

During the following year, H & W expanded to Longview. This enabled Mr. Wetzel to serve Eastman Chemical's northeast Texas operations better. Eastman later reciprocated this goodwill by giving H & W its "Supplier Excellence/Service Award," for 1993, 1994, and 1995. Similarly, Exxon has praised H & W as its "Most Successful Branded Wholesaler" for the last four years.

Recently, H & W made additional strategic acquisitions. In 1994, for example, H & W purchased a Waxahachie facility to gain better access to the Dallas and Waco markets. A year later, H & W bought the Exxon distributorship in Angleton. This further strengthened its presence in Texas.

Concurrently, Mr. Wetzel achieved more notoriety. He began serving on the National Quality Control Council in 1995. Then, in 1996, the U.S. Chamber of Commerce, Nations Business, and MassMutual selected H & W as a "1996 Blue Chip Enterprise Company."

Because H & W's founders and second generation family members Bill Harkrider II, Kay Wetzel, and Sharon Harkrider-Lambert, have remained committed to their customers and employees, this high octane company, during the last seventeen years, went from five to fifty persons. With annual sales exceeding $20 million and plans to expand its distributor network, a turbo-charged H & W Petroleum will continue to be Exxon's wholesaling tiger.

Above: 1996 Bulk Plant.

Below: Lubricants and Petroleum Specialties Tank Farm.

UTEX
INDUSTRIES

Joel and Fred Pippert, President and Vice President of Engineering/Manufacturing Operations, of Utex Industries, formerly Universal Packing and Gasket, cannot remember a time when the company did not loom large in their lives.

One of the earliest memories for both Joel and Fred was going with their fathers at night down to the old Clinton Road plant to fill an emergency order. They would mess around with the typewriters, adding machines and telex machines while their dads would fill orders for gaskets, packings or seals for a customer in the oil patch. Then they would go down to the bus station and send the part off to some faraway place in West Texas or Louisiana.

Joel stated, "I remember the special smell of the place. The plant had a smell I've never encountered anywhere else. It was like a signature - the smell of molded rubber from our production lines."

The two company leaders were not yet born in 1940 when Joel's mother and father joined forces with two friends to form a new enterprise, Universal Packing and Gasket. In the early days, the company was basically a distributor, buying and reselling cut gaskets. Joel says, "They had barely begun to build a clientele when the war sidelined their efforts. Mom & Dad spent the next five years finding

parts for the Liberty ships being constructed along Galveston Bay."

In 1945, Universal reorganized, moving from distribution to production and introducing a new, patented product. That product, a special shaped Chevron ring, received the company's first patent according to Joel.

"The urge to innovate and to design better products has always been the spirit of the company since its founding. It is incorporated into its every fiber," says Joel. "We have never had a 'me too' mind set. We've always been on the lookout for problems, knowing they represent an opportunity and a chance to find a way to do things better than they have been done before."

This fascination with innovation set a milestone in the late 1950's with the introduction of a new molded plunger pump packing. During this time, pressures in a lot of the oil fields discovered in the 30's and 40's had decreased substantially and oil could no longer be produced by conventional means. Secondary recovery was introduced using high pressure plunger pumps to pump water into the formations and floating the oil to the surface. There needed to be an improvement in the packings because the higher speeds and pressures shortened the life of the packings substantially.

Studying the problem closely, Utex engineers saw that improvements in materials and applications were necessary to improve the life cycle of the packing. New materials and a new design were invented to take the place of the Chevron ring and Compression Packings. Since part of the problem of premature failure was improper adjustment, Utex invented a "non-adjustable packing." This took the guess work out of the equation on how much to adjust packing. This packing became a huge success and today is still the number one packing used in plunger pumps worldwide.

This packing, along with other innovative approaches to designing parts, launched Utex into the forefront of the oil field market. In the early 60's, Utex built a manufacturing plant in Humble, Texas. From that time on, Utex began to establish its reputation as a custom rubber molder. "When somebody had a problem we couldn't solve with our proprietary

Clinton Drive

products," Fred explains, "we'd set to work designing completely new designs and assemblies. We were good at it."

Like all other oil industry suppliers, Utex enjoyed "experimental growth" during the energy-hungry 1960's and 1970's. Unlike many others, however, Utex weathered the crash of the 1980's with no major scars.

"The early 1980's, excluding 1981 and 1982, weren't boom years by any means," Joel recalls, "but we didn't really feel the pinch until 1986. Even then there was never a doubt that we would survive."

The company had entered the 1980's with large bank reserves. It used those reserves during the crash to diversify, purchasing two mechanical seal-producing plants in Odessa, Texas, and one plant in Nevada, a producer of braided packings. Utex consolidated the Odessa operations into one plant and transferred the production equipment from the Nevada purchase to a new plant in Weimar, Texas. "Those acquisitions," Joel says, "were a spur to the company's inherently innovative spirit."

"Since we bought the seal companies, we've introduced a half dozen new mechanical seals and a dozen or more new industrial packings," he says. "We've also added a full line of industrial maintenance products, everything from lubricants to cleaners to paint - anything a company needs to keep a plant and its equipment in good repair."

These products have given the company easy access to a wider market, including food and chemical processors and pulp and paper production plants.

"In 1985, 95% of our business was with oil field related companies," Joel says. "Today that percentage has dropped to around 55%, with another 20% of our sales being petrochemical processors. The rest of our sales, somewhere between 20% and 25%, are with non-petrochemical industrial processors."

Since he assumed the presidency in 1992, Joel has focused on moving the company into the international arena. His first overseas marketing trip, in 1992 just after the Gulf War, established the Middle Eastern market. Since then, Utex has developed distribution relationships in 40 different countries in South America, Africa, Europe and along the Pacific Rim.

The Pipperts describe their 500-employee operation as "being on the verge of growing by megabounds."

"Part of that growth will come from the continued expansion outside the oil field, part of it will come from growing markets overseas, part of it will come from the introduction of several new products within our traditional line," says Joel, "and part of it will come from a revolutionary new concept we're not quite ready to reveal."

While refusing to discuss the details, the Pipperts agree that this new product, which is scheduled for field testing in the very near future, continues the family tradition.

"Like all Utex innovations, it utilizes the latest technology to solve a problem that is wide-spread throughout the industry," Joel says, "and like all our innovations, this one is going to be around for a long time."

Above: Manufacturing plant in Weimar, Texas

Below: Corporate office in Houston

AMERICAN EXPLORATION COMPANY/ LOUIS DREYFUS NATURAL GAS

Above: Mark Andrews, Chairman and CEO of American Exploration Company.

Top right: Drilling rig in the Texas State Waters of the Gulf of Mexico.

When Mark Andrews decided to follow in his father's footsteps in the oil business, the elder Andrews gave his son this advice: "Success in this industry depends on money and technology. You have to be conversant in both and an expert in at least one."

"I chose the money side," the younger Andrews recalls. The wisdom of that decision can be seen in the success of the company he founded, American Exploration. While many other independent oil companies floundered in the mid-1980s during the industry downturn, Andrews' financial know-how kept American from suffering the same fate.

After graduating from Harvard College and Harvard Business School in 1975, Andrews landed a job with Rotan Mosle, a Houston-based brokerage firm that is now a subsidiary of Paine Webber. Then he spent the next five years securing equity and debt financing for oil and gas, drilling and other energy-related companies.

"I developed a knowledge about financing small energy-related ventures," he remembers.

Armed with that experience, in 1980 Andrews started an oil company of his own. The mission of American Exploration Company was "to be a bridge between the oil center of the country in Houston and the capital center of the country in the East," he explains. "There were good opportunities here that were hungry for money — and a lot of money there looking for good opportunities."

Initially, Andrews didn't operate any projects himself. Instead, he raised capital for exploration ventures operated by industry players he knew through his father.

Within a few years, though, he had shifted his strategy. After convincing such big-name institutional investors as New York Life, Phoenix Mutual, Provident Mutual, Connecticut Mutual and American General to become his partners, he began purchasing producing properties in Texas and becoming more involved as operator and principal.

"We formed a partnership each year from 1983 to 1990," Andrews remarks. "We bought a package of properties from Union Texas Petroleum, Britoil's U.S. holdings,

Transco's onshore production, Tesoro's oil and gas properties, a package from Oryx, and the Sawyer field from Enron Oil and Gas. During that period we bought over $500 million worth of properties with approximately 10,000 producing wells."

When the oil industry took a nosedive, Andrews' relationships with these investor partners prevented American from fully feeling the blow. "Our capital was still flowing," he recalls. "That kept us going through the tough times. From 1980 to 1990, despite the troubles in the industry, American was a very upbeat, exciting place to work."

By the beginning of the next decade, American had 450 employees and was one of the fastest-growing players in the oil industry. Then the company shifted its strategy.

"Though we had some modest activity outside Texas, our focus had been on the Gulf Coast," Andrews says. But in 1990, the company acquired Hershey Oil, which was based in California and had reserves primarily in Canada. And in 1991, it bought Conquest Exploration which had properties all over the U.S.

"We bought them for our own account, without partners," Andrews recalls. "We also borrowed heavily to pay for these acquisitions—just as the price of natural gas was beginning to drop. For the first time, the company was struggling."

But Andrews regrouped, selling some properties, cutting costs and raising some additional equity. He also refocused the company.

"We returned to our original plan of concentrating on Texas and the surrounding region," Andrews says. "We concentrated on large-scale projects where we could develop a competitive advantage. Typically, these were in areas 3-D seismic had not yet been shot. We initiated 3-D surveys and moved aggressively to establish dominant acreage positions."

American chose to concentrate on three key operating areas. One was the Yoakum Gorge, a vast, shale-filled subterranean chasm in South Texas. The company acquired 67,000 acres in Lavaca County, South Texas, which made it the largest acreage holder in the area.

Using advanced three-dimensional seismic technology, which provides a more detailed picture of the earth's subsurface, it discovered what Andrews calls "a treasure trove of opportunities" there. American's initial deep Wilcox test was successful, and the company has more than 20 exploratory prospects to drill in the area over the next two years.

American also teamed up with another oil company to venture into East Texas' Cotton Valley Pinnacle Reef Trend, one of the hottest exploration plays in the country. "Advanced 3-D seismic is enabling companies to target small but highly prolific reefs at depths of 15,000 feet," Andrews says.

In addition, the company intensified and focused its activity in the Gulf of Mexico. "We had some offshore acreage, a patchwork of activity across the Gulf," Andrews explains.

"But we zeroed in on one area: the Gulf's transition zone, the shallow waters along the Texas coastline. Our goal is to have seamless 3-D seismic coverage along the coast from Mexico to Louisiana."

Very little three-D seismic had been shot in this region previously because of the cost involved. But the advent of ocean-bottom cabling, which allows for cost-effective, high-quality data gathering in transitional environments, enabled the company to obtain data and establish a dominant acreage position there.

"We became aggressive participants in state and federal lease sales," Andrews adds. "As a result, we have leased over 50,000 acres on 20 significant prospects in the Texas State Waters so far."

Finally, the company capitalized on its expertise in horizontal drilling to recover additional oil reserves from existing wells in the Smackover Trend in southwestern Arkansas.

In 1995, American sold its Sawyer field to Louis Dreyfus Natural Gas, a rapidly growing domestic energy company based in Oklahoma City. "That deal ran so smoothly that we asked Dreyfus to be our partner in the Yoakum Gorge project," Andrews says.

Then in June 1997, American and Dreyfus announced plans to merge; the merger became final in mid-October. Collectively, the two entities had proven reserves of more than a trillion cubic feet of gas and 33 million barrels of oil at year-end 1996, plus interests in 2.8 million undeveloped acres, making the combined company one of the top 15 independent oil and gas companies in the country. Andrews explains, "Bigger is better in our business, and Dreyfus' lower-risk development portfolio is a good balance with our exploration opportunities."

The combined company, called Louis Dreyfus Natural Gas, has considerable financial and operating strength, Andrews adds. "We're optimistic about the future, because we have the capital, the technology, the people, the acreage and the prospects to be successful. We have a winning hand, and we're looking forward to playing it over the next few years."

Above: Seismic data acquisition in South Texas.

Bottom, left: Drilling operations.

GLOBAL MARINE

GLOBAL MARINE: AN ENERGY INDUSTRY SUCCESS STORY

A half-century ago, history was made when a well drilled in 20-foot-deep waters off Louisiana marked the oil industry's first venture beyond the coastal swamps and transition zones and into the open sea. Since then, explorationists have extended their search for petroleum into deeper, more challenging offshore environments around the globe. As each chapter in the history of the offshore oil industry's development has unfolded, Global Marine has played a prominent role.

The company's own history began in 1946, a year before the landmark well was drilled. Anticipating expansion of the offshore oil industry, Continental Oil Company (Conoco) and Union Oil Company of California (Unocal) formed a consortium to collect seismic data and conduct geologic surveys off California's coast. Soon, Superior Oil and Shell joined the venture, which became known as the CUSS Group.

The consortium began building a drilling fleet and creating tools and techniques for exploring and developing offshore petroleum reserves. By 1958, it had become incorporated as Global Marine Exploration of California; Global Marine Drilling was its major operating subsidiary.

As offshore activity began to boom, Global Marine Exploration signed drilling contracts with such clients as Chevron, Shell, Texaco and Humble Oil (now Exxon). Other industries began using its floating drilling technology, too. The Navy, for example, tapped Global Marine Exploration to install underwater test facilities for the Polaris missile; the National Academy of Science sought its help in a feasibility study of ultra-deepwater drilling that would lead to the Mohole program, a plan to penetrate the earth's crust.

By the mid-1960s, Global Marine Exploration owned seven drilling vessels; five larger ships were added over the next three years. The com-

pany's customer list included all the major oil companies. To eliminate potential conflicts of interest, its original owners sold their interests in the company, which was reorganized in 1964 as Global Marine Inc.

An industry downturn beginning in 1966 prompted the company to diversify its operations. It began securing rights for gold and other minerals in such locations as the Canadian Arctic, Baja California and The Philippines. In addition, its Glomar Explorer — the first vessel designed to lift heavy weights from deep water — conducted feasibility studies for mining manganese from the deep-ocean floor. Global also built and operated a dynamically positioned ultra-deepwater scientific coring ship, the Glomar Challenger, for the U.S. National Science Foundation. As a result of these activities, the company became a major force in ocean energy and engineering and Arctic-related endeavors.

An improving energy market in the early 1970s led Global to resume its fleet expansion. But mid-decade, another market downturn dampened its financial picture. One bright spot, though, was two contracts to build a next-generation drillship, the Glomar Atlantic and the Glomar Pacific — contacts that helped sustain the company and fuel its next expansion phase.

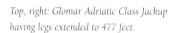

Top, right: Glomar Adriatic Class Jackup having legs extended to 477 feet.

Below: Glomar High Island VI Jackup crew tripping drill pipe.

Renewing its commitment to contract drilling, during the late 1970s Global Marine borrowed heavily to modernize and expand its fleet. It also established subsidiaries to support its other activities: Challenger Minerals for oil and gas development, Applied Drilling Technology Inc. (offshore turnkey drilling), Oceanographic Services Inc. (oceanic instrumentation) and Global Marine Development Inc. (marine engineering and construction).

"We knew that independent oil companies would be moving offshore, particularly in the Gulf of Mexico, as the majors moved overseas in search of larger projects," David A. Herasimchuk, vice president, market development, explains. "They would be looking for engineering services because most of them had lean drilling staffs."

In 1982, Global Marine relocated its headquarters to Houston. Expansion continued as explosive growth in the offshore drilling market boosted the company's revenues and earnings to unprecedented levels. By year-end 1982, it had a fleet of 28 rigs, $450 million in sales, $1.3 billion in assets and debts of $680 million.

But the mid-1980s brought one of the deepest downturns in energy industry history as oil prices plummeted from $32 to under $12 per barrel. After suffering financial losses in 1984 and 1985, in January 1986 Global Marine declared bankruptcy.

In 1989, it emerged from bankruptcy with its fleet intact, an experienced and capable board of directors and strong operating and control systems in place. Significant cuts in staff and overhead and a recapitalization in 1992 improved its financial position. This enabled the company to regain strength to compete competitively.

Today, Global Marine is a major international offshore drilling contractor that provides services on a day rate basis to oil and gas companies worldwide. Its fleet — the most modern and well-maintained in the industry — comprises 31 rigs: 23 cantilevered jackups, five semisubmersibles, two deepwater drillships and a concrete island drilling system. The company is converting a 5,000-foot semisubmersible and a 7,500-foot

drillship to enter service in 1997 and 1998.

In mid 1996, Global Marine received a five-year commitment from a major oil company to drill in water depths to 7,500 feet. To fulfill the commitment, it entered into a 30-year lease with the U.S. Navy to use the Glomar Explorer, the largest drillship currently in operation, which Global Marine had designed for the government. Once completed in 1998, the Glomar Explorer will be one of the most advanced deepwater drilling unit in existence.

In addition to contract drilling, Global Marine ranks as the world's leading provider of offshore turnkey drilling services, a business which it pioneered in 1979 with the formation of Applied Drilling Technology Inc., (ADTI). With approximately 55% of the market in the Gulf of Mexico, ADTI has drilled over 3,850,000 feet of hole under turnkey contracts.

As the oil industry continues to improve, Global Marine's future looks brighter than ever. With a modern and flexible fleet, quality crews, dedicated management and employees and a sound bottom line, it's well-positioned to tackle any challenges that lie ahead.

Above: Glomar High Island III Jackup on location offshore, Gabon, West Africa.

Below: Glomar Explorer being converted to dynamically positioned drill ship rated to 10,000 ft. water depth.

ICO

No company better embodies Houston's dynamic entrepreneurial spirit than ICO, Inc. One of the fastest growing publicly-held companies in Houston, ICO has won recognition world-wide for the quality of its services and its innovative approaches to supporting both the upstream and downstream segments of the energy sectors. A company that began in 1970 with a single facility, ICO has grown into a truly global enterprise providing state-of-the-art equipment and services throughout North America, Europe, the Far East, and Latin America.

From its early beginnings as a small West Texas oil service company, ICO has evolved into two main areas of business: ICO Oilfield Services and ICO Petrochemical Processing Services. The Oilfield Services Division provides specialized high technology state-of-the-art equipment and services designed to

help prevent costly down-hole tubular or rod failures in oil wells and to help reduce production and exploration costs. The Petrochemical Division provides a variety of equipment and services to the plastics industry and is recognized as a world leader in these services. ICO's revenues have grown rapidly over the past five years to more than seven times over 1992 revenues. Growth has been accomplished by the development of new products and services and by acquisitions of companies that were already leaders in niche markets.

ICO's growth has been driven by an ever-present spirit of innovation. The Company's first oilfield services plant was designed with the novel concept of reducing customers' costs of production by reclaiming used sucker rods. Over the years, ICO has further reduced its customers' operational expenses by preventing faulty tubular goods from being placed downhole (Exploration Services), by reconditioning used tubular goods and sucker rods (Production Services), and by preventing premature failure of tubular goods and sucker rods from occurring due to the corrosive downhole drilling environment (Corrosion Control Services). These innovations have positioned ICO as one of the two largest providers of inspection, reconditioning and coating services for tubular goods in the United States. The Oilfield Services Division has over thirty locations, including operations in Houston, Corpus Christi, Lone Star, Denver City, and Odessa,

Texas; as well as in Alabama, California, Colorado, Louisiana, Mississippi, New Mexico, North Dakota, Ohio, Oklahoma and Wyoming. International sales and services include Canada, Mexico, Italy, Latin America and the Far East.

ICO entered the petrochemical processing business in 1995 through acquisitions of leading companies in the U.S. and Europe. The first company acquired was WEDCO, the largest provider in North America and Europe of high technology equipment and services which are able to reduce plastic particles and minerals down to usable, consistent sizes for various applications for such products as the powdered resin used in molds, adhesives, or pigments and for food and pharmaceutical additives. WEDCO has locations in Texas, California, New Jersey, Tennessee, Indiana, Illinois, England, France, Holland and Sweden. ICO's Petrochemical Division also offers plastic compounding and distribution services in Europe through ICO Polymers; Rotec, a highly esteemed color compounder and distributor to the rotomolding industry, and Verplast, the leading provider of size reduction, compounding, and distribution services to the rotomolding industry in Italy. Bayshore Industrial in LaPorte, Texas, services the North American market in the man-

ufacturing of various additives and concentrates used by major plastic producers.

ICO anticipates rapid global growth in its petrochemical processing, as well as in its oilfield services segments. The company is well-funded to continue its external expansion through new markets and products, as well as acquisitions. Because of its proven leadership roles in both segments of the energy sector, upstream and down, ICO feels it still has outstanding opportunities for significant growth.

Above: Oil Field Services: high technology inspections.

Bottom, left: Oil Field Services: wellsite sucker rod delivery.

ARAMCO SERVICES COMPANY

About one-fourth of the world's oil reserves lie buried beneath the sands of Saudi Arabia. Since the country's national oil company, now known as Saudi Aramco, was founded six decades ago, it has become the world's largest producer of the hydrocarbons that fuel the economies of the globe.

Saudi Aramco's origins trace back to 1933, when Standard Oil Company of California, Chevron's predecessor, began exploring for oil in the Arabian desert. Texaco, Mobil and Exxon's predecessor, Standard Oil of New Jersey, later joined the venture, and the Arabian American Oil Company (Aramco) was born.

The government of Saudi Arabia negotiated a gradual buyout of the company, which culminated in the creation of the Saudi Arabian Oil Company (Saudi Aramco) in 1988. Today, Saudi Aramco is a fully integrated international oil company, with not only exploration and production capabilities but also refining, marketing and distribution facilities and even its own tanker fleet.

Saudi Aramco counts on Houston-based Aramco Services Company (ASC) to support its activities in this hemisphere. "We provide everything from technical services for engineering and design projects to purchasing, contracting and finance, and legal, public affairs and medical services," a company executive explains. "Those services vary greatly, depending on our parent company's needs.

"For example, we might arrange for a 300-ton structure to be towed across the Atlantic from Houston to Saudi Arabia. Or we might fill an urgent request for an unusual medicine needed to treat an employee. We also have an emergency response team ready to act in case the company should ever be involved in an oil spill in this hemisphere."

Through its own subsidiary, Aramco Training Services, ASC brings hundreds of Saudi students to North America to prepare for positions in Saudi Aramco ranging from physician to firefighter. ASC also arranges for Saudi Aramco employees to work on temporary training assignments at other U.S. companies. In addition, it recruits highly qualified North American professionals for Saudi Aramco, ranging from specialist engineers to health-care personnel for its hospitals and clinics, to teachers for its industrial training schools.

A second ASC subsidiary, Aramco Associated Company, owns and operates a U.S.-based DC-8 aircraft and leases approximately 40 aircraft to Saudi Aramco.

Another ASC subsidiary, Saudi Petroleum International Inc., provides marketing support to Saudi Aramco and arranges the scheduling, loading, storage, transportation and delivery of about a million barrels of crude oil sold daily by Saudi Aramco to North American refiners. Between fifteen and twenty percent of the oil imported into the United States comes from Saudi Arabia.

Another subsidiary, Saudi Refining, Inc., manages Saudi Aramco's share of Star Enterprise, a refining and marketing joint venture with a Texaco affiliate. Aramco Financial Services Company, a subsidiary of Saudi Refining, provides financial services to Saudi Aramco affiliates, primarily with respect to the tanker fleet.

Saudi Aramco's success has played a pivotal role in transforming Saudi Arabia into an industrial society and a major player in the world's economy. By supporting Saudi Aramco's activities in the United States and throughout the Western Hemisphere, Aramco Services Company makes a valuable and continuing contribution to its parent company's own success story.

Top, right: ASC administers engineering/design project teams at locations throughout the United States.

Below: Video-conferencing links ASC with its parent company in Saudi Arabia.

A joint venture formed by two oil industry giants in 1989 added a new star to the list of leading petroleum refiners and marketers in the United States. Houston-based Saudi Refining, Inc. (SRI), a subsidiary of Aramco Services Company (ASC), joined forces with an affiliate of Texaco Inc. to create Star Enterprise. Its goal: to refine, distribute and market petroleum products on America's East and Gulf Coasts.

ASC is itself a subsidiary of Saudi Aramco, the world's largest producer of crude oil. The move marked Saudi Aramco's first investment in international downstream oil processing. Saudi Refining, which was established to manage the new joint venture, acquired a 50 percent stake in the partnership.

"The formation of Star Enterprise assured the new U.S. joint venture access to oil at market prices over the next 20 years," a company executive recalls. "Coincidentally, it also strengthened Saudi Aramco's ties with Texaco, whose connections in Saudi Arabia reach back more than 50 years."

With assets of $2.5 billion, Star Enterprise quickly became a leading competitor in the American petroleum products marketplace. Today it ranks seventh among U.S. petroleum refiners. Its refineries, situated in Delaware City, Delaware; Convent, Louisiana; and Port Arthur, Texas, produce a daily total of approximately 600,000 barrels of gasoline, road diesel, aviation fuels, heating oils, residual fuel and lube-

base oils.

"In recent years, we've made major investments to upgrade our refining capabilities," a company engineer explains. "At Port Arthur, for example, we added a new coker to improve the quantity of gasoline being produced, and we installed a new wastewater treatment system. At Convent, we built a new oxygenate plant and diesel hydrotreater. We also built a new oxygenate plant at Delaware City and upgraded the control systems there. We'll continue to invest in these refineries as needed to make them more competitive."

Star Enterprise markets products under the Texaco brand in 26 states and the District of Columbia. It owns about 1,200 service stations and associated convenience stores and supplies petroleum products to about 7,500 others. As a result, it ranks as the sixth-largest retail gasoline marketer in this country and the second in its market territory.

As Saudi Aramco continues its expansion into the international petroleum refining and marketing arena, Saudi Refining will play a critical role in identifying and evaluating opportunities for further downstream integration in the Western Hemisphere. As of late 1997, SRI and Texaco were in negotiations to potentially merge their Star Enterprise assets with similar East and Gulf Coast downstream assets of Shell Oil Company.

SAUDI REFINING, INC.

Top, left: SRI's joint venture is assured a supply of Saudi Arabian crude.

Below: SRI manages Saudi Aramco's share of a refining and marketing joint venture.

PHILIP
SERVICES
CORP.

Philip Service Industrial Services Group offers complete fluid catalytic cracker unit turnarounds.

Although Philip Services Corp. is based in Canada, it has far reaching roots in the Houston area. In 1997, Philip acquired Allwaste and Serv-Tech, both Houston-based companies that were founded in 1978. Although serving many of the same clients, Allwaste and Serv-Tech rarely competed, as their service line offerings were different.

Allwaste was founded by a former Browning Ferris Industries (BFI) vice president, R. L. "Bubba" Nelson, Jr., whose family business, Nelson Industrial Services, was acquired by BFI in 1971. Bubba began with one air-moving truck in Sugar Land, Texas. Growing rapidly through acquisitions, Allwaste had expanded to 130 locations with revenues of $400 million.

Serv-Tech's roots run along a similar path, as its founder, Richard Krajicek co-founded a chemical cleaning company, Cesco, in 1961 and sold it to BFI in 1972. In 1978, Mr. Krajicek and several former Cesco employees set out on their own to form Serv-Tech. Prior to merging with Philip, Serv-Tech had grown to 20 locations with revenues of $175 million.

The operations of Allwaste, Serv-Tech, Philip's Environmental Services and Philip's By-Products Recovery were merged to form Philip's Industrial Services Group (ISG). Philip's ISG provides more than 70 service lines and processes to its industrial client base of more than 50,000. Houston is home to the ISG's main support group office, as well as several of its operating locations. Houston's strong industrial presence combined with its strategic geographic location made it the natural choice for Philip's ISG.

The ISG is one of two main divisions of Philip Services, the other is the Metals Recovery Group. While the ISG focuses on providing a broad range of industrial services and processes to its clients, the Metals Recovery Group offers a full complement of vertically integrated collection, processing and distribution systems.

Philip Services and all of its operations are not only committed to providing the best possible service to its clients, but also to providing a rewarding place for its employees to work and grow. This commitment flows out-side the boundaries of Philip's physical locations into the communities in which Philip operates. As such, Philip's ISG looks forward to making tomorrow's history today in Houston and will continue to be a visible supporter of this great city.

Philip Services Corp. is a fully integrated industrial services and resource recovery company with operations throughout the United States, Canada and the UK, providing steel, copper and aluminum processing and recovery services, together with diversified industrial outsourcing services to all major sectors. These services are delivered via Philip's ALLIES ® Approach, which works in tandem with its client base of more than 50,000 to continually identify value-adding processes and services within its industrial clients' facilities. Philip is publicly traded on the New York, Montreal and Toronto Stock Exchanges under the symbol "PHV."

THE POWER SOURCE:
WARREN ELECTRIC COMPANY

Keeping the wheels of industry turning around the world is a 24-hour-a-day commitment. That's why so many domestic and international businesses rely on the Warren Electric Group. Founded over 78 years ago, Warren today operates from more than 30 locations and specializes in the heavy process, pulp and paper and chemical industries. The company also serves the utility and telecommunications markets, with special emphasis on the energy and communications industry.

According to Chairman of the Board and CEO, Cheryl L. Thompson, "Experienced people, quality products and a total commitment to customer satisfaction has made Warren one of the nation's leading independent electrical distributors." Add to those attributes the company's $25 million inventory, which includes products from more than 250 manufacturers, and it's easy to understand why Warren is acknowledged as the largest electrical distributor in the Gulf Coast and Caribbean Rim. The company even has the distinction of being the largest woman-owned electrical distributor in the United States. Of course, Warren's presence isn't limited to the U.S. The company has also become one of the premier exporters of electrical supplies with global operations in industrial markets that include Mexico, South America, the Middle East, the Far East, and Russia.

"Because many of our customers need sophisticated inventory management solutions," notes Ms. Thompson, "Warren offers customized vendor stocking programs (VSPs) and a number of automation tools, such as bar coding. As pioneers of integrated supply management, Warren also continues to assist customers in developing innovative methods to reduce or eliminate their inventories. But most importantly, each branch stocks a full inventory of products and is linked to the company's Total Inventory Management system to ensure Warren will have the equipment our customers need, when they need it."

As for Warren's commitment to quality, the company has spent years building a quality culture that guides every aspect of its business. ISO 9002 certified, Warren continually tracks and measures company performance as it relates to customer service, vendors and internal activities.

Finally, Warren offers national account capabilities through its association with more than 100 top independent distributors nationwide. Through this network, the company provides uniform pricing, consolidated reports and expertise matched to any customer's operations.

"From our counter sales, to our fleet of delivery vehicles, to our full range of integrated supply capabilities, Warren will adapt its strengths to fit our customers' needs," says Ms. Thompson. "Of course, at the bottom line, our ability to best serve our customers all comes down to people. And Warren people are simply the best there are."

WARREN ELECTRIC COMPANY

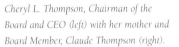

Cheryl L. Thompson, Chairman of the Board and CEO (left) with her mother and Board Member, Claude Thompson (right).

TIDELAND SIGNAL

Top, right: Houston headquarters.

Below: Solar-powered navigation buoy.

Bottom: Major lighthouse rotating beacon.

LIGHTING THE WAY

Loneliness characterized the lives of the lighthouse keepers of centuries past who climbed their towers each evening to light the beacons and again each morning to extinguish them. Danger threatened their existence, too, when storms churned the surrounding surf. Without these lights, though, the vessels that sailed in coastal waters at night or in bad weather risked running ashore or colliding with sunken rocks.

Today, high-tech lanterns and radar beacons have replaced those hand-lit beacons in lighthouses, on buoys that mark harbors and channels and, with the addition of fog signals, on the oil rigs that dot the world's coastal waters. Thanks to Tideland Signal Corp., these mariners' aids are more reliable and effective than ever.

Founded in 1954, Tideland provides light and sound signals for the maritime industry. It became a market leader in 1965 by offering navigational aids that incorporated automatic lamp changers and ran on transistorized flashers with electric batteries, which were more reliable than other offshore power sources. Two years later, it introduced a 300mm injection-molded acrylic-lens lantern that was more powerful and had a longer-range beam of light than competitors' products.

The lantern's popularity among offshore oil rig operators enabled Tideland to expand its international operations. Then in the 1970s, it established the first photovoltaic cell manufacturing operation in the southern hemisphere in Australia. These cells, which last 10 to 20 years, provide an inexhaustible, independent power source to continually recharge storage batteries. Continuing its string of successes, in 1985 Tideland introduced its SeaBeacon line of frequency-agile radar beacons, which can provide range and bearing to the worldwide mariner to safe waters in all weather conditions, signal a structure's position and identify it by using codes that are printed on seamen's charts.

By mid-decade, rig operators comprised the bulk of Tideland's business, so the oil industry's downturn took a tremendous toll. "To survive, we cut staff and closed offices," Tideland's chairman, Samuel N. Sprunt, recalls, "but we continued our product development and market expansion. As a result, we remained a leader in our industry."

The crisis, however, prompted Tideland to shift its focus from the oil industry to lighthouse, port and harbor authorities. "Before the downturn, the oil industry comprised 80% of our sales and ports and harbors 20%," Sprunt says. "Now it's the other way around."

Today, Tideland Signal Corp. has regained its strength and has 95 employees at its 60,000-square-foot facility in Houston, and around the world. We've been successful because of our continuing dedication to new product development and product improvement. "We're devoted to quality," Sprunt says of his company, which received its ISO-9001 certification in 1993.

Tideland's products can be found in locations ranging from the coast of Spain to the riverine waterways of Bangladesh. "Recently, our rotating beam lighthouse beacon was selected to mark the westernmost navigation point of the Hebrides, which is a critical tanker passageway," Sprunt reports.

Tideland's buoys, made of a plastic polyethylene that doesn't break down in sunlight, are the fastest-selling ones in the world for protected waterways. Now it's developing a bigger buoy with a more powerful light that can be used in the open sea.

Looking ahead, Sprunt sees even more opportunities for expansion and growth. As long as ships travel the waterways of the world, Tideland's future will be bright.

Decisions made in the early days of the petroleum industry were often based on nothing more than a gut feeling and a good sense of smell. Field scouts attempted to gather drilling and production information on wells with a pair of binoculars and barroom conversation. The energy sector of today, however, relies on the timely, high-tech information services of Petroleum Information/Dwights, LLC (PI/D). Petroleum Information/Dwights, LLC was formed as the result of a merger of two long-time oil and gas information service companies, Petroleum Information Corporation and Dwights Energydata, Inc.

In the early days of the century, the increasing number of wells being drilled provided a demand for better information on oil and gas activity. In 1928, Petroleum Information was founded in Denver, Colorado, to provide drilling reports for the Rocky Mountain region. Petroleum Information developed a national presence by acquiring other regional information service companies and by adding product lines needed by their clients. The expanded product lines included not only drilling and production data, but well log reproduction and distribution services, mapping services and automated computer services for clients.

PI formed a division to provide additional services to the natural gas industry. This division developed a mappable file of natural gas pipelines in the U.S. The file also contains important pipeline characteristics, including capacity, ownership and standard tariffs. Additionally, a database of major industrial users of natural gas was built.

The other part of the newly merged company, Dwights Energydata, Inc., was also formed in 1934 as a regional oil and gas service company. Interestingly enough, Dwights later formed a drilling information service company called the Panhandle Oil Explorer, which was eventually acquired by Petroleum Information in the 1960s.

Dwights initially focused on providing oil and gas production volumes in the Texas Panhandle, later expanding to include Oklahoma, Kansas, Arkansas, the remainder of Texas and the Gulf Coast region. Re-entering the drilling activity market in 1984 with the purchase of Hotline Energy Reports of Casper, Wyoming, Dwights was able to complement its production database with historical and current drilling information. At the same time, Dwights purchased a national database of field/reservoir characteristics which had been developed by the University of Oklahoma in cooperation with the US Geological Survey.

In 1989, Dwights was acquired by SoftSearch Holdings, Inc., whose subsidiary, Energy Enterprises, was a primary on-line distributor of Dwights production data services.

The January 1997 merger of Petroleum Information and Dwights Energydata created an information services company which provides comprehensive reporting of oil and gas data, software systems for data management and retrieval, sophisticated mapping applications and services and a suite of engineering and geological analysis software for the industry. The combined databases of Petroleum Information/Dwights contain more than 2.9 million drilling records of wells around the world and 1.3 million production entity records. Specialized data sources include 1.1 million square miles of photogeologic-geomorphic mapping, leasehold chain-of-title information on 300,000 federal leases, another 100,000 state and fee land records and detailed regional geological databases.

The new PI/Dwights continues to be in the forefront of technology for information services. With offices throughout the U.S. as well as in Calgary and London, the creative use of expanding information resources has truly made PI/D an international company. PI/D's data management system, P2000, is based on relational database technology being used by companies around the world. New Internet applications will offer opportunities for unparalleled timeliness of data delivery. Petroleum Information/Dwights utilizes state-of-the-art technology to provide dependable, usable databases and software services as a partner to the energy industry.

PETROLEUM INFORMATION/ DWIGHTS, L.L.C.

ROSE METAL RECYCLING, INC.

The chief executive officer of Rose Metal Recycling, Inc. describes his company as the "beneficiary of a blended heritage of business experience."

"We depend daily on the wisdom and advice of the older men, who have been in the business for decades," says Eliot Rose, whose grandfather, Edward, began the family business in 1939. "The younger generation – my cousin David Rose and myself — contribute our enthusiasm for change and familiarity with modern management philosophies."

In Edward's time, the old Houston Junk Company occupied a "very small piece of property" at Bell Street and Dowling Avenue and specialized in collecting metal, rags and bones from nearby homes and businesses. The modern Rose Metal Recycling plant occupies some six acres, employs 75people, and processes more than 200,000,000 pounds of scrap metal annually.

"Houston had not completely entered the automobile age in my granddad's day," Rose says. "Some suppliers still drove mule carts."

One supplier stopped for lunch one day, leaving his mule tied loosely outside. "The mule broke loose and, knowing the route, headed for our place," Rose says. "By the time the man realized his mule was gone and finally caught up, Granddad had completed the weigh-ins and unloaded the cart. All the man had to do was collect his money and his mule and go home."

Heavy equipment makes easy work of a mountain of scrap at Rose Metal Recycling.

Edward's son, Irving, was a mechanical innovator. Among his inventions was a metal shredder powered by a diesel engine from a World War II submarine. That prototype has been replaced by a $5 million state-of-the-art model (one of only a dozen in the country) capable of shredding an automobile and separating it into its component metal parts in less than a minute. Irving also founded Rose Steel Center, which operates as an adjunct to the recycling yard, selling new prime steel, factory rejects and other slightly blemished or used iron and steel products at reduced prices.

Jules Rose, Irving's brother, joined the business when he was only eight years old, operating a winch trunk and other equipment. As he matured, he developed into the family's financial specialist, implementing the company's first formal cost control and marketing programs.

The younger Roses form a tight-knit management team guided by a clear vision of the future.

"The first thing David, who is chief financial officer, and I did was compose a mission statement, one that recognizes people as our most precious commodity and commits us to creating a safe, family environment for our customers and employees," Rose says. "In keeping with that philosophy, we have introduced an employee profit-sharing plan."

Augmenting that plan is a new incentive plan for the small army of "across the scale" providers — one-truck, one-man operations — responsible for 60 percent of the yard's supply. "We still cater to our corporate clients, however, sending salesmen out to help them make metal recycling as easy and convenient as possible," Rose explains.

The pair has also "re-engineered" the company's six-acre campus, adding automated scales and developing traffic and holding patterns that have boosted the yard's capacity from 60 trucks a day to close to 300.

"What we do is a tremendous benefit to the environment and the country's natural resources," Eliot says. "Additionally, we make every effort to approach recycling in an environmentally reposnsible way"

Rose Metal Recycling is a Houston family business success story of how recycling can work to everyone's benefit.

Browning-Ferris Industries, Inc.

Top, right: BFI takes pride in the design and operation of its environmentally sensitive landfill sites, making them community assets.

Below: BFI's blue trucks are a familiar sight in Houston nieghborhoods.

Bottom: Browning-Ferris Industries is the leading recycling services company in the world.

From dare to dream... it all started in 1967. Residents of Willowbrook gathered to resolve their trash collection problems — missed pickups, surly personnel, high prices.

By the end of the meeting, Tom Fatjo, president of the subdivision, had accepted his neighbors' dare to "get a pickup truck and take care of this community's garbage." It was a decision that was to revolutionize the refuse collection and processing industry worldwide.

Within weeks Fatjo and his cousin, Thomas Deane, had begun to make good on that commitment, forming American Refuse Systems (ARS). Their new company pledged to provide cost-efficient, courteous and timely service neighborhoods want and need.

Only two years later, the fledgling firm was able to acquire controlling interest in Browning-Ferris Machinery Company, an established distributor of heavy construction equipment. The merger that accompanied that stock purchase created Browning-Ferris Industries (BFI) — today the second largest waste service company in the world.

The founders' can-do attitude is stronger than ever today, infusing BFI with a vital, entrepreneurial spirit unusual in a multi-billion dollar, multi-national firm.

"From the beginning, BFI focused on applying the latest technology to address the increasingly complex requirements of solid waste management," says Bruce E. Ranck, who joined the firm in 1970 and was elected CEO in 1995. "In 1975, when BFI was still a mid-sized firm, operating in only 100 American cities, we introduced forklift front-end loading collection vehicles. Those labor-saving, cost-efficient vehicles have since become an industry standard."

BFI's history throughout the 1970s and 1980s was a continuing chronicle of growth and innovation. The company expanded throughout North and South America, Europe and the Far East, introducing ecologically sensitive, cost-effective procedures.

In 1984, this emphasis on progress motivated BFI to create a new company, American Ref-Fuel, dedicated to the marketing of waste-to-energy (WTE) conversion

facilities. By 1989, Ref-Fuel had proven its staying power, opening its first conversion plant. Today, with its partners, Duke Energy Systems and United American Energy, Ref-Fuel operates seven WTE plants.

In 1986, as AIDS awareness was sweeping the health care industry, BFI purchased two companies which specialized in the disposal of medical wastes. BFI is now the premier medical waste services company in North America.

As the environment became a preeminent public concern, BFI began its investment in recycling, purchasing a fiber recycling company and offering residential and commercial recycling programs. By 1992, the company was serving more than 3,000,000 households, with curbside collection of paper, aluminum, bi-metal and plastic recyclable materials. Today, BFI is the leading recycling services company, its recycling trucks a familiar sight in many business and residential neighborhoods.

The company celebrated its 30th anniversary in 1997 with the adoption of the BFI Way for defining value which empowers every employee to participate in maximizing customer satisfaction and shareholder value.

"BFI stands today competitively poised to meet the future," says CEO Ranck. "We have the resources. We have the technology and the ideas. But most important, we have the commitment and motivation to make a difference in the quality of life."

MEREX
CORPORATION

Hans Roeschel, President

The Houston headquarters of Merex Corporation bubbles with conversations in a variety of languages as employees work to supply engineers and contractors around the world with the specialized equipment and materials they need to bring their projects in on-time and under budget.

"In the past few years, we've participated in six substantial projects, supplying all equipment and materials to build huge power generation plants and refineries in remote locations around the globe," says Hans Roeschel, president. "Each plant was completed ahead of time, in great part due to our timely delivery of materials, always meeting customer specifications. That's some track record, one of which we are justifiably proud."

That record, the Austrian-born Roeschel explains, is no accident. It represents, instead, the maturation of a management plan he envisioned when he formed the company in 1978 and which he works daily with his brother Robert, the company's executive vice president, to realize.

"From the beginning, I saw Houston as a city that nurtured entrepreneurial talent, that encouraged hard work and investment," Roeschel says. "I was inspired to invest heavily in my business, building an infrastructure that allows us to be totally responsive to customer needs and able to guarantee our work."

That infrastructure begins with a network of carefully-tended relationships with hundreds of manufacturers. These relationships, Roeschel says, make it possible for Merex to serve its customers in true professional fashion. "We work closely with vendors, actually assisting them in developing new products to meet customer needs," he says. "Recently our engineers helped a valve manufacturer design and fabricate an unusual double block and bleed plug valve for a demanding project in Mexico. The result was a purchase order for more than $1 million."

Merex's infrastructure allows for quick response to emergencies. "We inventory a wide variety of basic materials. We have the capacity to lift up to 33,000 pounds in our warehouse, so we can properly handle, export crate, and ship from our facility with ease," Roeschel explains. "What we don't have immediately available, we can usually find fast through our computerized world-wide access and order system. The goal is to make delivery on all emergency orders within 24 hours."

An even more critical component of the company's infrastructure, however, is its professional staff.

"Our sales staff consists almost entirely of engineering professionals, people with years of technical and procurement experience," he says. "They understand what our customers' businesses need, often saving them time, money — or both."

The advantages of that expertise are evident daily, Roeschel says, offering one "very small" example to illustrate. "Recently, we received an urgent request for a large amount of electrical cable for a time-critical operation in Venezuela," he recalls. "The customer insisted he needed a very specific type of cable. Because our engineers understood his operation, they were able to advise him of technically appropriate alternatives — ones that would allow for immediate delivery at a slightly lower cost."

Within five days, the Venezuelan operation was back on-line and another customer had learned to appreciate the Merex Corporation slogan: "We bring a world of experience to work for you."

In recent years, the Gulf of Mexico has become the world's busiest offshore basin for energy industry activity as oil and gas companies have intensified their efforts to find the vast petroleum deposits that lie buried there. For Walter Oil & Gas Corporation, operating in the Gulf isn't new. In 1984, when plummeting oil prices forced others to abandon the waters off America's Gulf Coast, this company was moving aggressively into the area. Today, it's one of the Gulf's most prolific natural gas producers and ranks consistently among the top 20 companies in wells drilled there each year.

The company was founded in 1981 when Houston Oil and Minerals Corp. merged with Tenneco, and its founder, J. C. Walter, Jr., started a new enterprise. His timing couldn't have been worse. A few years later, oil prices dropped to unprecedented lows. Many energy companies were forced to reduce their operations and overhead.

Being well capitalized, Walter Oil & Gas was able to begin acquiring leases that major oil companies were farming out to cut their operating costs. Although its focus was initially onshore Texas and Louisiana, it soon became one of the first independents to begin operating in the Gulf. As a result, it developed working relationships with major oil companies operating there, seizing the opportunity before its competitors had the chance.

That strategy set the pattern for the company's future as an industry pioneer. It formed gas and oil trading companies in 1985 and 1991. Then as competition in the Gulf began to build, it became one of the first independents to explore overseas.

"We sought opportunities that were too small for the majors to pursue profitably," J. C. "Rusty" Walter III, the company's president, chairman and son of its founder, recalls. "The same strategy that had worked so well for us in the Gulf worked well for us internationally, too."

Today, Walter Oil & Gas and its affiliates have about 60 employees. It owns, wholly or in part, and operates over 100 producing wells that yield about 300 million cubic feet of gas and 17,000 barrels of oil daily.

Recently, the company established another precedent when it formed Walter Power, LLC, becoming one of the first U.S. companies to build small electrical power generation plants in Europe. "There's a niche market there that's too small for the industry's big players but too big for local providers," Walter says, "and the European political climate is excellent for this kind of venture."

Walter credits the company's success, in part, to its team of geologists, geophysicists and engineers. "They are highly qualified," he says, "and they've worked long enough to understand each other's strengths and weaknesses. There's good chemistry among them."

The use of such advanced technology as 3D seismic also has contributed to the company's performance. In addition, Walter Oil & Gas assisted in the development and use of subsea production systems, which represented a major advancement in offshore technology.

But it's the ability to move fast and first that has made the biggest difference, Walter believes. "We're privately owned, so we make decisions based purely on economics rather than on public market evaluations," he concludes. "That enables us to respond quickly when opportunities arise.

"The key is to stay ahead of the herd. If you lag behind, you lose your chance."

QUALITY OF LIFE

*healthcare companies, educational institutions,
and historical and civic organizations
contribute to Houstonians' quality of life.*

184   The Methodist Hospital, Houston

*187   Greater Houston
Preservation Alliance*

188   Rice University

*190   Greater Houston
Convention & Visitors Bureau*

192   University of Houston

Texas Dental College, 1911.

COURTESY HOUSTON METROPOLITAN RESEARCH CENTER,
HOUSTON PUBLIC LIBRARY

THE
METHODIST
HOSPITAL,
HOUSTON

The tradition of excellence in medical care which began at The Methodist Hospital in Houston almost 80 years ago has established Methodist as a leading health care institution in the Bayou City and around the globe.

The hospital's roots go back to 1908 when Dr. Oscar L. Norsworthy, a prominent physician, built a 30-bed health center in downtown Houston to accommodate his growing practice. Eleven years later, he and his wife sold the facility to the Methodist Episcopal Church for less than half its appraised value—on condition that the church would agree to erect a new hospital building.

The new Methodist Hospital opened in April 1924. During its first year of operation, it admitted 1,620 patients who paid $3 a day for a bed on a ward or $6 daily for a private room with a bath and closet. Within three years, its patient census had almost doubled. By 1929, the hospital was filled to capacity and forced to turn patients away.

Then the bottom fell out of the stock market, ushering in the Great Depression. Since few people could afford to pay for health care, the hospital found itself in desperate financial straits. Still, it continued operations and

Top, right: Advances in surgical procedures originated at Methodist in the 1950's and 1960's are still widely used today.

Below: The Methodist Hospital's original location in downtown Houston, circa 1925.

opened a school of nursing in September 1934 to meet the growing demand for graduate nurses.

The facility's financial picture began to brighten, and by 1943 Methodist was debt-free for the first time in its history. In late 1944, the M. D. Anderson Foundation, which managed the $20 million estate of cotton magnate Monroe D. Anderson, offered land to the institution in the newly created, 134-acre Texas Medical Center on what was then the outskirts of town. A $1 million gift from Houston oilman Hugh Roy Cullen and his wife Lillie, followed by a $500,000 challenge grant from M. D. Anderson Foundation trustees, financed construction of a hospital on the site.

The Methodist Hospital's reputation took a major leap forward in 1948 with the arrival of Dr. Michael E. DeBakey, a noted heart surgeon who became chairman of Baylor College of Medicine's Department of Surgery and began practicing at Methodist.

In June 1950, Methodist and Baylor agreed to affiliate. After Methodist moved into a new 300-bed facility in the Texas Medical Center in November 1951, it quickly filled to capacity as patients arrived from around the world to benefit from its cardiovascular capabilities and other technological advances.

By 1954, the hospital had a regular staff of almost 300 physicians. Its annual patient census had grown to almost 16,000, and once again it was forced to turn patients away for lack of space. Although a new wing was added in 1963, the hospital was again operating at capacity within a year.

As The Methodist Hospital's reputation for excellence continued to grow, even more space was required to meet the expanding service demand. The Herman Brown and Ella F. Fondren buildings, totaling 273,000 square feet, were opened in December 1968 to house the Fondren and Brown Cardiovascular and Orthopedic Research Center.

By the beginning of the 1970s, The Methodist Hospital had 1,040 patient beds. The decade saw substantial growth in such areas as teaching, research and outpatient services. As part of a $100 million expansion that began in 1972, the hospital built a Neurosensory Center to house the institutes of Ophthalmology, Neurology and Otolaryngology, and expanding special services offered by the hospital. A $2 million contribution from the Alice and David C. Bintliff Foundation financed construction of the Bintliff Blue Bird Building within the Neurosensory Center to accommodate the hospital's growing pediatric neurology clinic. In 1980, the Total Health Care Center, which includes Scurlock Tower, its garage and the Marriott Hotel, was opened, offering facilities to meet the needs of patients and their families outside the hospital. The 1978 construction of Alkek Tower, a four-floor addition to the Brown Building, was made possible by a $3 million donation from Mr. and Mrs. Albert B. Alkek of Victoria, providing space to house research facilities and services for cardiovascular inpatients. A $7.4 million grant from the Fondren Foundation in 1976 financed the six-floor expansion of the Fondren Building to add patient beds and more research and medical service facilities.

By the next decade, rising medical costs, increased competition, falling patient census figures and growing government involvement in the health care field encouraged hospitals to share facilities and expertise. In October 1980, The Methodist Hospital board authorized formation of a community hospital network. By 1984, 15 hospitals with a total of 3,840 beds had joined the network. Methodist eventually purchased San Jacinto Memorial Hospital in Baytown, one of the original 15 in the network.

Continuing its expansion, Methodist launched a $196.9 million construction project in November 1984, boosting the bed total in its Texas Medical Center facility to 1,527. The three-phase endeavor included a 10-story hospital facility, the 25-story Smith Tower professional building, a 1,400-car parking garage, and renovation of the original buildings and concourses to link the buildings in the Methodist complex. In addition, a matching grant from the Cullen Trust for Health Care and a gift from the Hamill Foundation funded construction of a Multi-Organ Transplant Center. Concurrent with this physical growth, researchers at Methodist and Baylor continued to make major medical advances. Achievements including the development of ultrasonography for imaging prostate tumors, research into the chemical treatment of Alzheimer's disease, and experimentation with Tissue Plasminogen Activator, a drug for treating heart attacks, enhanced the institutions' reputations as research leaders.

Today The Methodist Hospital has more than 4,000 employees and 893 physicians on its active medical staff. It ranks among the most distinguished medical institutions in the world, with a reputation for excellence in such vital areas as cardiac care, cancer, neurosurgery and orthopedic care.

As patient care continues to evolve along social and economic fronts, Methodist has

Above: In the 1950s and 1960s, Methodist anchored the expansion of institutions within the Texas Medical Center.

Below: Many of Methodist's 893 active staff physicians are internationally recognized in their respective specialties.

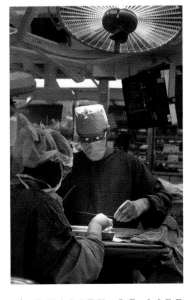

Above: Renowned for his breakthroughs in cardiovascular surgery at Methodist in the 1950s, Dr. Michael DeBakey remains a medical ambassador to the world.

Below: The Methodist Hospital complex today.

kept pace by contracting with a number of managed care providers. Through these contracts, the hospital serves more than 1.6 million people in the greater Houston area.

With this increased demand, Methodist continues to grow and expand beyond the hospital's walls and the confines of the Texas Medical Center. The hospital is the hub of a system that includes Diagnostic Center Hospital adjacent to the Medical Center, and San Jacinto Methodist Hospital in Baytown. Through an affiliation with the Visiting Nurse Association of Houston Inc., Methodist administers care to patients at home and in transitional care facilities.

These expanded services are offered under the umbrella of the Methodist Health Care System, a wide-ranging enterprise designed to make Methodist's high-quality services more accessible to people in communities outside Houston's urban core. Near-term plans for this expansion include the opening in early 1998 of the first Methodist Health Center in Sugar Land. Other community health centers are in development in the Memorial area of Houston and in The Woodlands and Clear Lake areas. These centers will allow many more people access to Methodist quality without the drive to the Texas Medical Center.

The System has also formed its own health maintenance organization (HMO) available throughout Southeast Texas through a select group of insurance carriers and managed care organizations. Two physician groups, Methodist Medical Group and Baylor-Methodist Primary Care Associates, pool the services of a network of primary care physicians located throughout the Houston area and surrounding communities.

In addition to developing signature services, Methodist has committed more than $96 million to community benefit programs, including $18.9 million for the care of financially and medically indigent people throughout the Houston area. Working with local agencies such as the Good Neighbor Healthcare Center, the American Red Cross and Interfaith Ministries, this money is used to create and manage direct patient care programs for expectant mothers, the homeless, senior citizens, AIDS patients, children with serious diseases and many others.

As it approaches the 21st century, Methodist continues to grow and expand its patient access with a truly global vision. As always, the heart and central focus of this vision is the patient. Methodist is dedicated to serving people and providing for their medical, health and wellness needs, not merely within the hospital itself, but in the community beyond.

Throughout its history, the Methodist Health Care System and The Methodist Hospital have remained true to their mission to provide high-quality, cost-effective health care that delivers the best value to the people it serves in a spiritual environment of caring. The tradition of excellence that has characterized the organization for almost 80 years will continue as it strives to achieve its vision—to be Houston's leading health system.

The history of Houston is a rich and varied tale – told not only by the stories of the men and women who made our city what it is today, but by the places they created and the buildings, neighborhoods, and communities they left behind. For nearly twenty years, the Greater Houston Preservation Alliance, or GHPA, has worked to preserve the best of our architectural and cultural heritage.

Committed action by GHPA has been instrumental in saving some of our most precious historic resources. For example, when the historic Pillot Building was threatened with demolition in the late 1970s, GHPA began an effort to save it. The building, built in the 1850s, was one of the oldest surviving structures in downtown Houston. It was owned by the county, but it had been abandoned for many years and was in serious disrepair. Through a campaign of determined advocacy, GHPA finally persuaded the county to issue a ground lease that would a private developer to save the building, which was finally renovated in the late 1980s through a combination of restoration and reconstruction. It opened in 1990 and now houses several law offices and a restaurant.

GHPA has also been active in urban and neighborhood revitalization. In 1986, GHPA completed an historic resource survey for the Old Sixth Ward neighborhood, located just northwest of downtown. Using the survey as a base, GHPA conducted a series of bi-weekly meetings with the neighborhood that ultimately led to a neighborhood cleanup, the rehabilitation of 18 low-income historic houses, the creation of a neighborhood park, and the formation of a neighborhood association. In 1990, we took title to two small shotgun houses in the neighborhood. Using a combination of donated labor and public and private funds, the houses were rehabilitated and sold in 1995 as affordable housing under the City of Houston HOMES program.

In the late 1980s, GHPA took the lead in developing the first Urban Main Street program, a project of the National Trust for Historic Preservation initiated in Texas by the Texas Historical Commission. The program is designed to facilitate downtown revitalization in large cities through preservation and was already operating successfully in smaller towns throughout the state. GHPA, in partnership with the Downtown Houston Association, developed the program for Houston and raised the money through a combination of private funding and a grant from the City of Houston, thus spawning what is now the Downtown Historic District, Inc.

In 1995 GHPA, in partnership with representatives of Houston's historic neighborhoods, successfully led the effort to secure passage of the Historic Preservation Ordinance at City Council. Our efforts in neighborhood revitalization continue today through our Historic Neighborhoods Council, which brings neighborhood representatives to bring about positive change that will help all of us to maintain the quality and character of Houston's neighborhoods.

Since it was formed in 1978, GHPA has provided training to individuals, neighborhoods and communities through providing workshops and educational forums. Our on-going educational programs include monthly walking tours of historic neighborhoods, a newsletter, and the Preservation Breakfasts, a quarterly series which focuses on the economic impact of preservation as a tool for inner city revitalization. Our heritage education program provides information for teachers to help them use the historic places in our community as a teaching resource. Each year we recognize the best in preservation through our annual Good Brick Awards program.

Houston is an intricate fabric of homes, businesses, diverse cultures, public places, and monuments. As a built artifact, our city is not only a repository of our common heritage and memory, but it is also the stage for our daily life. It is important that we preserve our collective past, not only as a reminder of where we have been, but as a foundation to spring forward into our collective future. The preservation of our built environment does not simply mean saving old buildings and spaces, but is also concerned with preserving the quality of life and the sustainability of our neighborhoods as living communities.

GHPA remains dedicated to the appreciation and preservation of Houston's cultural and architectural historic resources through education, advocacy, and committed action and thereby to the creation of economic value and a greater sense of community.

GREATER HOUSTON PRESERVATION ALLIANCE

Above, left: Texas Avenue looking west - the rear of Union Station is shown on the right and Annuciation Church is on the left. (c. 1920) Houston, Texas

POSTCARD COURTESY OF RANDY PACE

Below: Entryway to Historic Gulf Building (1929), now home to Texas Commerce Bank and the Greater Houston Preservation Alliance.

PHOTO COURTESY OF GERALD MOORHEAD, FAIA

Bottom: Private home in Houston's Old Sixth Ward Neighborhood Historic District (built ca. 1862; restored 1996).

PHOTO COURTESY OF GERALD MOORHEAD, FAIA.

RICE UNIVERSITY

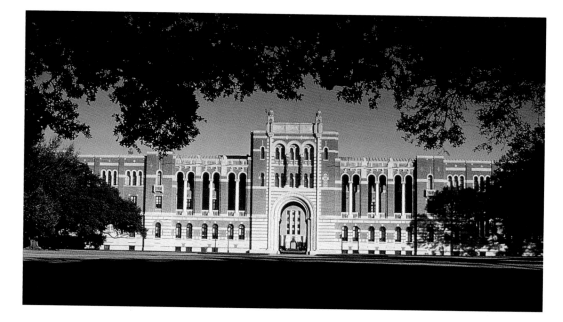

Top, right: Lovett Hall.

Below: Student Life.

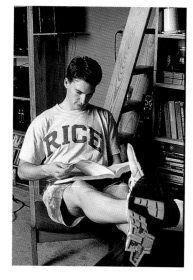

The history of Rice University, the premier private research university of the Southwest, is a story of foresight, resourcefulness, and dedication to the highest academic ideals. Yet it is a history that nearly failed to come into existence because of an elaborate scam to defraud its benefactor's estate. The William M. Rice Institute for the Advancement of Literature, Science, and Art was chartered in 1891 by merchant William Marsh Rice. Mr. Rice, a native of Massachusetts, came to Houston in 1839, made a fortune, then retired to New York City. Childless, appreciative of the opportunities Houston had provided him, and contemplating what he might do for posterity, Mr. Rice decided to establish an academic institute.

He secured the incorporation with a note of indenture, gathered a group of trustees, and specified that after his death they should proceed with establishing the school. But an unscrupulous lawyer, Albert Patrick, devised a scheme to write a fake will giving himself most of Mr. Rice's fortune and have an accomplice murder Mr. Rice in September 1900. An alert bank officer noticed a discrepancy in a check and telegraphed Captain James A. Baker, Mr. Rice's Houston lawyer and chair of the trustees. Baker rushed to New York, spearheaded an investigation that resulted in Patrick being convicted, and saved Mr. Rice's fortune for The Rice Institute.

The endowment became available in 1904, but the trustees moved deliberately in plan-

ning the new university. In January 1908, at the urging of Woodrow Wilson, Edgar Odell Lovett, a mathematician and astronomer at Princeton University, was appointed president. Lovett was an inspired choice. He soon set forth on a trip around the world visiting universities, interviewing scholars, and publicizing The Rice Institute. A noted architect was hired to design the campus, an international academic convocation was organized to celebrate the opening, and classes began on September 23, 1912, with seventy-seven students and ten faculty hired from famed centers of learning. Lovett envisioned Rice as a world-class university, with outstanding undergraduates, distinguished graduate work (the first Ph.D. was granted in 1918), and research and scholarship of the highest order.

If President Lovett could visit Rice today, he would be gratified at the ways in which the university has developed while, at the same time, adhering to its founding vision. After a period of austerity in the 1920s and 1930s, Rice expanded its facilities and programs in the late 1940s and again in the late 1950s. William V. Houston, president following Lovett's retirement in 1945, oversaw these developments. Kenneth S. Pitzer became president in 1961, and he increased the size and quality of graduate programs and enhanced the humanities and social sciences.

Norman Hackerman took the reins in 1970, consolidated the gains of the previous decade, slowly expanded the enrollment, and established the schools of administration and music. George E. Rupp, the first president without a science background, led Rice from 1985 to 1993. He promoted interdisciplinary research institutes and elevated the recognition of the university. Economist Malcolm Gillis became Rice's sixth president in 1993. He is a strong advocate of Rice's interdisciplinary centers, the diversity of its student body, and the internationalization of its teaching, research, and outreach programs.

Rice today has over fifty architecturally consistent buildings shaded by stately live oak trees on a campus of three hundred acres. The ensemble of buildings, characterized by arches, red tile roofs, and detailed masonry, is widely recognized as one of the nation's most handsome campuses. Because of its academic distinction and architectural beauty, Rice was chosen as the site of the 1990 Economic Summit of Industrialized Nations.

Rice enrolls approximately 2,700 undergraduates, all members of eight residential colleges - there are no fraternities or sororities - and 1,400 graduate students. An honor code is a revered part of student life. The student body is among the most select in the nation, with the highest percentage of National Merit Scholars of any college or university. The middle 50 percentile of students have SAT scores between 1350 and 1500. Rice is the smallest university competing in Division IA sports, but its women's 4x400 relay team won the NCAA national championship and its baseball team advanced to the College World Series in 1997.

Full-time faculty exceed 450 and include many who are internationally acclaimed. Rice's strengths in the sciences and engineering are well known, but its schools of architecture and music are equally distinguished, and the programs in the humanities and social sciences are renowned. Rice graduates include a Pulitzer Prize-winning novelist, Nobel laureates in physics and chemistry, and seven astronauts.

From the very beginning, Rice has sought to balance teaching and research, technical and humanistic scholarship, pure research and service to society. Recent developments demonstrate a continued devotion to excel-

lence. In 1991, two major buildings were opened, George R. Brown Hall for Biosciences and Bioengineering and Alice Pratt Brown Hall for the Shepherd School of Music. In 1996, Rice professors Bob Curl and Rick Smalley received the Nobel Prize in Chemistry for their discovery of a third form of carbon. Their discovery occurred at Rice, and their research continues in the new Dell Butcher Hall and Center for Nanoscale Science and Technology.

Also recently completed are Anne & Charles Duncan Hall, a stunning facility for Rice's pioneering interdisciplinary program in computational engineering, and James A. Baker III Hall, home of the Baker Institute for Public Policy, where academic scholars and leaders from government and business interact to study policy issues ranging from international relations to health care.

A major research university with a commitment to the highest standards of instruction, Rice is an asset to the entire state of Texas. As President Edgar Odell Lovett envisioned in 1912, Rice is taking its place among the world's leading academic institutions.

❦

Above: Campus Life.

Below: Rice is known for its beautiful campus.

GREATER HOUSTON CONVENTION AND VISITORS BUREAU

Ed Hall was tired but happy the day he spoke with *Historic Houston*.

He and his staff of professionals and volunteers at the Greater Houston Convention and Visitors Bureau had just spent the better part of a week displaying the charms of their city to a group of 550 travel agents and writers from Latin America and Europe. And, they had done the job extraordinarily well.

"Our staff and volunteers have been going from early morning to late at night for five solid days," explained Hall, the bureau's vice president for tourism sales and marketing. "We toured the museum district, the theater district, and the Galleria. We took in the freshwater activities up north and the saltwater attractions down south, along the bay. One evening was devoted to a barbecue at the George Ranch. The next morning began with an organized trip to Space Center Houston. We showed our visitors that it is impossible to stereotype Houston."

The bureau, a non-profit organization dedicated to promoting Houston as a tourist destination around the country and the world, started life more than a quarter century ago as a special project of the old Chamber of Commerce. Today, its staff and volunteers are instrumental in attracting more than 16,000,000 visitors (and some $5 billion) annually to the city.

"Every tour we host is carefully planned to provide a sense of the amazing range of choice Houston offers," Hall said. "Our visitors — the two or three million who pass through each year — go home knowing that the city's new motto, 'Expect the Unexpected' is more than a graceful collection of happy words. It's a perfect description for the vibrant multi-cultural energy that moves this town."

According to Hall, the Houston metroplex offers "a Chinese menu" of entertainment opportunities. "The diversity of activities here is simply staggering, there is no other word to describe it," he said. "We have world class art, world class museums, ballet, symphony, theater in every possible format, special events, festivals, theme parks, history – the list is virtually endless." The city also offers a dizzying selection of eateries, with more than 8000 restaurants featuring the cuisines of every country in the world. "We're talking not just good eating, we're talking great eating," Hall insists. "Did you know Houston has more restaurants recognized as gold culinary award-winners than any other city in the country?"

Adding to the city's already-impressive attractions is the imminent rebirth of its downtown area. Projected for completion in 2005, the re-development of downtown will include the delineation of a grand prix race track, the expansion of the George R. Brown convention center, completion of an entertainment and shopping complex along Buffalo Bayou, dedication of a new stadium and the opening of several new hotels.

"What Houston is experiencing downtown is not just an awakening, but a virtual renaissance," Hall said. "The city's commitment to the transformation of its central core into a center of community activity heralds Houston's arrival among the elite cities of the world."

When the transformation is complete, Hall predicts, Houston will be a city that magnetizes people from all over the world, all eager for an opportunity to feel the heartbeat of civilization in Houston's unique signature style — a style that will never be duplicated anywhere else in the world.

UNIVERSITY OF HOUSTON SYSTEM

Near the heart of the University of Houston's main campus on the city's southeast side stands a three-story structure, built of Texas limestone with a red tile roof, where the university's English classes are held. More than an educational facility, the Roy G. Cullen Building is also the symbol of the generosity of three families whose contributions put the university officially on the map.

Its history — and the history of the UH main campus — dates back to 1936, when the Settegast family heirs and Capt. Ben Taub agreed to donate two adjacent plots of land, totaling 108 acres, for the university's permanent home. Until then, the fledgling institution had been holding day classes in downtown churches and evening sessions at San Jacinto High School. From its beginnings in 1927 as Houston Junior College, with 230 students and eight faculty, it had grown into a four-year college with an enrollment of 909. But it needed a home of its own.

The Settegast/Taub pledges moved this dream closer to reality, but they were given on condition that construction of a new building would begin by January 1,1938. When that stipulation couldn't be met, oil man Hugh Roy Cullen personally guaranteed that the structure would be completed. He and his wife Lillie launched the university's first fund drive, raising $325,000. They also contributed $335,000 of their own— the first of the Cullens' many contributions to the university system totaling more than $100 million. That first building, which was dedicated on June 4,1939, was named after their only son.

The Cullens' gift, too, had a stipulation: "The University of Houston must always be a college for working men and women and their sons and daughters."

SHAPING A UNIVERSITY

The main campus, its faculty and student body continued to grow. Then in 1942, a Downtown Business School was formed in the heart of Houston's central business district. Eventually becoming UH-Downtown in 1975, it now provides undergraduate education for the most diverse student body in the state as well as credit and continuing education for business and professional workers.

In 1973, UH expanded beyond the city, opening a campus in Victoria. Today, UH-Victoria is the only baccalaureate and master's degree-granting university serving a 15-county area. To meet the demand for educational courses in the community surrounding the Johnson Space Center, UH-Clear Lake opened in 1974.

Although it's a state institution, the UH System receives less than half of its income from the State of Texas. To support its rapid growth, in 1989 the UH System universities launched an ambitious endowment campaign with a target of $350 million, the largest fund drive ever undertaken in Houston. The six-year effort exceeded its goal, raising $358 million, primarily for endowments for scholarships, fellowships, faculty chairs, library resources and new programs.

Further broadening its boundaries, in the late 1980s UH established a West Houston Institute in Cinco Ranch and a North Houston Institute near Bush Intercontinental Airport. In 1995, it also opened a multi-institution teaching center in Fort Bend County, one of the fastest-growing counties in Texas. All four UH system universities now offer courses and degrees in Fort Bend County.

Stimulated by the legislature's establishment in 1995 of the Telecommunications Infrastructure Fund, which is enabling UH to acquire instructional hardware and software and to launch projects that enhance on- and off-site learning, the UH System has strengthened its commitment to long-distance education.

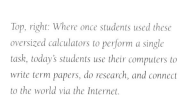

Top, right: Where once students used these oversized calculators to perform a single task, today's students use their computers to write term papers, do research, and connect to the world via the Internet.

PHOTO COURTESY OF UNIVERSITY ARCHIVES,
M.D. ANDERSON LIBRARY, UH

Below: The newly opened 800-seat Moores Opera House boasts a striking interior with a large hanging mural. It was designed by Frank Stella and is one of two of his works in the building.

PHOTO BY AKER/ZVONKOVIC PHOTOGRAPHY L.L.P

Already, the UH main campus has the highest enrollment in long-distance education courses of any university in Texas.

CROWNING ACHIEVEMENTS

Since they were founded, the four universities that comprise the University of Houston System have a long list of accomplishments to their credit. The main campus, for example, ranks as Houston's largest public research university; with 31,602 students in the fall of 1997, UH has one of the largest enrollments in the country. Its 14 colleges offer 281 bachelor's, master's and doctoral degree programs; more than 5,500 degrees were awarded in 1996-1997.

The main campus has the only optometry school in the Southwest, one of the top five hotel and restaurant management programs in the United States and one of the nation's largest and most productive creative writing programs. Its College of Education received recognition recently as the Distinguished Program of the Association of Teacher Educators, the only national competition for excellence in teacher education. UH is the home of the Texas Center for Superconductivity, the nation's most comprehensive university superconductivity effort, which is directed by National Medal of Science winner Paul Chu. Pulitzer Prize-winning playwright Edward Albee also calls UH his faculty home, along with many members of the National Academies of Sciences, Engineering and the Arts. The UH Law Center has national rankings in both health law and intellectual property, and the College of Business Administration is the primary source of top business professionals in the region.

A $71.8 million campus-wide renovation project involving almost 1,700 projects is underway; it represents one of the most ambitious capital renewal programs ever undertaken by a university.

UH-Clear Lake, which enrolled more than 7,000 students for the fall 1997 term, holds a leadership position in the application of quality management principles. University-industry partnership are an important focus for this campus.

A collaboration between the university and Rockwell Space Operations, for example, allows graduate students in computer science and software engineering to work on real-life aerospace projects with faculty and Rockwell engineers. A

joint effort with IBM in Austin enables IBM engineers to pursue degrees in software engineering— the only such degree program in Texas — from their own facility through long-distance learning.

UH-Clear Lake's Environmental Institute of Houston, a collaborative with UH, brings experts together to improve the environment. And its economic development efforts include the 14-state NASA Mid-Continent Technology Transfer Center and Research Institute for Computing and Information Systems. In 1995-96, more than 1,600 degrees were awarded through 72 degree programs at UHCL's four colleges.

An open-admission university, UH-Downtown attracted 8,194 attendees in fall 1997. The university's four colleges offer 25 undergraduate degree programs.

With a mix of Hispanic, white, African American and Asian students, this campus reflects the ethnic composition of its service population more accurately than any other state university. Recently, *U.S. News and World Report* described UH-Downtown as the most ethnically diverse liberal arts university in the Western United States. The Houston Resource Center, which helps economically disadvantaged students, is located here.

To expand its services for working adults, UH-Downtown began a Weekend College in 1994-95, enabling students to attend weekend classes toward degrees in interdisciplinary studies, purchasing and materials management and general business.

At UH-Victoria, almost 1,500 students enrolled in its arts and sciences, business administration and education colleges for the fall 1997 semester. This university's Center for Professional Development and Technology provides in-service training to teachers, with a focus on helping them incorporate new technologies into their instruction. About 85% of its alumni have remained in the area, contributing to both its economy and cultural life.

The University of Houston System has undergone sweeping changes since its flagship university was founded seven decades ago. Today, it has the technology, endowments, research and leadership required to fulfill its vision: to become the foremost metropolitan university system of the next century — a driving educational force in the future of this city, this country and the world.

Top: The Gerald D. Hines College of Architecture Building at UH.

Middle: Graduate biology students study a molecule's structure using 3-D computer technology.
PHOTO BY MARK LACY

Bottom: Students in the early 1950's look on as a professor conducts a simple chemistry experiment. Today, the University of Houston is a leading research force in superconductivity, molecular design, and virtual environment technologies, among others.
PHOTO COURTESY OF UNIVERSITY ARCHIVES, M.D. ANDERSON LIBRARY, UH

SERVICE & NETWORKS

Houston's service sector businesses enhance Houston's Dynamic business climate

196   *Stewart Title*

198   *Walter P. Moore & Associates*

200   *Dean & Draper Insurance Agency, Inc.*

201   *Houston Creative Connections*

202   *Houston Chapter, Texas Society of Certified Public Accountants*

203   *Semasys*

Stewart Abstract & Title Co., 1911.

COURTESY HOUSTON METROPOLITAN RESEARCH CENTER,
HOUSTON PUBLIC LIBRARY

STEWART TITLE

When William Henry Stewart, a young Maryland-born attorney, stepped ashore on Galveston Island in 1844, he had no reason to expect that his role in the development of Texas would be such a profound one. Nor could he know his descendants would continue that development for generations to come.

William H. Stewart settled in Gonzales, established his law practice, and after serving as the town's mayor, was elected to the Texas Legislature. During the War Between the States, Stewart served as a major in the Army of Northern Virginia in Hood's brigade. Upon his return to Texas, he made Galveston his home.

As a delegate to the convention in 1876 which formulated the Texas Constitution still in use, he wrote the resolution to finance construction of the present State Capitol building. For this contribution, William H. Stewart was named "Father of the State Capitol of Texas." In 1876, he was named judge for the Tenth Judicial District in Galveston, a position he held until his death in 1903.

Judge Stewart's descendants would also play major roles in the growth and development of Texas. In 1892, Maco Stewart, then 20, an attorney, established his Law and Land Title office in Galveston to examine titles statewide. In 1893, he purchased a Galveston abstract company, marking the beginning of the Stewart companies. Ever visionary, Maco Stewart recognized the importance of providing greater security and guarantees to property owners, and with his brother Minor, founded the Maco and Minor Stewart Title Guarantee Company in 1905. Maco was instrumental in encouraging legislation to allow title insurance to be written within the state, and in 1908, Stewart Title Guaranty Company was chartered with capital stock of $150,000, and issued the state's first title insurance policy. Original directors included Maco and Minor Stewart and their brother-in-law, W.C. Morris, who began working with the company in 1897.

In 1905, Maco Stewart purchased the Kauffman and Runge Building. The impressive Neo-Renaissance red pressed brick structure became Galveston's premier busi-

ness address when the Stewarts introduced on-premise wireless telegraph, an innovative interior atrium design, a "bird-cage" elevator, and the first postal letter drop in an office building in Galveston. To this day, Stewart Title maintains its offices in the historic building.

Stewart Title Guaranty and its subsidiary, Stewart Abstract company — later renamed Stewart Title Company — began to expand in 1910. Offices were opened in Dallas, San Antonio and Houston, and operations expanded to El Paso and Fort Worth in the 1920's. W.C. Morris assumed an ever-increasing role in the expansion, directing day-to-day operations and setting up new companies statewide. By the end of World War II, Stewart Title Guaranty Company was the largest title insurance company in the state, a distinction it still holds.

After the deaths of Maco Stewart in 1938, and of W.C. Morris and Maco Stewart, Jr., in 1950, the continuity of family involvement was perpetuated by the election of Carloss and Stewart Morris, sons of W.C. Morris, as presidents of Stewart Title Guaranty Company and Stewart Title Company, respectively. Under second-generation leadership, Stewart Title first ventured outside Texas into neighboring New Mexico in 1956. By 1960, the company had issuing offices throughout the Sun Belt states and began a vigorous nationwide expansion.

Stewart Information Services Corporation was formed in 1970 to allow the company to

Right: Carlotta Barker painting of Stewart Title Building in Galveston

Below: Carlotta Barker painting of Stewart Title's corporate offices in Houston

form new real estate information companies. At this time, the third generation assumed their roles in operations when Malcolm Morris and Stewart Morris, Jr., sons of Carloss and Stewart Morris, joined the management team. In 1972, Stewart Information became a publicly-traded stock with its first offering providing capital for further expansion. Few publicly-held international companies can boast of three generations of family leadership to provide total consistency of vision. With offices and agents throughout the United States and new international ventures each year, the company carries an "A Double Prime" rating from Demotech, the highest rating available for the field of 100 title insurance companies.

Stewart's commitment to leadership in technology for the real estate closing process has top priority. Productivity and electronic commerce in the real estate process is the task of the Landata group of companies. Landata has become the industry leader and continues developing technology to reduce costs and speed transfer of title to real estate safely.

Other subsidiaries provide ancillary products essential to the real estate transfer process. Landata Geo Services provides digital geographic information systems for government agencies, engineering firms and real estate developers. Stewart Mortgage

Information interfaces with mortgage lenders to provide electronic data interchange (EDI) for real estate settlements, to provide flood determination information, document preparation and other real estate information, and to develop a paperless, yet protected, conveyance process, and reliable document storage system.

Stewart Information International, Inc., leads the organization as experts in global real estate, as they help other countries enhance and manage geographic information systems, and introduce good land records and a secure land title conveyance process.

As evidence of their commitment to the enduring value of real estate, the Morris family and the Stewart companies have been active in the historic preservation movement for decades. In 1979, the National Trust for Historic Preservation awarded the prestigious Gordon Gray Award to Stewart and Joella Morris and Stewart Title Guaranty Company for the painstaking restoration of the landmark Stewart Title building in Galveston. The company proudly dedicated the William H. Stewart Room to house treasured historic documents relating to the history of the company and of Galveston. Among those items available for viewing are the original 1838 Menard Grant providing for establishment of the City of Galveston, signed by Sam Houston; the first title policy issued in 1905 by Maco and Minor Stewart Title Guarantee Company; the Galveston City Company safe which houses original minute books and records of the City's early history; and many valuable old maps.

In keeping with its emphasis on historic preservation, the company sponsors symposia and holds special events in historic structures throughout the United States, and periodically presents the Stewart Title Historic Preservation Award to deserving projects.

Bonding past to present while building for the future has been a Stewart tradition for more than a century. Three generations have provided management continuity in ensuring the company remains true to its mission: to *Enhance the Real Estate Closing Process.*

Left: Company principals (left to right): Carloss Morris, Malcolm Morris, Stewart Morris, Jr., Stewart Morris., Sr.

Below: Gordon Gray Award from the National Trust for Historic Preservation

WALTER P. MOORE & ASSOCIATES

Top: Rice Stadium, Houston, Texas.

Middle: Astrodome, Houston, Texas.

Bottom: Miller Theater, Houston, Texas.

Walter P. Moore, Jr. can gaze across the skyline of Houston and see the evolution of the engineering firm his father formed in the heady days of the early Bayou City.

Long-time city landmarks such as the Astrodome, Rice Stadium, Miller Theater, The Warwick Hotel and Jesse H. Jones Hall bear the mark of Walter P. Moore and Associates. Well-known Houston venues such as Hofheinz Pavilion and The Summit are also associated with his name, along with many of the institutions in the Texas Medical Center and the corporate headquarters for Brown & Root, Prudential Insurance and American General. The vast array of buildings, separated by style, age and purpose, all represent the achievements of Houston's most prominent structural engineering firm.

Walter P. Moore, Sr. launched his structural engineering firm in 1931, selling his Stutz Bearcat automobile for capital. His earliest job was designing foundations for homes in the posh River Oaks neighborhood for $10 apiece. But by 1950, he would sign onto a local project that would mark the turning point of Moore's firm: Rice Stadium.

The massive concrete stadium, nestled comfortably between some of Houston's most beautiful tree-lined boulevards, is still regarded as one of the most elegant and functional sports facilities in the country. Although many other more complex engineering projects would follow in Houston and across the country, Walter P. Moore, Jr. still regards Rice Stadium as one of the ground-breaking achievements of Walter P. Moore and Associates because of its scale and enduring importance to the city and to the then-Rice Institute, now known as Rice University.

During the decades that followed the construction of Rice Stadium, Walter P. Moore and Associates would serve as structural engineer to most of the major architectural firms in Houston. Walter P. Moore, Sr. was mentor, collaborator and friend to many local architects who gave Houston its distinctive architectural character.

Moore's finished products stand as a testimony to the evolution of Houston from a small Gulf Coast town to a major urban hub, not the least of which is the Astrodome. The Harris County Domed Stadium would be meticulously designed and revamped by teams of engineers which included Moore in 1961, years before number-crunching computers were in widespread use by engineering firms.

When the domed stadium, dubbed the Eighth Wonder of the World, was finally completed in 1963, observers stood nervously as steel erection towers supporting the roof during construction were removed. The 642-foot clear span domed roof performed beautifully, sagging 1/16-inch less than predicted by the design team. As a structural engineer responsible for the Dome, Walter P. Moore and Associates had performed what other structural engineering firms only dreamed could be accomplished.

It would not be Moore's only triumph in the sports world. The firm would build on the stadium, designing major sporting venues nationwide which have included The Ballpark in Arlington and the Frank C. Erwin Special Events Center in Austin, as well as sports arenas in more than a dozen other states. Today the firm is noted as one of the country's top design firms for major sports facilities.

Walter P. Moore, Sr. was joined in his firm by his namesake son in 1953, and the two worked alongside each other until the elder Moore's death in 1983. The junior Moore's own first design project was replacing the Miller Outdoor Theater in Houston's Hermann Park. The structural engineer, who now teaches at Texas A&M university, admits he is probably one of the few Houston natives who remembers that the stately columns which now stand in a circle in Hermann Park near the Mecom Fountain were actually the original columns from the city's open-air theater.

Only a stone's throw away from Hermann Park, Walter P. Moore and Associates' designs are the underpinning of most of the Texas Medical Center, now the world's largest health care center. Over the last 47 years, the firm has designed structural systems and infrastructure for more than 60 major buildings for 21 different Texas Medical Center institutions. Milestones include all the buildings in the M.D. Anderson Cancer Center, Texas Children's Hospital, Baylor College of Medicine, Ben Taub Hospital and the original Methodist Hospital and its neurosensory clinic. The firm was also

an integral part of the team that designed Houston's Veterans Administration Replacement Medical Center, the world's largest VA hospital.

Space exploration continues to play a prominent role in Houston's economy, and Walter P. Moore and Associates has supported the city's emergence as one of the nation's major centers for the aerospace industry. Design work has included numerous facilities at NASA's Johnson Space Center, notably the Mission Control Building, the Astronaut Training Building and, most recently, Space Center Houston. Similarly, the firm has designed many of Houston's major governmental and justice buildings, such as the award-winning Harris County Jail, the Harris County Administration Building and Family Law Center and the downtown County Justice Center, now under construction..

As Houston's growth and success fueled more cultural and entertainment facilities, Walter P. Moore and Associates was again called to contribute. The firm's design work on Astroworld, Busch Gardens, Sea World, the Houston Zoo and Fiesta Texas in San Antonio established the firm as a leader in the new world of entertainment design. Today, Walter P. Moore and Associates continues to support Galveston's Moody Gardens, the Houston Museum of Natural Science and the Museum of Fine Arts/Houston with major ongoing expansion programs. Walter P. Moore's elegant design of Moody's Tropical Rain Forest and the Butterfly House at the Houston Museum of Natural Science have helped cement these buildings as new Houston-area landmarks.

Recognizing the need to diversify, the firm branched out to civil engineering services in the mid-'60s, designing roadways, utility and water systems and drainage structures throughout the city and state. With such a broad area of spe-

cialization, the firm was often called upon by the City of Houston to assist in dealing with its mobility challenges through traffic analyses and designs. Another facet was effected in 1997 with the addition of a highly experienced parking consulting group. Moore's designs have sped the city's traffic and made parking easier in many of the city's major employment centers, including the Texas Medical Center, Greenspoint, Greenway Plaza, Uptown Houston and downtown Houston.

Taking that experience a step further, the firm was commissioned to complete a high-profile graphic identity program for the world-famous Galleria area, complete with signposts, utility relocation and traffic improvements.

In many ways, the rise of Walter P. Moore and Associates as one of Houston's best-established structural, civil, traffic and parking engineering firms reflects the growth of the City of Houston itself. As the city has grown, expanded and reached out to a global market, so has Walter P. Moore and Associates. With regional offices in Dallas, Tampa, Atlanta and Orlando, the 66-year-old Houston-based firm has completed work in 35 states and 13 countries to date.

Ray Messer was named president of Walter P. Moore and Associates in 1993 and has guided the firm's transition from a family-owned and operated business to a modern organization with broad horizons and diverse ownership. For the last 26 years, the quality of Walter P. Moore's design work has been consistently recognized with state and national awards, including Texas' highest award for engineering excellence in four consecutive years, from 1990 to 1993. More than 90 percent of the firm's work is with repeat clients.

Left: The ballpark at Union Station, Houston, Texas. Groundbreaking in late 1997. Projected opening is March, 2000.

Below (top to bottom):

Aerial view of Texas Medical Center, Houston, Texas

Walter P. Moore, Sr. with H.M. Sanford, his employer, January, 1931.

Uptown Houston

Bottom, inside: Aerial view of Moody Gardens, Galveston, Texas

DEAN & DRAPER INSURANCE AGENCY, INC.

Top Right : R.F. (Bob) Dean, President & CEO (right) and J. Mace Meeks, Vice President (left).

Left: Providing service with a personal touch.

INSURING THE GROWTH OF TEXAS

The insurance business, says R.F. (Bob) Dean, founder, president and CEO of Dean & Draper Insurance, is a microcosm of the larger economy, mirroring the revolutionary changes that have swept through all aspects of the nation's business life in the past 20 years.

"In 1980 when I started in business, there were approximately 65,000 independent agents across the United States," Dean says. "Today, there might be 40,000. At least 25,000 agencies have disappeared, victims of the increased competitiveness and reduced profit margins that have become so characteristic of American business since 1985."

Within this chaotic environment, Dean & Draper has emerged a clear winner. The company ranks as one of the largest agencies in Texas specializing in commercial and personal property and casualty coverages and also has considerable expertise in preparing life insurance and employee benefit packages. Dean & Draper has 40 employees, premiums of more than $25,000,000 annually and plans are for rapid expansion in the near future.

"We've managed to increase our market penetration every year by adhering to a few simple, but unshakable tenets," the founder says. "Throughout the company's history, I've emphasized careful hiring practices, continuing education, and automation. With these three practices, we've been able to negotiate some pretty stressful changes in the industry."

The agency employs service-oriented, as well as marketing-oriented people, often pairing them to assure the finest customer relations.

"A recent industry survey indicated that commercial customers look for three things in an insurance provider," he says. "They want their providers to understand their particular industry, they want us to be able to translate that general understanding into a policy tailored to the individual company's needs, and they want us to respond immediately to any problem or concern."

To meet these demands, the agency retains individuals with strong technical backgrounds. "If members of my technical staff are talking to an electrical contractor, I want them to have access to any information they might need to put them a level above our competition," Dean says. "When we sign on a new policyholder, I insist our

employees go out of their way to give more than the customer thought he was getting. I'm never satisfied with 'okay' service. Our response to our personal and commercial policy holders has to be extraordinary in order to be good enough."

The company offers insurance shoppers access to as many as 40 different carriers, including CNA, Chubb Insurance Group, Hartford, Safeco, and the Traveler's Insurance Co., and can produce non-standard, custom contracts tailored to highly-individual or highly-technical needs through its rich network of brokers.

Dean and his vice president, J. Mace Meeks, recently completed a strategic alliance for management and possible acquisition of Draper and Associates, a regional agency founded in 1968. This is the latest development in a history of growth that began in 1983 when the firm acquired the insurance division of the former Drew Mortgage Company.

Further growth is anticipated through what Dean calls "branch partnerships," combining Dean & Draper's formidable access to insurance markets with the personal contacts of established agents throughout the Houston metropolitan area and the State of Texas.

"We recently insured some office properties valued at $120,000,000 through our branch partnership with a suburban agent," he says. "That agent had the contacts, ones I could never have developed on my own. But, he didn't have access to a carrier for such a large account, which is what we contributed to the partnership."

Dean says he expects his firm to double in size in the next five years.

"The toughest work has been done. We've built a stable structure that can sustain and support our staff," he says. "We're ready and able now to do some really creative things to produce rapid growth."

Sue Jackson, CEO

Trey Click, President

When Sue Jackson decided to create her own future against the odds, she also created a future for other downsized and outsourced professionals caught in the headlights of Houston's bust.

It was 1985, when falling oil prices forced energy companies across Houston to slice staff. After more than 10 years in the oil and gas business in drafting and drafting management, Jackson saw the layoffs, the fear and . . . the opportunity.

"Houston wasn't closing down," she says. "It was paring down." She recognized that when the dust settled, the same companies laying off long-term professionals would need short-term talent to supplement the cuts and accomodate leaner budgets. When the market improved, which Jackson believed it would, those companies would need help with overflow work during peak periods. She came up with the idea of Houston Creative Connections — the city's first placement network specializing in drafting, graphic design and technical personnel.

She started the company with a $20,000 line of credit secured by $12,000 in severance pay from her own industry layoff. At her celebratory open house in 1985, most of the guests had been recently laid off. They wouldn't remain jobless.

After 10 years in design and management, Jackson discovered she had a knack for sales. She signed Shell, Chevron and Marathon oil companies as clients and received an assignment from Texaco that was one of the biggest graphic design projects in Houston at the time. Houston Creative Connections, born of the bust, began to boom.

Today, Houston Creative Connections and Houston Creative, the graphic design component of her outfit, has more than 200 temporary technical creative personnel and more than 200 clients. Its biggest account is the Houston Chronicle, which has 120 workers under contract. The graphic design side of the business has grown as well, evolving into an award-winning advertising and public relations agency.

Sue Jackson's success is based on three beliefs. "Anyone can operate a computer, but a creative, thinking individual can provide the problem-solving edge our clients are looking for. It is really a more holistic approach to placement."

A second belief has held steady for 20 years. Marketplace trends continue to drive firms to choose short-term, short-notice placement; farm out sporadic projects, or use more contract personnel to maximize flexibility and minimize overhead. "There is no permanent employment in this economy," says Jackson. "There are, however, companies that still need the resources of talent and talented people who can do the best work."

And finally, she believes in reinvesting in success, consistently plowing profits back into Houston Creative Connections' personnel, computer systems and software.

For example, hearing that one oil company would be upgrading a great deal of its documentation, Jackson had powerful desktop publishing software installed. When the company called about the work, the system was in place and Houston Creative personnel knew how to use it.

The company that had to create its own place in the city two decades ago has expanded beyond the marketplace. Houston Creative Connections reaches into the community by donating design and artwork annually to non-profit organizations and fundraisers. Jackson is a board member of Literacy Advance and is committed to "painting out" illiteracy. "Being in business in Houston means being involved with the whole city," says Jackson.

HOUSTON CHAPTER, TEXAS SOCIETY OF CERTIFIED PUBLIC ACCOUNTANTS

≈

Since its organization in 1928, the Houston Chapter of the Texas Society of Certified Public Accountants (TSCPA) has been a leader in defining the profession's present and expanding its future, changing as the needs of the business community it serves have changed

"In the early years, we were primarily a social organization," says Nancy Rutledge, executive director. "As late as 1978, our members – most of whom were employed by local and national CPA firms — still met monthly for dinners that attracted as many as 600 people. This social emphasis was responsive to the needs of our membership during the city's growth and development period. As the city matured, so has our organization. Our primary focus now is on continuing professional education. Our membership has changed, too — the original composition of public practitioners has shifted to include an ever-growing group of industry-based CPAs."

Since the 1970s, Rutledge says, the chapter has evolved into a highly structured organization. Hundreds of member/volunteers staff 45 standing committees, two task forces and a student auxiliary to fulfill the chapter's mission — "to educate, inform and lead." Ten staff/team members work full-time to keep the organization aligned with its vision statement, which calls for it to be "Houston's leading forum utilizing its size, structure, and diversity to address issues of importance to its members, the accounting profession, and the community,"

"The chapter is a dynamic organization, empowering its members to meet the challenges of the future," says Rutledge.

The most rapid phase of the chapter's evolution began in 1980-81 when the Texas State Board of Public Accountancy mandated a minimum of 40 hours of continuing education annually for all CPAs in the state. "That's a remarkable requirement," Rutledge explains. "I don't know of another profession that places such a premium on continuing education." To help members fulfill the new mandate, the chapter moved from its original 600 square-foot downtown office to the heart of the Galleria. Today, the organization occupies an 8500 square-foot facility with three training rooms, state-of-the-art audio-visual, computer and

CPAs Helping Schools

kitchen facilities, and an executive board room featuring a panoramic view of the downtown and Greenway Plaza areas. A special committee is currently researching the feasibility of using advanced technology to expand the organization's educational capacities still further.

The chapter, Rutledge says, sees itself as an integral part of the Houston community. "Our health as a profession is directly tied to the social and economic health of the community we serve," she says. "It's in our self-interest to work to insure the well-being of the community in anyway we can."

Included in the chapter's on-going community service efforts are two major annual charity fund-raising events — a golf tournament and a black tie dinner — participation in the Houston/Galveston Head Start program, work with senior citizens at the Wesley Community Center and provision of pro bono services to local non-profit agencies.

The chapter promotes educational excellence at the primary and secondary levels through its CPAs Helping Schools Committee, which sponsors annual Outstanding Teacher, Principal, and Volunteer Awards and provides a $1000 scholarship to one outstanding high school senior each year.

The chapter's future, Rutledge says, looks bright. Being the largest chapter in Texas and the third largest in the United States, the Houston Chapter TSCPA is excellently positioned to continue its growth, meeting its goal of 9000 members just about the time Houston enters the new millennium.

Many other point-of-purchase companies in the United States offer some of the services provided by Houston's family-owned SemaSys, Inc. But none, according to president Gary Watts, offer the same range and coordination of services.

"We serve the retail industry, designing and constructing point-of-purchase merchandising programs," Watts explains. "The United States has more retail stores per capita than any other country, making retail one the most competitive arenas in business, today. Our response has been to position ourselves as the full service provider, the one to call when you want someone who can take care of the whole job."

To dozens of national customers (including such giants as TruServ and Ace Hardware, Sears and Wal-Mart, Eckerds and Walgreen drugstores, and Anheuser Busch and Miller Brewing) the "whole job" means designing, manufacturing and installing all the interior decor and signage necessary to direct a store's customers to appropriate locations and to provide them with essential merchandise information in a format that will encourage them to buy and want to return.

"Decor graphics, signing, sizing, pricing, point-of-purchase displays and fixtures are important parts of a store's identity," Watts says. "Notice, for example, the difference between an Albertson's and a Randall's Flagship store. They each have a distinct signature atmosphere. An individually tailored ambiance created in part by our company's attention to a thousand tiny details. The real challenge is to be able to do this, as we do, on a large national scale."

The Heights-area company was started during the Depression as Fit-All Pricing Corporation, a name it retained after its purchase by John Watts, Gary's father, in 1975.

"Our father, John, is a highly entrepreneurial personality, owning manufacturing businesses at one time or another in Spring Branch, the Summit area, and here in the Heights," Watts says. "Houston offered him the perfect climate, giving him the freedom and encouragement to express and develop his unique type of business creativity."

John Watts took the company through the expansive 1970s and well into the consolidating 1980s, developing long-term relationships with anchor customers like K-Mart and Western Auto. In 1986, he turned the business over to his four children, Gary, Bob, Marty and Natalie. The "defining point" in the company's evolution into a full-service operation occurred in 1993 when the Houston operation purchased Central Sales Promotion, Inc., in Oklahoma City.

"We were the best at what we did prior to 1993, but we were still operating as Fit-All Pricing Corporation, focused almost exclusively on producing extruded plastic fixtures," Watts says. "The Oklahoma purchase added 160 employees with extensive experience in the design and production of a variety of printed materials. We were motivated to expand, not just our resources and our revenues, but our sense of who we are and what we do."

The company's expanded capacities are reflected in its new name, SemaSys — a name which combines the Greek word "sema," meaning "sign" with "sys," an abbreviation of "systems."

"Our new name defines perfectly who we want to be in the competitive retail market that prevails today and is expected to prevail well into the twenty-first century. We are determined to be recognized as the vendor of choice for retailers who need high-quality, systematized services," Watts says. "By providing those services, we will keep our customers and our employees happy."

The Watts family is happy, too, the company president reports: "We are doing what we love in Houston — the innovative, adaptive, and freedom-loving city where it all began."

Top left: (From left to right) Natalie, Marty, Gary, Bob and John Watts gather for a year-end celebration.

Bottom Right: SemaSys is ideally situated near downtown Houston.

Sharing the

SOURCES OF PHOTGRAPHS USED IN
HISTORIC HOUSTON

Baytown Historical Museum, Baytown
Center for American History, University of Texas at Austin
Gilcrease Museum, Tulsa, Oklahoma
Greater Houston Partnership
Houston Chronicle
Houston Endowment, Inc. Archives
Houston Metropolitan Research Center, Houston Public Library
Institute of Texan Cultures, University of Texas at San Antonio
Keightley, Patricia John, Houston
Library of Congress, Washington, D. C.
Masonic Grand Lodge Library & Museum of Texas, Waco
Museum of Fine Arts, Houston
National Aeronautics and Space Administration
Office of George Bush, Houston
St. Luke's Episcopal Hospital/Texas Heart Institute, Houston

Salvado, Jean D. B., Victoria, Australia
San Jacinto Museum of History, La Porte
Southwestern Writers' Collection, Southwest Texas State University, San Marcos
Special Collections & Archives, University of Houston Libraries
Special Collections Division, University of Texas at Arlington Libraries
State Preservation Board, Austin
Texas General Land Office, Austin
Texas Medical Center, Houston
Texas State Library, Austin
Texas Trailblazers Preservation Association, Houston
The Heritage Society, Houston
The Methodist Hospital, Houston
The Torch Collection of Torch Energy Advisors, Inc., Houston
The Witte Museum, San Antonio
Woodson Research Center, Rice University, Houston

SPONSORS OF
HISTORIC HOUSTON

American Exploration Company/Louis Dreyfus Natural Gas
Aramco Services Company
Baker & Botts, L.L.P.
Browning-Ferris Industries, Inc.
Computer Station Corporation
Continental Airlines
Dean & Draper Insurance Agency, Inc.
El Paso Energy Corporation
Fayez Sarofim Company
Fiesta Mart
Global Marine
Greater Houston Convention & Visitors Bureau
Greater Houston Preservation Alliance
H & W Petroleum
Houston Chapter, Texas Society of Certified Public Accountants
Houston Creative Connections
Houston Distributing Company
Houston Trust Company
ICO
Lancaster Hotel
Landry's Seafood Restaurants, Inc.
Merex Corporation
Mesa Southwest Construction Company
The Methodist Hospital, Houston
MetroBank
MHI
Mohle, Adams, Till, Guidry & Wallace, L.L.P.
Molina's Restaurants
Nils Sefeldt Volvo

Pennzoil
Petroleum Information/Dwight's, L.L.C.
Philip Service Corporation
Randall Davis Properties, Inc.
Reading & Bates Corporation
RELO.net
Rice University
Rose Metal Recycling, Inc.
Sanders Morris Mundy
Saudi Refining, Inc.
Schlumberger Oilfield Services
Semasys
Southern National Bank
Southwest Airlines
Stewart Title
The Way Companies
The Westlake Group of Companies
Tideland Signal
TIW Corporation
Torch Energy Advisors, Incorporated
United Business Machines, Inc.
University of Houston
UTEX Industries
Visible Changes
Walter Oil & Gas Corporation
Walter P. Moore & Associates
Warren Electric Company
Waukeshaw Pearce Industries, Inc.

SELECTED BIBLIOGRAPHY

BOOKS

Barker, Eugene C. *The Life of Stephen F. Austin*. Austin: Texas State Historical Association, 1949.

Baron, Steven M. *Houston Electric: The Street Railways of Houston, Texas*. Lexington, Ky.: Steven M. Baron, 1996.

Beeth, Howard and Cary D. Wintz, ed. *Black Dixie: Afro-Texan History and Culture in Houston*. College Station: Texas A&M University Press, 1992.

Berlandier, Jean Louis. *The Indians of Texas in 1830*. Trans. Patricia Reading Leclercq. Ed. John C. Evers. Washington, D. C.: Smithsonian Institution Press, 1969.

Carleton, Don E. *Red Scare: Right-wing Hysteria, Fifties Fanaticism and Their Legacy in Texas*. Austin: Texas Monthly Press, 1985.

Chipman, Donald E. *Spanish Texas, 1519-1821*. Austin: University of Texas Press, 1992.

Covey, Cyclone, trans. and ed. *Cabeza de Vaca's Adventures in the Unknown Interior of America*. Albuquerque: University of New Mexico Press, 1983.

DeLeón, Arnoldo. *Ethnicity in the Sun Belt: A History of Mexican Americans in Houston*. Houston: Mexican American Studies, University of Houston, 1989.

Dresel, Gustav. *Gustav Dresel's Journal: Adventures in North America and Texas, 1837-1841*. Trans. and ed. Max Freund. Austin: University of Texas Press, 1954.

Feagin, Joe R. *Free Enterprise City: Houston in Political and Economic Perspective*. New Brunswick, N. J.: Rutgers University Press, 1988.

Fehrenbach, T. R. *Lone Star: A History of Texas and the Texans*. New York: American Legacy Press, 1983.

Foster, William C. *Spanish Expeditions into Texas, 1689-1768*. Austin: University of Texas Press, 1995.

Gray, Millie Richards. *The Diary of Millie Gray, 1832-1840*. Houston: Fletcher Young Publishing Company for the Rosenberg Library Press, 1967.

Hatch, Orin Walker. *Lyceum to Library: A Chapter in the Cultural History of Houston*. Houston: Texas Gulf Coast Historical Association, 1965.

Haynes, Robert V. *A Night of Violence: The Houston Riot of 1917*. Baton Rouge: Louisiana State University Press, 1976.

Hogan, William Ransom. *The Texas Republic: A Social and Economic History*. Norman: University of Oklahoma Press, 1946.

Holley, Mary Austin. *The Texas Diary, 1835-1838*. Ed. James Perry Bryan. Published by the Humanities Research Center, University of Texas. Distributed by University of Texas Press, 1965.

Houghton, Dorothy Knox Howe, Barrie M. Scardino, Sadie Gwin Blackburn, and Katherine S. Howe. *Houston's Forgotten Heritage: Landscape, Houses, Interiors, 1824-1914*. Houston: Rice University Press, 1991.

Hurley, Marvin. *Decisive Years for Houston*. Houston: *Houston Magazine*, 1966.

Johnston, Marguerite. *Houston: The Unknown City*. College Station, Texas A&M University Press, 1991.

King, John O. *Joseph Stephen Cullinan: A Study of Leadership in the Texas Petroleum Industry, 1897-1937*. Nashville: Vanderbilt University Press, 1970.

Krenek, Thomas H. *Del Pueblo*. Houston: Houston International University, 1989.

Larson, Henrietta M. and Kenneth W. Porter. *History of the Humble Oil and Refining Company: A Study in Industrial Growth*. New York: Harper, 1959.

Lipartito, Kenneth J. and Joseph A. Pratt. *Baker and Botts in the Development of Modern Houston*. Austin: University of Texas Press, 1991.

Lubbock, Francis Richard. *Six Decades in Texas*. Ed. by C. W. Rains. Austin: Ben C. Jones & Co., 1900.

Macon, N. Don. *Monroe Dunaway Anderson: His Legacy*. Houston: Texas Medical Center, 1994.

McComb, David G. *Houston: A History*. 1st ed., rev. Austin: University of Texas Press, 1981.

Morris, Sylvia Stallings, ed. *William Marsh Rice and His Institute: A Biographical Study*. Houston: Rice University Studies, 1972.

Muir, Andrew Forest, ed. *Texas in 1837*. Austin: University of Texas Press, 1958.

Platt, Harold L. *City Building in the New South: The Growth of Public Services in Houston, Texas, 1830-1915*. Philadelphia: Temple University Press, 1983.

Ricklis, Robert A. *The Karankawa Indians of Texas*. Austin: University of Texas Press, 1996.

Roemer, Frederick. *Texas: With Particular Reference to German Immigration and the Physical Appearance of the Country*. Trans. Oswald Mueller. San Antonio: Standard Printing Co., 1935.

Sibley, Marilyn McAdams. *The Port of Houston: A History*. Austin: University of Texas Press, 1968.

Timmons, Bascom M. *Jesse H. Jones: the Man and the Statesman*. New York: Henry Holt & Company, 1956.

Tyler, Ron, ed. *The New Handbook of Texas, Vol. 1-6*. Austin: Texas State Historical Association, 1996.

Von der Mehden, Fred R., ed. *The Ethnic Groups of Houston*. Houston: Rice University Studies, 1984.

Wheeler, Kenneth W. *To Wear A City's Crown: The Beginnings of Urban Growth in Texas, 1836-1865*. Cambridge, Mass.: Harvard University Press, 1968.

Wilson, Ann Quin. *Native Houstonian: A Collective Portrait*. Norfolk, Va.: The Donning Co., 1982.

Wooster, Ralph A., ed. *Lone Star Blue and Gray: Essays on Texas During the Civil War*. Austin: Texas State Historical Association, 1995.

Works Projects Administration, Writers' Program in Texas. *Houston: A History and Guide*. Houston: Anson Jones Press, 1942.

PERIODICALS

Civics for Houston

Houston Chronicle

Houston Morning Star

Houston Post

Houston Review: History and Culture of the Gulf Coast

Houston Telegraph and Texas Register

Progressive Houston

Southwestern Historical Quarterly

INDEX

A

Abercrombie, James 65
Adams, K. S. "Bud" 99
Adams-Onis Treaty 11
Addicks 81
Looscan, Adele 51
Aeros 99
African-American 106
Alamo 17
Aldrin, Edwin E. 101
Allen, Augustus Chapman 19
Allen, John Kirby 19, 22, 28
Alley Theater 100
Allies 72
American Red Cross 70, 86
American Sugar Refining Company 69
Anahuac 17
Anderson Foundation 92
Anderson, Clayton and Company 72, 92
Anderson, Frank E. 72
Anderson, Monroe D. 72, 92
Andrews, Mrs. E. A. 31
Apollo 101
Appalachia 88
Appomattox Courthouse 41
Arizona 33, 41
Arkansas 12, 40
Armour 67
Armstrong, Neil 101
Arrowhead Park 104
Astros 99
Atlanta 40
Audubon, John James 24
Austin 11-17, 20, 23, 28, 35, 80, 88
Austin, John 15, 20
Austin, Moses 11
Austin, Stephen F. 11, 15, 16, 20, 80
Austin, William T. 21
Australia 91
Azteca 83

B

Baker, Botts, Baker and Lovett 48
Baker, James A. 47, 79
Baker, William R. 35, 55
Baldwin, Charlotte 19
Baldwinsville 19
Ball, Tom 60, 65
Ballet Russe de Monte Carlo 76, 99
Baltimore 66
Barbers Hill 64
Barbirolli, Sir John 99
Barker 81
Barrymore, Maurice 54
Bates, W. B. 92
Baylor College of Medicine 102
Baylor University's School of Medicine 92
Bayou Bend 100
Baytown 81, 87, 91
Baytown-LaPorte Tunnel 91
Beauchamp Springs 25
Beaumont 36, 61, 62, 63, 64
Belgium 91
Bellaire 83
Bering, Anna Margaret 38
Bering, John 38
Bertner, Dr. E. W. 92
Big Inch 88
Biggers, John 100
Black Tuesday 79
Blaffer, Robert E. 64, 100
Blitz, Julian Paul 75
Bloodgood, William 16
Blue Ridge 64
Boeing 101
Booth, Edwin 54
Borden, Gail 22
Borden, Thomas 22
Boston 30, 35, 46
Botts, Walter Browne 47
Brady, John T. 59
Brady, William 46
Braes Heights 89
Braeswood 83
Braniff 82, 90
Brashear, Samuel 57
Bray's Bayou 69, 83
Brazoria 15, 20, 100
Brazos 6, 12, 13, 16, 17, 20, 23, 26, 27, 29, 35
Bremond, Paul 35, 36, 38, 45
Brinson, Enoch 16
Briscoe, Andrew 17, 29, 61
Broadacres 83
Brown Foundation 100
Brown Shipbuilding 87
Brown v. Board of Education 96
Brown, George 87, 92, 93
Brown, Herman 87, 92
Brown, John 16
Brownsville 49
Brunner suburb 54
Buff Stadium 82
Buffalo Bayou Ship Channel Company 44
Buffalo Bayou 6, 13, 14, 15, 16, 17, 20, 21, 22, 25, 26, 27, 28, 35, 36, 37, 38, 40, 42, 44, 54, 57, 58, 59, 60, 65, 79, 81
Buffalo 21
Buffs 82
Buick 73
Buna-S rubber 87
Burke, Andrew J. 55
Burnet, David G. 17
Bush, George 108
Business League 65, 70

C

Cabeza de Vaca , Álvar Núñez 7, 8, 9, 10
Cadillac 73
California 33, 35, 94
Callahan, Moses 16
Cambridge, Massachusetts 68
Cameron Iron Works 65, 83
Cameron, H. S. 65
Camino Real 13
Camp Logan 71, 74
Camp Wallace 83
Cape Canaveral 101
Cape Kennedy 101
Capitol Hotel 52, 56, 57
Caribbean 90
Carlos, John 30
Carnegie Library 51
Carnegie, Andrew 51
Carpenter, David 16
Carter, Oscar M. 54
Caruso, Enrico 76
Catholic 12, 51, 76
Cayuga 17
Central America 90
Central Park 67
Chamber of Commerce 28, 68, 70, 79, 83, 90, 93, 105
Charleston 40
Cherry, Emma Richardson 80
Cherryhurst 83
Chew, William B. 48
Chicago 36, 55, 79, 83
Chihuahua 35
Chillman, James 76
China 91
Chocolate Bayou 13
Christ Episcopal Church 56
Chronicle 69, 79, 82
City Auditorium 76, 100
City Directory 46, 50, 55
City Park Commission 68
City Planning Commission 73, 74
Civil Aeronautics Board 90
Civil War 36, 38, 44, 45, 48, 50, 54, 61, 69
Clayton, William L. 72, 79
Clear Lake Ranch 93
Clear Lake 93, 101
Cleveland, William D. 48, 59
Clinton 44, 58, 59
Clopper, Joseph 20
Clopper's Bar 36, 44
Coahuila 16
Cobb, Arnett 76
Coke, Richard 43
Colorado Railway Company 35
Colorado 12, 27, 28, 34, 35
Colt .45s 99
Columbia 22
Columbus, Christopher 7
Comey, Arthur C. 68
Commerce 23, 28, 68, 70, 79, 83, 93, 105
Commercial National Bank 48
Confederacy 39, 42
Confederate 39, 40, 41, 42, 43, 48, 55
Congregation of the Sisters of Charity of the Incarnate Word 49
Congress Avenue 54
Congress Street 29
Connally, Ben C. 96
Connally, John 99
Constitution 17, 26, 31, 37, 77, 95
Constitution Bend 26
Constitution of the Confederate States of America 39
Contemporary Arts Museum 100
Cooley, Dr. Denton 102
Coronado 10
Corri, Henri 31
Corsicana 62, 63
Cotton Exchange 44, 52, 59, 83
Courthouse Square 30, 52, 55
Crespo, Manuel 78
Crotty, Charles 65
Cruz, Lauro 97
Cuba 8, 38
Culiacán 9
Cullen, Hugh Roy 75
Cullinan, Joseph F. 76
Cullinan, Joseph S. 62
Cullinan, Nina 100
Cushing, E. H. 35, 37
Cutrer, Lewis 94, 97

D

Dallas 79, 80, 82, 92, 104
Damon Mound 64
Davis Guards 41
Davis, Edmund J. 43
Davis, Jefferson 41, 80
de Menil, Dominique 100
de Menil, John 100
de Piñeda, Alonzo Álvarez 7
de Rubí , Marqués 11
de Zavala, Lorenzo 17
DeBakey, Dr. Michael 102
Democratic 77, 79, 95
Democrats 43, 79
Dempsey, Jack 82
Denison 45
Depression 77, 78, 79, 80, 81
Diana 42
Dickey, George 52
District of Texas 41
Dow 41, 52, 61, 87
Dowling, Dick 41, 61
Dreyer, Margaret 100
Duhig, John 78
Dun & Bradstreet 38
DuPont 87

E

Earle, Thomas 16
Eastern airlines 82
Eastwood 83
Economic Summit of Industrialized Nations 108
Eddy, Nelson 76
El Anunciador 82
El Tecolote 82
Eldorado Ballroom 76
Elkins, James A., Sr. 92
Ellington Field 71, 83, 84, 86
Ellington, Eric 71
Emancipation Day 42
Enfield rifles 41
England 34, 37, 55
Ennis, Cornelius 35, 38
Episcopal 56, 92
Europe 7, 8, 9, 19, 48, 54, 69, 70, 72, 76, 83

F

Fairgrounds 54
Fairview 54, 83
Fannin 17, 22
Farish, W. S. 79
Farish, William Stamps 64
Ferdinand, Franz 70
Fifth Ward 53
Finn, Alfred 80
Finnigan, Annette 76
First Manassas 40
First National Bank 48
Fisher, George 27
Floeck, Peter 41
Florida 7, 8, 26, 101
Foley Bros. 88
Fondren, Walter 64
Ford Motor Company 73
Fort Bend 6, 100
Fort Worth 82
Fortune magazine 81
Forum of Civics 74
Fourth Ward 53
France 10, 11, 91, 100
Freed, Frank 100
Freedmen's Bureau 50
Freedmen's Town 53
Freeman, John H. 92
Fuermann, George 85

G

Gabel, Peter 41
Galena Park 83
Galena Signal Oil Company 67
Galey, John H. 63
Galleria Vittorio Emmanuele 102
Galleria 102
Galli-Curci, Amelita 76
Galveston Daily News 40, 53
Galveston Wharf Company 37, 42, 44
Galveston 6, 8, 13, 17, 20, 21, 26, 27, 28, 29, 34, 35, 36, 37, 38, 40, 41, 42, 44, 49, 53, 56, 59, 60, 66, 67, 80, 82, 90, 98
Galveston, Harrisburg & Houston Railway 56
Garden Villas 83
Gardes, Henry 48
Garner, John Nance 92
Garrow, H. W. 59
General Electric 101
General Sherman 35
Gilbert and Sullivan 55
Gilded Age 45
Gladys City Oil, Gas, and Manufacturing Company 62
Gockley, David 99
Golf Villas 103
Goliad 11, 17, 22
Gonzales 17
Goose Creek 64, 78
Gould, Jay 47
Graham, George 20
Gray and Botts 46

Gray, Millie...28
Gray, Peter...46
Great Britain...91
Great Depression...80
Greece...83, 91
Greenway Plaza...102
Gregory Institute...50
Grovey v. Townsend...95
Grovey, R. R. ...95
Grumann...101
Guffey, James M....63
Guillemin, Dr. Roger...102
Gulf Building...83
Gulf Coast...70, 78
Gulf Freeway...90
Gulf Intracoastal Waterway...66
Gulf Oil Corporation...63
Gulf Refining Company...63, 67
Gulf ...7, 8, 9, 13, 16, 34, 37, 60, 62, 63, 67, 81, 83

H

Hamilton...21
Hamilton, Andrew Jackson...42
Hamilton, Hugh...62
Hamlet...54
Hare and Hare...73, 74
Harlem Grill...76
Harriet Lane...41
Harris County Democratic Executive Committee...77
Harris County Flood Control District...81
Harris County Houston Ship Channel Navigation District...66
Harris County Medical Association...50
Harris County ...9, 14, 16, 29, 30, 39, 41, 50, 66, 69, 70, 77, 80, 81, 84, 88, 95, 97, 99, 100, 106
Harris, David...16
Harris, Jane...17
Harris, John R....15, 17, 20
Harris, William...16
Harrisburg Railroad and Trading Company...29
Harrisburg Town Company...35
Harrisburg...6, 15, 17, 18, 20, 22, 26, 28, 29, 30, 35, 56, 73, 83
Havana...27, 41, 49, 66
Hebert, Walter...99
HEDC...105
Heights Boulevard...54
Heights...83
Heiner, Eugene...52
Hempstead...36
Hermann Hospital...92
Hermann Park...69, 82, 92, 99
Hermann, George...68, 76
Hermann, John...41
Herrera, John J....78
Higgins, Pattillo...62
Hines, Gerald D....102
Hobby, Oveta Culp...86, 98
Hobby, William P....98
Hofheinz, Fred...106
Hofheinz, Roy...94, 99
Hogg, Ima...76, 100
Hogg, James C. ...63, 74
Hogg, Will C....70
Holcombe, Oscar F....73, 76, 93, 94
Holland...38, 91
Hood, Dorothy...100
House, T. W....48
House, Thomas W....28, 34, 38, 40
Houston Academy...31
Houston Airport Corporation...82
Houston and Texas Central...36, 45, 47, 62
Houston Art League...76
Houston Ballet...99, 100
Houston Bar Association...48
Houston Board of Trade and Cotton Exchange...44
Houston Buffaloes...82, 99
Houston Business League...65
Houston Chronicle...79, 82
Houston City Directory...46, 50
Houston City Street Railway...54
Houston Club Building...86
Houston College for Negroes...75
Houston Colored Junior College...75
Houston Daily Post...46, 53, 54, 57, 66
Houston Daily Sun...56
Houston Daily Telegram...56
Houston Defender...82
Houston Direct Navigation Company...42
Houston East and West Texas Narrow Gauge Railway...46
Houston Economic Development Council...105
Houston Electric Light and Power Company...57
Houston Fat Stock Show and Livestock Exposition...83
Houston Gas Light Company...57
Houston Grand Opera...99, 100
Houston Harbor...67
Houston Heights...54, 83
Houston Ice and Brewing Association...62
Houston Independent School District...74, 98, 106
Houston Informer...77, 82
Houston Intercontinental Airport...91
Houston International Airport...90
Houston Junior College...75
Houston Labor Council...78
Houston Light Guards...56
Houston Lyceum...50, 51
Houston Magazine...79, 87
Houston Metropolitan Transit Authority...104
Houston National Bank...83
Houston Navigation Company...37
Houston Negro Chamber of Commerce...77
Houston Oilers...99
Houston Post...50, 72, 82, 85, 91
Houston Press...82
Houston Rockets...99
Houston School Board...75, 94
Houston Select School...31
Houston Sentinel...82
Houston Ship Channel...26, 66, 67, 72, 87, 91
Houston Shipbuilding Corporation...87
Houston Sports Association...99
Houston Symphony...75, 99, 100
Houston Tap...35
Houston Town Company...23
Houston Transit Co....103
Houston Volunteer Fire Department...51
Houston Waterworks Company...57
Houston, Sam...16, 17, 22, 23, 25, 27, 28, 39, 41, 58, 79, 80
Houston, the cruiser...81, 86
HouTran...104
Hughes Tool Company...64, 84
Hughes, Howard R., Sr....64
Humble Oil and Refining Company...64, 83, 93
Humble Oil Company...64
Humble ...62, 63, 64, 65, 67, 68, 79, 81, 83, 93
Hunter, Dr. Johnson...16
Huntington, Collis...47
Huntsville...47
Hupmobile...73
Hutcheson, Joseph Chappell...59
Hutchins, William J....35, 38
Hyde Park...83

I

Idylwood...83
Independence Heights...83
India...8, 9, 11, 38, 91
International Business Machines...101
Iowa...64
Ireland...43
Italy...91

J

J. M. Guffey Petroleum Company...63
J. S. Cullinan Company...62
Jack Yates High School...75
Jackson, Humphrey...16
Japan...70, 84, 87
Jefferson Davis Hospital...80
Jesse H. Jones Hall for the Performing Arts...100
Jet Era Ranch Corporation...90
Jews...76
John, Grace Spaulding...80
Johnson City...91
Johnson, Andrew...42
Johnson, Lyndon B....91, 92, 93, 99
Jolson, Al...76
Jones Hall...100
Jones, Anson...32
Jones, Jesse H....66, 79, 92
Jones, Martin Tilford...48
Jordan, Barbara...97
Juarez...83
Judge Humphreys...28
Julius Caesar...54
Juneteenth...42

K

Kansas City...73, 83
Karankawa...8, 9
Kendall, Belle...51
Kennedy, John...41
Kentucky...6, 11, 40
Kessler, George E....69
KGUL-TV...98
KHOU-TV...98
Kidd, George W....59
King Nottoc...66
King Retaw...66
Kings Forest...103
Kingwood...103
Kirby, John Henry...46
KLEE-TV...98
Klineberg, Dr. Stephen L....106
KPRC...82, 98
KPRC-TV...98
Kreisler, Fritz...76
KTRK-TV...98
Ku Klux Klan...76
KUHT-TV...98
Kurtz, Efrem...99

L

La Prensa...82
La Salle, Rene Robert Cavalier, Sieur de...10
La Traviata...54
La Tribuna...82
LAC...61, 78, 97
Ladies' Reading Club...50
Lamar Hotel...92
Lamar, Mirabeau B....28, 80
Langtry, Lillie...54
Lanier, Bob...106
Lapham, Moses...22
Larkin, Milton...76
Latin American Club of Harris County...78
Laura...22, 26, 27
Lavaca...13
League of United Latin American Citizens...78
Lee, Robert E....41
Lee, W. Albert...98
Lexington, Kentucky...11
Liberty...17, 70, 100
Lind, Jenny...54
Little Inch...88
Lockheed...101
Loew's State...83
London...30, 100
Long Reach...65
Lorehn, Olle...52
Los Angeles...81, 106
Louisiana...11, 13, 17, 22, 40, 78
Louisville...21
Lovett Hall...108
Lovett, Edgar Odell...75
Lubbock, Francis R....21
Lubbock, Thomas S....39
Lucas, Anthony F....62, 63
LULAC...78, 97
Lynch, Nathaniel...16, 17
Lynchburg...65

M

M. D. Anderson Foundation...92
M. T. Jones Lumber Company...48
Magnolia Park...67
Magruder, General J. Bankhead...40
Main Street...22, 27, 53, 54, 57, 65, 68, 86, 88, 89
Majestic...83
Malay Peninsula...87
Mallory, C. H....42
Manned Spacecraft Center...93, 101
Matagorda...22
Matamoros...41
Maxwell...73
McCarthy, Glen...89
McCarthy, Joseph...94
McConn, Jim...106
McCormick, Arthur...16
McCormick, Peggy...18
McDonald, Jeanette...76
McDonnell...80, 101
McDonnell, Angela...80
McFarland, Fannie...39
McGowen, Alexander...41, 43
McVey, William...80
Mellon...63
Memorial Park...74
Methodist Hospital...92, 102
METRO...104
Metropolitan Opera...55, 76
Metropolitan...55, 76, 83
Mexican...11, 12, 13, 16, 17, 33, 38, 77, 78, 80, 82, 97
Mexican-Americans...78, 97
Mexico City...108
Mexico...8, 9, 11, 12, 13, 16, 32, 33, 67
Meyerland...89
Milam...22
Milan...102
Miller Theater...82
Millican...36
Miss Mary B. Brown's Select School for Young Ladies...50
Mississippi...10, 11, 13, 40, 41, 42, 67
Missouri Pacific...47
Missouri...11, 12, 45, 47
Missouri, Kansas and Texas Railroad...45
Mitchell, George P....103
Mobile...21, 27, 40
Mohawk River Valley...19
Monsanto...87
Montgomery...100
Montrose area...83
Moore, John W....17, 30
Moore, Luke...16
Morgan, Charles...42, 44, 58
Morgan's Point...44
Morning Star...27, 31
Moscow...108
Municipal Annexation Act...102
Museum of Fine Arts...76, 100
Music Hall...80

N

NAACP...77, 95
Nacogdoches...11, 16, 19, 22, 46
Narváez, Pánfilo...8
NASA...93, 105
National Aeronautics and Space Administration...93
National Aeronautics and Space Council...93
National Association for the Advancement of Colored People...77
National Bank of Commerce...79
National Guard...71
National League...82, 99
Navasota...36
Neal, J. W....79
Nebraska...54
Neches...36
Nevada...33

New England 37
New Kentucky 6
New Mexico 33, 41, 71
New Orleans...6, 15, 17, 21, 25, 27, 30, 48, 49, 56, 59, 60, 66, 81, 91
New Washington 21
New York Times 79
New York ...6, 18, 19, 21, 25, 27, 28, 30, 34, 42, 57, 58, 59, 63, 75, 79, 81, 88, 91, 94, 99, 100, 106
Nichols, Ebenezer 28
Niels Esperson building 83
No-tsu-oh Carnival 66
Nueces 8

O

Oak Forest 89
Oberholtzer, E. E. 74
Oil Workers' Union of the Congress of Industrial Organizations 78
Oklahoma 9, 64, 72
Old Spanish Trail 104
Old Three Hundred 14, 15, 16
Olmsted, Frederick Law 61
Omaha and South Texas Land Co. 54
Omaha 54
Onodaga County, New York 19
Othello 31, 54
Overland 73

P

Pacific Ocean 67
Packard 73
Paderewski, Ignace 55
Pan American 90
Panama Canal 67
Panic of 1873 ....44, 55
Pánuco 8
Paris 100
Parker, Mrs. Edwin B. 76
Parrott, Mrs. T. F. L. 20
Pasadena 67, 70, 80, 83, 91
Pavlova, Anna 99
Pearl Harbor 84
Pecan Grove Plantation 103
Peden and Company 62
Peden, Edward A. 68
Pennzoil Place 104
Perkins Theater 39, 54
Perkins, Erastus 28
Philippine Islands 8
Pilgrim Temple 76
Pillot's Opera House 54, 56
Piney Point Village 13
Piney Woods 46
Pittsburgh 63
Political Association of Spanish-speaking Organizations 97
Popova, Nina 100
Port Arthur 63
Port Commission 78
Port Houston 67
Port of Houston 29, 33, 35, 60, 72, 79, 81, 84, 91, 104, 105, 106
Post Oak Boulevard 102
Post-Dispatch building 83
Potter, Hugh 74
Powhatan 21
Presbyterian 31
Princeton University 75
Progressive Houston 68, 69
Protection Company No. 1 51
Pubic School Art League 76
Public Works Administration 80
Puccini's *Madame Butterfly* 99
Putnam, Frank 69

R

R. G. Dun & Company 37
Rachmaninoff, Serge 76
Rankin, Frederick 16
Rayburn, Sam 92
Reconstruction Finance Corporation 80
Reconstruction 42, 43, 76, 80, 97
Red Fish Bar 36, 44
Red River Railway Company 36
Red Scare 94
Republic of Texas 21, 27, 32, 52
Republican 43
RepublicBank Building 104
Rice Institute 69, 75
Rice University 93, 106, 108
Rice, Horace Baldwin 65, 68
Rice, William Marsh 28, 35, 38, 75
Richards, Daisy 76
Richardson, C. F. 77, 82
Richmond 35, 40
Ring, Elizabeth 51
Rio Grande 10, 11, 33
River Oaks Community Center 83
River Oaks 74, 83, 103
Riverside Terrace 83
Rodriguez, Juvencio 78
Roemer, Ferdinand 35
Rogers, Will 76
Rolla 26
Romeo and Juliet 31, 54
Roosevelt, Franklin D. 84, 92
Runaway Scrape 17

S

Sabine 11, 41, 46, 61
Saibara, Seito 70
Saint Vincent de Paul Catholic Church 51
Sallyport 108
Salome 99
Saltillo 16
Sam Houston Coliseum 80
Sam Houston Park 58
San Antonio 11, 13, 17, 22
San Francisco 106
San Jacinto High School 75
San Jacinto Monument 80
San Jacinto 6, 11, 13, 14, 17, 18, 19, 20, 21, 22, 36, 66, 75, 80, 84
Santa Anna 17, 41
Santa Anna, Antonio López de 17
Santa Cruz 49
Santa Fe 35
Sarajevo 70
Saunders, Edna Woolford 76
Saxet 66
Scandinavia 91
Scanlan, Thomas H. 43
Schnitzer, Kenneth 102
School of Law of the Texas State University for Negroes 96
Scott, John T. 79
Scott, William 16
Scottsburg 21
Select Classical School 31
Semenova, Tatiana 100
Shamrock Hotel 89
Sharp, Frank 89
Sharp, Walter B. 64
Sharp-Hughes Tool Company 64
Sharpstown 89
Shearn, Charles 28
Sheffield Steel Corporation 83, 87
Shell Petroleum Corporation 67, 81
Shepherd, B. A. 35, 48
Sherman, Sidney 35
Shriners Hospital for Children 92
Sims Bayou 44
Sixth Ward 52
Skinner, Otis 54
Smalley, I. H. 76
Smith, Ashbel 50
Smith, Christian 16
Smith, Daniel 55
Smith, Dr. Lonnie E. 95
Smith, R. E. "Bob" 99
Somerset, England 34
Sour Lake 61, 63, 64
Sousa, John Philip 55
South America 8, 90
South Houston 83
South Main 69, 89
South Texas National Bank 48
Southern Pacific 48, 64
Southern 48, 64, 75, 90
Southside Place 83
Space City USA 93
Spain 8, 10, 11, 91
Spindletop 61, 62, 63, 64, 65
Spring Branch 13
Spring Creek 6
St. Joseph's Infirmary 50
St. Louis Cardinals 82
St. Louis 10, 36, 45, 60, 69, 82
St. Luke's 92
Stafford's Point 35
Standard Oil of Pennsylvania 63
State of Texas 32
Sterling, Ross S. 64, 79
Stevenson, Ben 100
Stokowski, Leopold 99
Strange, James 16
Straus, Percy 100
Strauss, Richard 99
Stude, Henry 41
Stutz 73
Sugar Land 69
Suite 8F 92
Summit, the 99, 102
Sunda Strait 86
Supreme Court 95, 96
Sweatt, Heman 95
Sweeney and Coombs Opera House 55

T

T. M. Bagby 42
Talfor, R. B. 59
Tanglewood 89
Taylor, John D. 13
Taylor, John 16
Tejas 10
Tekram 66
Telegraph and Texas Register 21, 22, 28, 31, 32, 35
Tempest, J. Arthur 52
Tenneco Inc. 88
Tennessee Gas Transmission Company 88
Tennessee 40, 88
Terry, Benjamin Franklin 40
Terry's Texas Rangers 40
Texas and New Orleans Railroad Company .. 36
Texas Centennial 80
Texas City 71
Texas Commerce Tower 104
Texas Company 62, 63, 67
Texas Constitution 31, 37, 77
Texas Eastern Transmission Company 88
Texas Freeman 82
Texas Fuel Company 63
Texas Heart Institute 102
Texas Highway Department 90
Texas League 82
Texas legislature 35, 39, 97, 102
Texas Medical Center 92, 102, 105
Texas Portland Cement Company 67
Texas Railroad Commission 47
Texas Southern University 75
Texas Southern 75, 96
Texas State Fair 104
The Gondoliers 55
The Woodlands 103
Thebes 21
Thomas, Albert 81, 93
Thomas, Ezekiel 16
Tidewater Oil Company 81
Tijerina, Felix 78
Tower Community Center 83
Tower 83
Trailblazer 104
Transco Energy Company 88
Transcontinental Gas Pipeline Company 88
Transylvania University 11
Travis 22
Tri-City Relief Association 80
Trinity 11, 36
Trovatore 54
Tuffly, Bartholomew 41
Tunney, Gene 82
Turning Basin 26, 66, 82, 91

U

U. S. News and World Report 102
Uhler, Ruth 80
Union Carbide 87
Union National Bank 66
Union 32, 39, 40, 42, 56, 78, 87, 94
United Service Organization (USO) 86
United States Army Corps of Engineers 43, 59, 81
United States 11, 12, 14, 16, 17, 19, 20, 22, 23, 27, 32, 33, 35, 38, 42, 43, 50, 56, 59, 61, 70, 71, 79, 81, 83, 87, 88, 90, 91, 94, 95, 96, 97, 103, 104, 106, 108
University of Houston 75, 98
University of Texas School of Dentistry 92
University of Texas School of Law 96
University of Texas 92, 96
Uptown Houston 102
Utah 33

V

Vance, Nina 100
Velasco 22
Veracruz 7, 41
Vicksburg 40
Village, the 83
Vince, Allen 16
Vince, Richard 16
Vince, Robert 16
Vince, William 16
Virginia 39, 40

W

W. M. Rice & Company 38
Wall Street 79
Washburn Tunnel 91
Washington 6, 17, 21, 22, 59, 65, 66, 91
Waterloo 28
WCAK 82
WEAV 82
Weekly Telegraph 39, 42, 53
Welch, Louie 94
West Columbia 64
West University Place 83
West Virginia 88
Western Union 56
Westmoreland 54
WEV 82
Whispering Pines 103
White Oak Bayou 22
White, Amy 16
White, Lulu B. 95
White, Reuben 16
Whitlock, William 16
Whitmire, Kathy 106
Wiley College 95
Wilkins, Horace 92
Wilkins, Jane 13
Wilson, James T. D. 55
Wilson, Woodrow 66
Winnie Davis Auditorium 55
Winton 73
Woman's Club, The 51
Women Airforce Service Pilots 86
Women's Army Corps 86
Women's Choral Club 76
Woodville 46
Works Progress Administration 80
World War II 84, 85, 87, 90, 95, 97, 102
Wortham, Gus 92
WPAN 82
Wyoming 34

Y

Yale University 50